IN
Readi...
and American Politics

IN "MEDIA" RES
Readings in Mass Media and American Politics

Edited by
JAN P. VERMEER
Nebraska Wesleyan University

McGraw-Hill, Inc.
New York   St. Louis   San Francisco   Auckland   Bogotá   Caracas
Lisbon   London   Madrid   Mexico City   Milan   Montreal   New Delhi
San Juan   Singapore   Sydney   Tokyo   Toronto

IN "MEDIA" RES
Readings in Mass Media and American Politics

Copyright © 1995 by McGraw-Hill, Inc. All rights reserved. Printed in the United States of America. Except as permitted under the United States Copyright Act of 1976, no part of this publication may be reproduced or distributed in any form or by any means, or stored in a data base or retrieval system, without the prior written permission of the publisher.

This book is printed on acid-free paper.

2 3 4 5 6 7 8 9 0   DOC   DOC   9 0 9 8 7 6 5

ISBN 0-07-067467-1

This book was set in Melior by Compset, Inc.
The editors were Peter Labella and Fred H. Burns;
The production supervisor was Leroy A. Young.
The cover was designed by Tana Kamine.
R. R. Donnelley & Sons Company was printer and binder.

Library of Congress Cataloging-in-Publication Data

In "media" res: readings in mass media and American politics / [compiled by] Jan P. Vermeer.
     p.   cm.
  Includes bibliographical references.
  ISBN 0-07-067467-1
  1. Mass media—Political aspects—United States. 2. Government and the press—United States. 3. Communication in politics—United States. 4. Public opinion—United States. 5. United States—Politics and government—1993– I. Vermeer, Jan Pons.
P95.82.U6I5   1995   94-21292
302.23′73—dc20

About the Editor

Jan P. ("John") Vermeer is presently professor of political science at Nebraska Wesleyan University, where he has taught since 1974. In 1990 he won the Sears-Roebuck Foundation Teaching Excellence and Campus Leadership Award. A graduate of the University of California at Santa Barbara, he received both his master's and Ph.D. degrees from the Department of Politics at Princeton University. He has previously published *For Immediate Release: Candidate Press Releases in American Political Campaigns* (Greenwood Press, 1982) and *Campaigns in the News: Mass Media and Congressional Elections* (Greenwood Press, 1987). Vermeer's research interests include public law as well as media and politics. He is currently a member of the editorial board of *The American Review of Politics*.

To Kurt and Mark

Contents

Preface — xiii

1. Introduction — 1

2. News Media Practices — 9

   1. Objectivity and the News Media
      The "Uncensored War"
      DANIEL C. HALLIN — 11

   2. Media and the Public Agenda
      Setting the Agenda: Mass Media and the Discovery
      of Famine in Ethiopia
      CHRISTOPHER J. BOSSO — 21

   3. Television and Print Media
      Amusing Ourselves to Death
      NEIL POSTMAN — 27

   4. Framing the News
      Freezing Out the Public
      ROBERT M. ENTMAN AND ANDREW ROJECKI — 35

3. Media Effects on Attitudes and Opinions — 45

   5. Political Socialization through Media
      Television Entertainment and Political Socialization
      JAMES M. CARLSON — 47

   6. Public Opinion and the Media
      How the Media Affect What People Think—
      and Think They Think
      ROBERT M. ENTMAN — 55

   7. Political Participation through Media
      Talk Radio
      DIANA OWEN — 60

4. Campaigns, Elections, and Media — 67

   8. Parties, Media, and National Nominating Conventions
      Cordial Concurrence: Orchestrating National Party
      Conventions in the Telepolitical Age
      LARRY DAVID SMITH AND DAN NIMMO — 70

9. Presidential Campaigns and the Press
   Media Politics: Do They Make a Difference? 76
   F. CHRISTOPHER ARTERTON

10. New Techniques in 1992
    Playing to a Friendly House: Narrowcasting and
    Politics 83
    LEE WILKINS AND PHILIP PATTERSON

11. Congressional Campaign Coverage
    Do Challengers Even Have a Chance? Media Coverage
    of Congressional Elections 87
    J. P. VERMEER

12. Endorsements in Local Politics
    The Papers Vote: Endorsement Politics 92
    EDWIN DIAMOND

5. Media and the Institutions of Government 96

13. Legislators and the News Media
    Making Laws and Making News 98
    TIMOTHY E. COOK

14. Presidents and Publicity
    Going Public: New Strategies of Presidential
    Leadership 108
    SAMUEL KERNELL

15. Clinton and the Media
    Letter from Washington: The Syndicated Presidency 114
    SIDNEY BLUMENTHAL

16. Covering the Court
    Press, Politics, and the Supreme Court 121
    RICHARD DAVIS

17. Governmental Bureaucracy in the Media
    The Care and Feeding of the Fourth Estate 129
    STEPHEN HESS

6. Media and Law 133

18. Prior Restraint and the Press 135
    New York Times Company v. United States

19. Libel and the Law 138
    Hustler Magazine v. Falwell

20. Opposing Viewpoints and the Press 142
    Miami Herald Publishing Company v. Tornillo

21. News Gathering and the Law 145
    Branzburg v. Hayes

7. Media and Controversy — 150

22. Anti-Abortion Activists in the Press
    Abortion Foes Stereotyped, Some in Media Believe — 152
    DAVID SHAW

23. Reporting News as It Happens
    A Matter of "Live" and Death — 157
    JEFF KAMEN

24. The Media in the Persian Gulf War
    Pools and the Press in the Persian Gulf War — 164
    DAVID STEBENNE

25. The Pentagon and the Press—Another View
    The Media and the Military — 169
    PETER ANDREWS

26. Interest Groups Using the Media
    Take Two Ads and Call Me in the Morning — 175
    HOWARD KURTZ

27. Privacy, Public Officials, and the Press
    Politicians and Privacy — 179
    CHARLES S. CLARK

8. Conclusion — 187

Index — 190

Preface

What most undergraduate students know about U.S. government and politics before enrolling in their first political science class they have learned through the media. What most of them will experience about politics in the years after graduation will revolve around news provided by the media. For students, the political world is the world of government and public affairs as reported by the media. Students' interest in political events is piqued by media coverage, and events that receive little mention in newspapers, newsmagazines, and television newscasts are shrugged off as insignificant. Most students interact with the political world around them through the media.

Students are intensely interested in media coverage of politics as a phenomenon. Discussions about media bias, about journalists slanting the news, about clashes between government officials and reporters grasp their attention and generate spirited debate. It seems that virtually every student has an opinion about the relationship between media and politics. Some argue vehemently about a liberal bias in the media, and others argue just as strongly that the media protect existing institutions and political practices by focusing blame for problems on mistakes by individual politicians instead of on the system. But few indeed are neutral.

This book builds on that interest to help instructors introduce students to the study of U.S. government and politics and to use the study of U.S. government and politics to present important issues about the mass media in society today. It should be useful, therefore, in introductory American Government, media and politics, and public opinion courses, as well as in mass media and society and political communication courses in departments of communication. The selections in this book, some by professional political scientists, some by journalists, and others by media scholars and commentators, guide students through the interactions among reporters and officials and provide a basis for judging how media affect politics in the United States. Clearly, the mass media have become important actors in the political system. The general theme running through these readings is that the conduct of politics and public affairs in the United States is greatly affected by the way in which the media report them. The media are in the middle of things in more ways than one.

After an introduction providing an overview of the issues raised in the readings and their interrelationships, Chapter 2 discusses the impact of news-gathering and reporting techniques on the picture of the world we see in the media. Chapter 3 explores the effect media may have on our basic attitudes and on our opinions on the issues of the day. Chapter 4 presents some perspectives on the news media's relationship to campaigns and elections, at the presidential level, the congressional level, and the state and local levels.

The readings in Chapter 5 provide some evidence that how media report the actions of government influences how public officials act. Their choices, their priorities, and their public actions all reflect their concerns with the media and their news accounts. Chapter 6 excerpts critical passages from important Supreme Court opinions about the legal status of news media, covering such issues as prior restraint, criticism of public officials, and access to the media. The final chapter includes some selections about several widely discussed issues: privacy, abortion, and the Persian Gulf War. A conclusion ties the package together at the end.

The criteria I had in mind when choosing selections for this reader were timeliness, flexibility, solid content, and the potential for generating student interest. Teachers of introductory courses in U.S. government and politics will find that the readings can be adapted to a variety of teaching styles and formats. Some present beginning students with perspectives they have not previously considered, for instance, that some government agencies seek news coverage while others do not. Others provide an opportunity to evaluate contemporary news coverage of political events: how are the media "framing" the president's latest domestic policy initiative? Still others introduce students to widely cited scholarly works, such as Kernell's *Going Public* and Arterton's *Media Politics*. Finally, some selections invite students to consider the nature of news and of news coverage, especially the selections from Postman's *Amusing Ourselves to Death* and Kamen's "A Matter of 'Live' and Death." In every instance, discussion questions after the readings help students focus their attention on some of the issues involved—these questions could form the basis for in-class discussion, journal entries, short written assignments, or a review for an examination. And of course these readings will be as useful, if not more so, to teachers of mass media and politics courses.

Instructors can profitably assign the readings in various sequences. Many of the selections go together well, even though they fall into different chapters. Reporting wars is covered in the Hallin selection, the Stebenne piece, and the Andrews article, as well as raised in the *Pentagon Papers* case, a part of which is also included. The Shaw article on abortion activists, the nuclear freeze piece about framing, and the Kurtz discussion of health care ads all deal with interest group activity in one way or another. The *Tornillo* case and Diamond's discussion of newspaper endorsements fit together nicely. I urge instructors to explore different combinations to adapt the materials to their courses. Such combinations may indeed help students draw connections they otherwise would not notice.

The selections are taken from a variety of sources, some popular, some scholarly. Overall, they are intended to inform as well as to engage students. In general, the pieces included here present perspectives, insights, and conclusions—with only a little of the supporting evidence on which those positions are based. That was a conscious choice. For introductory students, the arguments are more accessible and less technical when presented without the data the authors rely on. For advanced students, instructors can ask them to consider the kind of evidence required to buttress the arguments made in the readings and what evidence would contradict the conclusions the authors have drawn. On occasion, discussion questions at the end of each chapter raise the evidence concern.

My debts to others in preparing this book are great. Nebraska Wesleyan University provided me an E.C. Ames grant and a sabbatical. The Political Science Department at the University of Nebraska—Lincoln, where I spent that sabbatical, was most hospitable, and my discussions with colleagues there were most useful. Among individuals to single out for thanks are John R. Hibbing and Melissa Gates of the University of Nebraska—Lincoln; Michael K. Moore of the University of Texas—Arlington; Robert C. Oberst, Dennis Wakefield, Rick Cypert, and Leon Satterfield, all of Nebraska Wesleyan University; Jay Ovsiovitch, Fort Hays State University; Rebekah Herrick, Oklahoma State University; Trudy V. Selleck, University of California—Riverside; Thomas Patterson, Syracuse University; and the following reviewers: David Bell, Eastern Washington University; Christopher Berkely, Framingham State College; John Boiney, Duke University; Jeri Cabot, College of Charleston; Ken Collier, University of Kansas; John Crow, University of Arizona; David Freeman, Washburn University; David Allen Gawell, University of Texas; Forest Grieves, University of Montana; Theodore Mosch, University of Tennessee; Samuel Pernacciaro, University of Wisconsin–Parkside; Patricia Bayer Richard, Ohio University; Kathleen Ruszay, Kennesaw State College; Mark Wattier, Murray State University; Mark Weaver, Glendale Community College; and Christine Williams, Bentley College. Several years' worth of students at Nebraska Wesleyan University gave me candid responses to these (and other) selections along the way; their insights helped tremendously. At McGraw-Hill, John Bakula, Bert Lummus, Peter Labella, Bill Barter, Fred Burns, and Marsha Scott have been professional, competent, and enormously helpful.

Finally, family: To my father, thanks, for life and love and the opportunity to pursue my dreams. My mother, too, had she lived, deserves my deep gratitude. To Kathy, Kurt, and Mark, who have helped shape who I am and softened the edges in the process, thanks are also due. They've made it possible for me to develop this book. They've made me proud of them; each has contributed something special to my life. This book would not have been the same without you all.

I'll share any credit for this book with every single one of you, but I'll retain all the blame for errors, mistakes, and misstatements. Let's hope there are but few.

Jan P. Vermeer

IN "MEDIA" RES
Readings in Mass Media
and American Politics

CHAPTER 1
Introduction

Images of tanks, tents, and troops in Saudi Arabia flashed on our television screens nightly during the recent war in the Persian Gulf, thanks to satellites and videotape. We heard the sounds and saw the scenes experienced by U.S. troops deployed thousands of miles away from home. Even local newscasts regularly gave their viewers a weather report for the Gulf area: hot and dry, with little prospect for cooling. And as we watched, we imagined what it must have been like for our friends, relatives, and fellow citizens serving in the middle of the Gulf war. We began to form our own opinions about President George Bush's decision to take military action to force Iraqi forces from Kuwait.

Would our opinions have been different if we hadn't received nightly images, the regular "Gulf War Updates," the on-camera interviews with soldiers struggling with the conflicting demands of patriotism and duty on the one hand and worry about their personal safety on the other? Would we have considered the situation less critical if we hadn't developed the feeling of immediacy that the extensive broadcast news coverage generated? Would we have been more willing to accept a compromise settling the war if we hadn't gotten hourly updates? Was public opinion, in this case regarding support for the Bush policy in the Arabian Gulf, affected by the fact of media coverage? Do media make a difference?

Obviously, you wouldn't be holding this book in your hands if I thought that media do not make a difference. They do, and in a broad range of areas. In fact, I think it is helpful to think of media as being *in medias res,* Latin for "in the middle of things." A great deal of politics in the United States (and, indeed, elsewhere) today is conducted through the media or is affected by the way the media operate. Some things are not done or they are done differently because of media activities. For instance, a member of the House of Representatives with two simultaneous committee hearings may choose to attend the one more likely to be televised so his or her constituents do not see an empty chair behind the nameplate, even if the member feels the other hearing will deal with more important issues. When officials' choices are so affected, the media definitely have an impact.

But it is an unintentional impact. We need, right from the start, to differentiate media attempts to influence political choices and outcomes from the effect media have when they are reporting events and developments using their standard procedures. An effect then comes as a by-product, nothing more. The difference lies in intent. A lot of commentators will see intent behind any media impact, but media impact is much more likely to occur without any such intent. Media personnel are not unaware of their potential impact, but their decisions are not guided by a choice among different effects. Rather, they make their decisions guided by professional and economic criteria common to journalists: What is news? How much of our resources can we devote to covering this development? How can we keep an audience interested in this story? Reporting the news is the intent; other effects are by-products.

A consensus has developed among reporters about what constitutes news. Although many never succeed in putting it into words, journalists consider developments that involve conflict, have significant impact, involve recognizable people (celebrities, VIPs, and so forth), have recently occurred, and were unexpected as newsworthy. Such events have a much greater chance of being reported as news than developments missing one or more of these elements. Further, the closer to home the event took place, the more likely it will be reported. A car accident that claims one life is news at home, but it would have to claim three lives somewhere else in the state, ten lives elsewhere in the nation, and even more abroad, to be reported as news in our hometowns. Finally, predictable events are more likely to be reported as news than unpredictable ones, because news directors then have time to send television cameras and editors can save space on the paper's front page for the story.

How news is reported can also have an impact. Journalistic norms call for developments to be reported objectively. In effect, objectivity calls for reporters to leave out their personal preferences and perspectives, to report events neutrally, to report both (what if there are more than two?) sides of each issue. As some have said, objective reporting holds a mirror up to reality, so that the public can know what happened by seeing what is reflected in the mirror. Unfortunately, people act differently in front of mirrors than they do elsewhere. (If you doubt that, put a mirror up in an unexpected place and observe how people behave.) And it is impossible for reporters not to be affected by their personal outlooks. For instance, isn't a decision about whether a statement is important enough to be included in a news story affected by a reporter's judgment about what is important and what is unimportant? Objectivity is an ideal, at best.

Media personnel have to make judgments about importance all the time. Some story has to be first on the evening news; some stories have to be put on the front page and others near the classified ads. Those kinds of decisions cannot be avoided, even when journalists recognize that choices about priorities and importance have an impact. That impact, generally, is on us, on what issues and concerns we consider important and which we consider minor. As Bernard Cohen said years ago, "The press is unable to tell us what to think, but it is stunningly successful in telling us what to think about."[1] In other words, the media may be able to influence our perceptions about what is important enough in our surroundings, the locality, the state, the nation, and the world, for us to take into account. We call this effect of the media, "agenda setting." The agenda-setting function of the media refers to the media's ability to generate a list of the issues the public ought to be considering. And I do not see how the media cannot have that effect, even if they wished not to.

Sometimes, too, the media have an effect on how we view the world. Political socialization, transmitting political culture (basic attitudes about the nature of politics and government and about the individual's place in society) from generation to generation, operates through the media as well as the family and schools. When media broadcast criticisms of government policy, we may absorb their implicit standards ourselves, usually without recognizing it. When media portray some political events as exceptions, we begin to form a picture of what "normal" politics consists of. If it is unusual for a local congregation to take a political position, a news story reporting such an action as extraordinary subtly emphasizes for us that churches rarely take public positions. And since we have nationwide media, people in all regions of the country begin to respond to similar perceptions of what it means to be American and what criteria we should apply in judging government activity.

It is not as clear that media can influence public opinion directly. The success of public information campaigns (for instance, "Just Say No," don't smoke, use seat belts, and so forth) varies tremendously. But it is clear that you and I use the media to get information in support of the positions we hold on public issues and that we talk to others about media discussions of issues we are interested in. In addition, interest groups, public relations officers, and people with axes to grind try to get access to news columns and stimulate television coverage in order to influence what we think of the issues of concern to them. And sometimes they are successful. Bankers, for instance, managed a public relations campaign to get Congress to reconsider automatic income tax withholding of savings account interest.[2] When that happens, we have a media impact that is really the product of other people using the media as a channel to reach the public. But the media are an essential element in that process.

Since we know pretty well how media make their choices of developments to report as news (a whole industry—public relations—is built on

---

[1] Bernard C. Cohen, *The Press and Foreign Policy*, Princeton, N.J.: Princeton University Press, 1963, p. 13.
[2] For a discussion of this incident, see Jeffrey M. Berry, *The Interest Group Society*, 2d ed., Glenview, Ill.: Scott, Foresman and Company, 1989, p. 114.

that knowledge), it is not too difficult to find ways to generate news coverage. National nominating conventions, to cite one major example, have evolved over time into quite different events than they were fifty or a hundred years ago. They have adapted themselves to the need to conduct their business in a way that generates favorable media images, attracts a television audience, and still gets the work of the party done. Although they are still "party events," national conventions are "media events," too, and significantly so.

Generating news coverage is nowadays the essence of campaigns. You are probably most familiar with the role of the mass media in elections and in presidential elections specifically. Here candidates plan extensive campaigns to solicit electoral support, and reaching voters through the media is the focal point of their efforts. In winning the nomination, candidates must try to distinguish themselves from other hopefuls, build name recognition, gather momentum, and influence the media's expectations about the outcome of primary elections. It doesn't do much good to win 40 percent of the vote, more than any other candidate in the primary, and be considered a loser because reporters expected you to win 50 percent or more.

Presidential campaigns orchestrate advertising campaigns (paid media) and publicity campaigns (free media) to reach as many voters as possible while retaining as much control over the content of the messages they send as possible. Let me put that in different words: Presidential campaigners try to manipulate the media into reporting what they want them to report in a way most helpful to the campaign. And so advance people for campaigns will limit television cameras to locations that will yield the most favorable pictures for the campaign. And candidates will hop from television market to television market in their travels, appearing in telegenic settings that reflect the themes their campaigns are stressing. Of course, there's nothing new here, as the old picture of staid Calvin Coolidge looking unhappy in an Indian headdress in the 1920s indicates. What is new is the range of media available for exploitation: talk shows, viewer call-in shows, interview shows, even entertainment shows, such as *The Arsenio Hall Show*.

Generating news coverage is more difficult but no less important for candidates for Congress. They are substantially less prominent than presidential candidates. Frequently, aspiring legislators running against incumbents pose only minor challenges, with little chance to generate the kind of media coverage that will significantly increase their name recognition. For candidates for the House of Representatives, especially, the disparity between their district's boundaries and the reach of television stations in the area (the "media market") is great. A candidate for the House from a district in Manhattan who wants to use television will have to pay advertising rates based on an audience that includes all of New York City and its northern suburbs, a large segment of New Jersey, and a significant portion of Connecticut. Only a small portion of these people can vote in the candidate's district. The same rationale restricts news coverage local newspapers give the candidates—most of the paper's readers are not interested in the race.

When candidates have won office, when they have become legislators, governors, presidents, senators, and representatives, they quickly discover that the media still play a major role in their lives. The press especially likes to cover the president, reporting the trivial as well as the important. For instance, the morning of President Nixon's resignation on August 9, 1974, the media reported to the nation that their next president, then-Vice President Ford, fixed his own breakfast that morning: an English muffin and orange juice. Wherever the president goes, at least a small segment of the White House press corps goes too, known irreverently as the "body watch." Why? So that the media would be there to record anything newsworthy that might happen to the president, from a stumble over a curb to an assassination attempt. No other public official lives and works in such a fishbowl.

The impact of the media on the functioning of the presidency, however, is more important than this trivial reporting of a celebrity. The White House is a convenient "beat" to cover, with many significant developments occurring there regularly. The White House exterior makes an impressive backdrop for stand-up television news reports. What also makes the White House attractive to media reporters is the fact that there is a single spokesperson for the executive branch there—the president. In Congress, competing voices, usually from people the public doesn't readily recognize, make it more difficult for reporters to cover. And so there is an understandable tendency for the media to center their Washington reporting on the White House, and much of our national political news originates there.

For a president, that is convenient and useful. Whenever presidents want to make announcements they need only to walk out to the press center, and they can be sure of finding representatives of all major media (as well as a horde of reporters from less important outlets) eager to report the news. Because so much presidential news is generated within the White House, reporters assigned the White House beat rarely need to seek outside sources. Presidents, therefore, can be assured that their perspectives are likely to be dominant in the stories reporters file. The media's preoccupation with the presidency further increases the likelihood that the president's point of view will be emphasized in the news of the day. Press releases, briefings, and public statements, all coming out of the White House Press Office, are all carefully orchestrated to present the president's work in a good public light in order to build popular support for his or her policies and actions.

It doesn't always work, and some presidents wind up seeing the White House press corps as opponents. Critical reports and interpretations of the news that dispute official explanations can draw presidential fire. One way presidents try to retain control over the "spin" of the news they generate is to go over the heads of reporters to the public directly. Public appearances and national television addresses, even press conferences, allow presidents to speak to citizens without having their messages diluted, interpreted, and analyzed by the White House press. Members of local media tend to be much less critical of presidential actions and to report presidential actions favorably. Nowadays presidents do not restrict their efforts to reach the public to dealing with the White House press corps, despite the extra effort and resources required. President Clinton, especially, has gone to great length to exploit the potential in local media coverage.

In contrast, coverage of Congress is much more difficult for the media. The complexity of the legislative process, the large number of representatives and senators, and the ambiguity of much congressional action all contribute to the difficulty of the task. Unlike the White House, where the press secretary's office may delay releasing news about minor developments in order to focus press attention on what the president considers the major story of the day, a variety of events may occur simultaneously in Congress: a vote on final passage of a tax bill in the Senate, a conference committee meeting on reconciling competing versions of a House and Senate bill on controlling acid rain, a subcommittee hearing in the House, a press conference by the Senate majority leader, or a debate about a cabinet appointment in the Senate. And on all these and other matters, different legislators may be the "authoritative" source, the right person to quote. Few journalists know enough about all 535 representatives and senators to know who to see on more than four or five subjects, not to mention the hundreds of issues that arise in Congress every year. Further, the essence of Congress centers on its process, whereas journalistic conceptions of news center on results. A long, drawn-out debate in Congress may be important to the final form a bill may take, but that debate is rarely pithy enough, dramatic enough, newsworthy enough to warrant much press attention. Congress is therefore much more difficult for news media personnel to cover.

However, individual members of Congress need media coverage. In order to raise their policy concerns to a higher priority for their colleagues—in order, in other words, for members to force the House to take action on their bills—members frequently try to generate news coverage. The combination of factors that makes such action successful is hard to manipulate. When media concerns and member interests coincide, sometimes fortuitously, a senator or representative can successfully call enough attention to an issue to have it addressed by the chamber. When such a combination of circumstances arises, a member must strike quickly, or the window of opportunity will close.

Members need coverage of their activities by their state media as well. Here members hold most of the cards. It is exceedingly difficult for local media to obtain news reports of their local member's actions. Consequently, many local outlets rely heavily on member-produced communications. Senators or representatives will send out press releases, write weekly newspaper columns, and hold telephone press conferences regularly with the news media in their states or districts. Each chamber in Congress even has extensive television studio facilities to produce video news clips of the member to send to television stations back home. Since C-SPAN is widely available across the nation, many local stations will use excerpts from floor debate featuring the home-town representative in their news broadcasts. And since local media rarely have other sources in Washington to contact about their member's statements, whatever spin the member's press operation gives the story is likely to be adopted by the district media. The result: favorable coverage of the representative. What do the local media get out of it? These efforts by the representative make news coverage possible that they would otherwise not be able to provide.

The result is uniformly positive local media coverage for the district's representative in Congress. The views you and I form of our representatives' work in Washington on behalf of the state and constituency emanate from the representatives' offices, based on releases, actualities, columns, telephone calls, and interviews set up by the press operations in the offices. And, of course, local media want to provide us with news about our representatives' actions. However, local media just don't have the resources to seek out such information on their own. They rely heavily, therefore, on the member's own office to keep them informed about newsworthy developments. Is it any wonder that we may have negative impressions of Congress but favorable impressions of our incumbent?

State and local news coverage is different. Admittedly, we political scientists do not know as much yet about that coverage, but what we do know indicates that there is a great deal of attention paid by in-state newspapers and television news operations to the day-to-day activity of state legislatures and governors' offices. Both the executive branch and the legislative branch at the state level are more accessible to reporters than the presidency or Congress is, and so reporters manage to develop reliable sources of information on which to base their reports. Sometimes the situation in state legislatures is rather fluid, and journalists may not know who to contact (who the right "spokesperson" is) on an issue, but leadership structures and political patterns tend to be open enough—and conflict wide enough—for reporters to have little difficulty getting access to sources both knowledgeable and willing to be quoted.

Local coverage varies, much of it not very good. Frequently reporters here are young and inexperienced, and political leaders feel as if they are continually breaking a new group of journalists in. A journalist who finally learns the ropes and knows how city hall operates is promoted or moved to another beat, and a fresh face appears to ask all the same questions over again. Even more frequently, publishers and editors move in the same political and social circles as the civic and business leaders and understandably become reluctant to air dirty linen in public when issues of concern could just as easily be settled quietly behind the scenes. When downtown redevelopment is going to affect the newspaper as a business enterprise, a publisher may feel more comfortable working quietly with other political leaders than publicizing the disputes. Further, publishers may be thought of as taking unfair advantage of their media resources if they were to use the news columns in such a struggle—after all, the other participants don't have the same access to the public. The result: skimpy, uninformative coverage.

Clearly, these patterns differ from locality to locality. The point remains, however, that in most cities, news organizations are major political players on civic issues. To use or not to use the news columns becomes a political question that goes beyond considerations of good journalism. Publishers are major actors in the political arena of cities of every size.

Media actions are shaped and influenced by the contours of U.S. law. Under the First Amendment's guarantees of a free press, media have benefited from a number of U.S. Supreme Court decisions. One makes control of news before publication ("prior restraint") almost impossible. Another makes it difficult for public figures to sue for libel successfully, because the Court has felt that the normal give-and-take of democratic discourse shouldn't be inhibited by reporters' worry about whether they can prove the statements they make. And should people who are unfairly criticized in the newspaper be given the chance to respond?

The major outcomes of the political process are the policies that affect us. Media reports of these policy questions shape our perceptions of them. When these policies are controversial, the very way in which media approach them make a substantial difference. Are proponents of one side of the abortion issue extremists and the other side reasonable activists? Was reporting of the Gulf War unreasonably restricted by U.S. government policy? Should television have been more circumspect in its live coverage of the raid on the Branch Davidian compound in Waco, Texas? The more controversial the subject, the more difficult, it seems, it is for media to report objectively.

Because we view the political world through the perspective provided by media, contemporary journalism unavoidably colors our outlooks and our judgments. Only if we have sufficient alternative sources of information, or if we are sufficiently aware of how the news is made and reported, will we be able to make independent judgments about public affairs. The media are in the middle of things, and that affects us all.

CHAPTER 2
News Media Practices

The news you and I see on television and read in our papers reflects not only the events that come to reporters' attention but also the impact of how journalists practice their craft. How events are reported influence what we learn about them. Far from media being a mirror held up to reality where we see the whole world reflected, only part of the world's events are chosen for coverage. Far from media allowing us to see what happened where we cannot be in person, the presence of reporters changes the events that occur. Far from different media providing similar portrayals of the same events, print and electronic media report differently, and we respond to those reports differently. Journalistic routines affect what we learn of the political world.

I am not suggesting that media personnel consciously try to slant the news to support a particular partisan position. I do not mean that a journalist will choose to report a development in a specific way in order to build sympathy or undermine support for one candidate or another in order to further the reporter's political goals. I do not mean that journalists are conservatives and favor conservative causes or that they are liberals and support liberal causes. It is not a question of *partisan* bias (although some people maintain there is partisan bias among the media). It is a question of *structural* bias, a slant that emerges because of the way reporters do their jobs, even (some people would say "especially") when they try to be fair and impartial. Distortion is a result of the way news is reported, whether on television or radio or in print.

Objectivity is the standard to which journalists attempt to adhere in their efforts to report the news fairly and impartially. Objectivity should be contrasted to subjectivity, the notion people view and interpret the world from their own peculiar perspectives. Rather than speaking from partisan perspectives, reporters want to report from neutral perspectives. And to insulate themselves from charges of favoritism and bias, journalists follow procedures that ideally guarantee unslanted news reports.

These standards, described in Daniel Hallin's piece in this chapter, lead to their own difficulties. By relying on official sources, reporters see events through particular filters, although not their own. By focusing attention on breaking events, journalists cannot effectively describe long-term trends and therefore cannot place stories in those contexts. By choosing news stories on the basis of newsworthiness criteria (rather than on the basis of personal preference), news personnel leave themselves open to manipulation by sources who stage events primarily to stimulate news coverage. And the result is news that does not reflect what would have happened with no media present or what we would have observed had we ourselves attended a news event. It is news influenced by news sources, sources with their own biases and agendas.

Reporting on an event does not necessarily lead to public attention. Christopher Bosso explains how a peculiar convergence of factors led the Ethiopian famine to become a major issue on the public agenda. Vivid television images, elite attention, and follow-up reports by other media transformed the Ethiopian situation into a newsworthy story. And before the famine crisis had passed, the story dropped from public awareness. But in the meantime, public concern led to action by government. One major impact of media on politics is media's effect on the public agenda, what media scholars call "agenda setting." News coverage helps to place a concern on the public agenda.

News coverage alone is not enough—there was, for instance, substantial news coverage of the Nazi Holocaust in U.S. papers before and during World War II, but the problem never became an important item on the public agenda. You may want to consider what elements, besides news coverage, are needed for an issue to be taken up by decision makers in your locality, your state, or in the nation.

Perhaps vivid television images make a difference. Neil Postman argues that our responses to news reported on television and news reported in the press are markedly different, that each evokes modes of thinking that elicit different responses. News in print can be read and reread; it can present arguments that must be followed and paid attention to; it can provide detail and development, often in abstract terms. News on television, Postman argues, lacks context, juxtaposes unrelated developments, builds on emotional responses, and discourages abstract thinking. Since more Americans claim they get most of their news from television, Postman's argument is disturbing if correct.

Some recent research has suggested that the context within which an issue is presented (sometimes called "priming" or "framing") affects our responses. For instance, if a story on presidential approval ratings immediately follows a news item about a lackluster economy on network television news, we are more likely to evaluate the president in terms of economic performance than if the stories had been reported in separate newscasts. Whether that effect is long-lasting or disappears by the next week is still open to question. Nevertheless, the last selection in this chapter asks you to think about the effect of framing on your political views.

At any rate, which stories are reported, which facts are seen as relevant to the stories, how much emphasis stories are given, and how they are transmitted to us, all influence our conceptions of the political world. If media hold up a mirror to the world for us, it is a peculiar mirror, to say the least. Some things are reflected clearly and accurately, others are reflected as if in a carnival fun-house mirror, and others, like the vampires of mythology, are not reflected at all.

1. OBJECTIVITY AND THE NEWS MEDIA

In contrast to the avowedly partisan press of the nineteenth century, journalism in the twentieth century developed a set of principles that supposedly describe neutral reporting, separating conscious editorializing from accounts of news. What you and I learn from the media, then, would ideally reflect actual events, not the reporters' interpretations of those events. We would ideally have the facts at our disposal for us to use to reach our own conclusions—to form our own interpretations. But adhering to the demands of objectivity turns out not to be neutral reporting—objectivity results in a treatment of the news that emphasizes official explanations of events over other interpretations, and it leaves reporters subject to manipulation by sources who now know exactly how to get a story into print.

In this selection, Daniel C. Hallin uses his study of media coverage of the Vietnam War to explain how attempts to be objective colored press accounts of Vietnam and how television's version of objectivity varies from that of print media. For newspapers, official sources in Washington provided most of the facts and interpretations that the press dutifully reported as news. For television, objective journalism was practiced chiefly in what Hallin calls the Sphere of Legitimate Controversy, in contrast to both the Sphere of Deviance and the Sphere of Consensus. You may want to apply Hallin's analysis here to the selections in Chapter 7. What objectivity means in theory and what it means in practice differ significantly.

The "Uncensored" War
Daniel C. Hallin

[M]ost journalists would acknowledge the following principles, in one form or another, as central to modern American journalism. These principles, with a set of routines and assumptions which allow them to be put into practice in concrete situations, form the core of the ideological system that is referred to . . . as "objective journalism."

Independence. Journalists should be independent of political commitments and free of "outside" pressures, including pressures from government and other political actors, advertisers, and the news organization itself as an institution with economic and political interests.

Objectivity. The journalist's basic task is to present "the facts," to tell what happened, not to pass judgment on it. Opinion should be clearly separated from the presentation of news.

Balance. News coverage of any political controversy should be impartial, representing without favor the positions of all the contending parties.

These principles are deeply held by American journalists, and their impact on the practice of journalism is profound. But they cannot guide that practice by themselves. Their guidance is essentially negative: they tell the journalist *not* to allow political pressures to interfere with "news judgment," *not* to take sides in political controversy, *not* to let personal opinions color the reporting of news. But they do not say how "news judgment" should actually be exercised; they do not tell the journalist how to make the series of positive choices the production of news necessarily requires: which stories to cover—what, out of the seamless flux of human activity, should be singled out as news—which "facts" to include and which to emphasize, or how to present those facts in a way that will render them meaningful to the news audience. In part, these choices are guided by the cultural assumptions of the wider society.... And in part they are guided by a set of routines (themselves rooted in the dominant political culture, though modified by the particular demands of the journalists' activity) which form the real working infrastructure of the institution of journalism. . . .

OBJECTIVITY IN PRACTICE: THE GULF OF TONKIN

. . . Tom Wicker's right-hand lead [in the *New York Times*] on August 5 began:

Washington, Aug. 4—President Johnson has ordered retaliatory action against gunboats and "certain supporting facilities in North Vietnam" after renewed attacks against American destroyers in the Gulf of Tonkin.

In a television address tonight, Mr. Johnson said air attacks on the North Vietnamese ships and facilities were taking place as he spoke, shortly after 11:30 p.m.

This "positive reply," as the President called it, followed a naval battle in which a number of North Vietnamese PT boats attacked United States destroyers with torpedoes. Two of the boats were believed to have been sunk. The United States forces suffered no damage or loss of lives.

Mr. Johnson termed the North Vietnamese attacks "open aggression on the high seas."

Washington's response is "limited and fitting," the President said, and his administration seeks no general extension of the guerrilla war in Southeast Asia.

This was precisely how the administration wished its action to appear, as a "positive" but limited "reply" forced upon the president by the actions of the enemy, *not* related to any change in U.S. *policy* which might require public debate. This was also objective journalism: Wicker merely presented "the facts"—in this case primarily facts about what the president said in his

SOURCE: Abridged from *The "Uncensored War": The Media and Vietnam* by Daniel C. Hallin. Copyright ©1986 by Daniel C. Hallin. Reprinted by permission of Oxford University Press, Inc.

television address; he took no position on the truth or falsity of the president's remarks or on the policy itself. A right-hand lead on a major event, Wicker explained looking back on this story, was "supposed to be almost deadpan...as near absolutely—'objective' is too strong—it's supposed to have no content other than what is documentable and quotable fact. No interpretation of any kind. If the president says, 'Black is white,' you write, 'The president said black is white.' "[1] Of course, the reporter is doing more here than simply excluding interpretation. He is exercising "news judgment" according to several of the basic conventions of objective journalism, conventions which here make the *New York Times* essentially an instrument of the state. These conventions include the following

1. *The use of official sources.* The injunction to present "just the facts" leaves the journalist in a difficult position, for in politics the facts are almost always to some degree in dispute. As many studies of newsmaking have shown, American journalism resolves the problem, most of the time, by taking its facts from official sources.[2] This was certainly the case on August 5, 1964. Wicker's story contained official sources exclusively. Most were administration officials; the only sources outside the administration were senators Mike Mansfield, the majority leader, and Barry Goldwater, Johnson's opponent in the approaching 1964 election, both of whom supported his action. Indeed, every *Times* story on the Gulf of Tonkin incident that day was based on official U.S. sources exclusively, with the exception of a two-paragraph "shirttail" reporting Hanoi's contention that the naval battle of August 4 was "sheer fabrication" ([indeed], there is strong evidence that in fact there was no battle that night). One study of the *Washington Post* and the *New York Times* found not only that most of the sources in the two papers were official but that most stories were based on government/press contacts initiated by officials rather than journalists, especially press conferences and press releases. And, indeed, each of the *Times*'s three front page stories on the Tonkin Gulf incident on this day centered around officially initiated events: the right-hand lead, around the president's address; the other two stories, around two Defense Department press conferences.

The use of official sources, as many have pointed out, is convenient for reporters. The government is organized to provide a timely flow of information, geared to the demands of daily journalism; it is extremely efficient for news organizations to locate their personnel at the channels provided by government. But the use of official sources also fulfills another, perhaps more important function for the media: it fills a vacuum of authority left by the rise of "disinterested realism." Journalists cannot, without stepping outside the role of disinterested observer, decide on their own authority to favor one version of the facts over another because it seems to them, for instance, closer to the truth or more desirable in terms of its effect on public opinion. The principle of balance is no solution. The decision to weight equally conflicting accounts of political reality is no less a political act than the decision to report only one. For the *Times* to have given prominent play to Hanoi's version of the Tonkin Gulf incident would, in the political context of the time, have been a significant and highly controversial political statement, a challenge to the structure of political authority. The solution American journalism has adopted is to defer authority, justifying that choice as a decision to "let things be what they are," and hence a choice compatible with objectivity. Whether they are true or not, statements by top administration officials are unquestionably "newsworthy" because they come from people of power and authority.

2. *Focus on the president.* Whenever the president acts publicly, he is the focus of coverage; his "newsworthiness" overrides all other priorities. On the day of the Tonkin raids the right-hand lead was constructed around Johnson's address, the address itself was printed next to it, and above the address, beside the headline on the right-hand lead, was a photograph of the president speaking behind the presidential seal, with the caption, "DECISION: President Johnson, in a nationwide broadcast, tells of action he ordered taken against North Vietnam." The personal leadership of the president occupied the foreground of the coverage. Judging from what we know about public response to international events, this is probably very significant. People generally know little about policy, and their attitudes on foreign policy options tend to be ambivalent and unstable. But when a president appeals for unity in a crisis situation, popular support is generally forthcoming.[3]

3. *Absence of interpretation or analysis.* The principles of objectivity forbid editorializing in the news columns. But the status of interpretation, what journalists call news analysis, has been ambiguous since the rise of the ethic of objectivity.[4] Its role was particularly circumscribed during the early 1960s.

Here we encounter another important dilemma which the principle of objectivity creates for the journalist. Journalists are supposed to report the news "straight"—"just give the facts." At the same time they are inevitably teachers and storytellers: they must place events in some kind of framework that will make them meaningful to the news audience. Journalists have generally resolved this dilemma by focusing on the only sort of fact which really does "speak for itself"—facts about what people—in the case of political reporting, generally official people—*say*. Wicker's Tonkin story is a perfect example. All he does is to report what the president said. The president's words, however, are more than mere data being transmitted to the audience: they serve to place the day's events within a context the public can easily understand. American ships were attacked on the high seas; the president, as commander in chief, responded to the Communist challenge with military force; the United States seeks no wider war. Good and evil and cause and effect are clear—yet the journalist has remained strictly objective. Here again official sources fill an important void left by the ethic of objectivity: they fill the vacuum of meaning left by the journalist's renunciation of the role of interpreting reality....

4. *Focus on immediate events.* Closely related to the low priority American journalism places on analysis and interpretation is a strong tendency to focus on immediate events. The definition of *news*, as the term implies, involves a time dimension. In principle, journalists could report on phenomena of any duration, as long as demographic changes unfolding over decades or as instantaneous as individual deaths in battle. In practice, news is normally defined in terms of discrete "events" which unfold over the course of a day or less[5]—the period of time between one broadcast or issue of a newspaper and the next—and the historical or structural context of these events, unless it is made an issue by the newsmakers themselves, is relegated to the ambiguous realm of analysis—and generally to the back pages. A presidential speech or press conference is news; a gradual change in policy is not. A clash between

Buddhists and the South Vietnamese government is news; the power relations or cultural tensions that lie behind it are not.

The news on August 5, 1964, was the president's address and the raids on North Vietnam, which were described in great detail in the *Times*—the nature of the targets, the damage to them, and so on. Officials had described those raids as a response to the North Vietnamese attacks on U.S. destroyers, and those events were mentioned prominently in the *Times*. Beyond that, the *Times* contained only the slightest fragments of historical context. And this was true not only on the day of the event, but in the days that followed as well, as attention first turned to the passage of the Gulf of Tonkin resolution and then fell off. The *Times* contained, for example, only a few brief and ambiguous allusions to the intensification of covert operations against North Vietnam which had preceded the previous clash in the Gulf of Tonkin, the North Vietnamese attack—this one acknowledged by North Vietnam—of August 2. Little was said either about the implications the incident might have for the future, aside from the official statement that the United States sought no wider war. The closest thing to an independent assessment of the significance of the event was an ambiguous statement buried deep in Wicker's August 5 story, and stated virtually without elaboration: ". . . despite Mr. Johnson's assurances that the U.S. sought no 'wider war,' it was plain that the situation in South Vietnam and the surrounding area had reached new gravity." The absence of these elements of historical context cannot be explained by simple lack of information. The *Times* had reported in some detail on the covert operations against the North as recently as July 23;[6] and although the administration was giving out little information about its policy deliberations, it had . . . frequently gone public in the months preceding Tonkin with warnings to Hanoi that it might well expand its involvement—among other things by air action against the North—if North Vietnam did not cease its "aggression." By the conventions of objective journalism, however, none of this was news in August 1964.

THE PEACE OFFENSIVE AND THE BOUNDARIES OF OBJECTIVITY

The decision of July 1965 to raise the level of American troops in Vietnam to 175,000 was intended as the first of two phases, with approval of the second phase expected early in 1966. Phase II was originally planned to involve 112,000 additional U.S. troops. But the North Vietnamese were matching U.S. escalation. By November 1965, it had become clear that infiltration from North Vietnam had increased substantially, and Phase II had to be revised upward. By December, force levels of up to about 400,000 were being discussed for the end of 1966. Vietnam was going to be a big war. Political support would be a problem, and there was considerable sentiment in the administration that an escalation of this magnitude should not be undertaken without some major new peace effort which would, if nothing else, convince world and American public opinion that diplomatic channels had been fully explored. At the end of November, Secretary [of Defense Robert S.] McNamara wrote to the president:

It is my belief that there should be a three- or four-week pause in the program of bombing the North before we either greatly increase our troop deployments to Vietnam or intensify our strikes against the North. The reasons for this belief are, first, that we must lay a foundation in the mind of the American public and in world opinion for such an enlarged phase of the war, and, second, we should give North Vietnam a face-saving chance to stop the aggression.[7]

So on Christmas Eve 1965, a thirty-seven day pause in the bombing of North Vietnam began. It was accompanied by a moderately serious secret contact with the North Vietnamese through their mission in Rangoon, Burma.... It was also accompanied by a massive public peace offensive, aimed at both U.S. and world opinion. W. Averill Harriman, Vice President Humphrey, and other officials were dispatched to various capitals to carry the message of American willingness to negotiate; Arthur Goldberg did this at the United Nations; Secretary [of State Dean] Rusk released the first formal statement of American peace proposals, known as the Fourteen Points. Not everyone was convinced by the peace offensive. Perhaps most important, J. William Fulbright, chairman of the Senate Foreign Relations Committee and at one time the president's key Capitol Hill supporter on foreign policy, went public with his opposition to U.S. policy in Vietnam, holding hearings in February which could be considered the first major congressional debate on the war. But on television, the peace offensive was an unqualified success.

In order to understand television's reporting from Washington during this period, we need to consider a more complex view of American journalism. The model of objective journalism introduced [above] does not apply: the television journalist presented himself, in this case, not as a disinterested observer, but as a patriot, a partisan of what he frequently referred to as "our" peace offensive. It is useful to imagine the journalist's world as divided into three regions, each of which is governed by different journalistic standards. These regions can be represented ... [as two] concentric circles.... The province of objectivity is the middle region, which can be called the Sphere of Legitimate Controversy. This is the region of electoral contests and legislative debates, or issues recognized as such by the major established actors of the American political process. The limits of this sphere are defined primarily by the two-party system—by the parameters of debate between and within the Democratic and Republican parties—as well as by the decision-making process in the bureaucracies of the executive branch. Within this region, objectivity and balance reign as the supreme journalistic virtues.

Bounding the Sphere of Legitimate Controversy on one side is what can be called the Sphere of Consensus. This is the region of "motherhood and apple pie"; it encompasses those social objects not regarded by the journalists and most of the society as controversial. Within this region journalists do not feel compelled either to present opposing views or to remain disinterested observers. On the contrary, the journalist's role is to serve as an advocate or celebrant of consensus values.

And beyond the Sphere of Legitimate Controversy lies the Sphere of Deviance, the realm of those political actors and views which journalists and the political mainstream of the society reject as unworthy of being heard. It is, for example, written into the FCC's guidelines for application of the Fairness Doctrine that "it is not the Commission's intention to make time available to Communists or to the Communist viewpoints."[8] Here neutrality once again falls away, and journalism... plays the role of exposing, condemning, or excluding from the public agenda those who violate or challenge the political consensus. It marks out and defends the limits of acceptable political conflict.

It should be added that each "sphere" has internal gradations, and the boundaries between them are often fuzzy. Within the Sphere of Legitimate Controversy, for example, the practice of objective journalism varies considerably. Near the border of the Sphere of Consensus, journalists practice the kind of objective journalism we encountered [earlier], where objectivity involves a straight recitation of official statements. Farther out, as the news deals with issues on which consensus is weaker, the principle of balance is increasingly emphasized, and then, still farther out, the "adversary" ideal of the journalist as an independent investigator who serves to check the abuse of power. . . .

Which of these various models of journalism prevails depends on the political climate in the country as a whole. But there is also considerable variability within American journalism. And at the beginning of 1966 there was a dramatic contrast between television and the "prestige" print media in Vietnam coverage. The prestige press, for the most part, continued to practice the kind of objective journalism that lies just outside the Sphere of Consensus, though there had perhaps been a little movement outward within the Sphere of Legitimate Controversy [since the war's escalation]. Most press reports, particularly on the front page, still simply reported official statements at face value. There were, however, considerably more front page reports on congressional criticism of administration policy. There were more stories in which a number of different sources, some from inside the administration and some from outside (almost always in Congress), were used more or less equally, with the journalist constructing a synthesis. And nonelite opposition was beginning to be reported in a "straight" way, that is, stories on opposition figures, like those on the administration, would be centered around the sources' own statements.

On television, on the other hand, the peace offensive appeared as a kind of morality play: while the coverage of a paper like the *Times* had a dry and detached tone, television coverage presented a dramatic contrast between good, represented by the American peace offensive, and evil, represented by Hanoi. In part, the effectiveness of the peace offensive in creating a powerful television image of American virtue might be considered a result of the familiar ironies of objective journalism, somewhat modified by the nature of television presentation. It has often been observed that American television coverage is more "thematic" than print reporting.[9] Because television news is organized in time rather than space, the television audience must be "carried along" from the beginning of the story to the end. It cannot be allowed—as a newspaper audience can—to shift its attention from story to story. A definite theme or story line is therefore essential to a television report (or even, at times, will structure a whole broadcast) in a way it is not for a newspaper article. . . .

In 1966, . . . when contrasting interpretations were rarely being reported, what jumped to the foreground in television's simple, thematic presentation was the administration's own rhetoric. Television's version of objective reporting looked something like this:

David Brinkley. President Johnson's peace campaign continues, and there has been no bombing of North Vietnam for more than ten days now. But radio Hanoi called the whole campaign a swindle and there is no public sign of any peace talks. [Hubert

Humphrey is then shown speaking at a news conferences, after which Brinkley "wraps up."] What Humphrey did was to deliver a brief, simple list of this country's efforts to end the war and a quick explanation of what the United States is after in Vietnam. It says among other things: the U.S. wants no bases there, will happily pull out its troops, will give economic aid to all sides, will accept a neutral Vietnam if that is what the people there freely decide they want. In short, Humphrey said, we have offered to put everything into the basket of peace except the surrender of South Vietnam. As yet, again, there has been no favorable response from the North.[10]

What Brinkley does here is not so different from what a newspaper reporter might do: he structures the story around the vice president's remarks. The difference is that on television the story is boiled down to a single image, the contrast between the American peace offensive—"everything in the basket of peace except surrender"—and North Vietnamese failure to respond, an image sharpened by Brinkley's simple, expressive language....

But in drawing the contrast between America and its enemies—between good and evil—television journalists did not always confine themselves to reporting the official proceedings of the peace offensive. Their role was much more active: they moved back and forth between "straight" reporting and commentary; their language was peppered with phrases strongly charged with moral and ideological significance. Television treated the peace offensive largely as a matter of consensus, to which the injunctions of objective journalism did not apply. Here are a few excerpts:

ABC, January 4, 1966, Peter Jennings. Hanoi, commenting for the first time on the halt in U.S. bombing of North Vietnam, snapped that the U.S. had no right to make any conditions for ending the war except on Hanoi's terms. Ambassador Goldberg talked again of negotiating peace.

NBC, January 21, 1966, David Brinkley. As for the peace campaign, the Communist side has repeatedly called it a sham. If it is, they could come to the bargaining table and expose it. But they haven't.

Chet Huntley. The Communists in Vietnam demonstrated today that they attach no more solemnity to a truce than to their politics. [Huntley then reported on charges of violations of the Tet truce, which received prominent and dramatic coverage on all three networks that day. On the cease-fire, the *New York Times* reported, "Most cease-fire violations have been of 'minor significance,' a United States military communique said, and casualties suffered by allied forces have been light."[11]]

ABC, February 1, 1966, Jennings (making a transition between a report from the U.N. and another from Paris). The uncompromising position of North Vietnam was also made clear today in a different quarter....

Following the February 1 report from Paris, Jennings continued, "The stubborn defiance of the North Vietnamese leadership in Hanoi is often evident in the Communist prisoners captured in the South." Jennings then reported on North Vietnamese prisoners, being returned to the North in an exchange, who had thrown into the river packages given them as a "goodwill" gesture by the South Vietnamese. This kind of connection between different stories usually does not exist in newspaper coverage. It is one of the things that makes television a more ideological medium than the newspaper: television forces much more of the news into the unity of a story line—and therefore of a world view. . . .

TV and the prestige press perform very different political functions. The prestige press provides information to a politically interested audience; it therefore deals with *issues*. Television provides not just "headlines," as television people say, nor just entertainment, but ideological guidance and reassurance for the mass public. It therefore deals not so much with issues as with symbols that represent the basic values of the established political culture. This difference is certainly not absolute. Newspapers too can play the role of moralist; much of the *Times*'s coverage of Vietnam in the early 1960s, before Vietnam moved into the Sphere of Legitimate Controversy, did this, albeit in a more sophisticated way for its more sophisticated audience. And television has always been torn between a desire to belong to the inner circle of serious journalism and its other identity as storyteller-moralist. Since the mid-1960s the balance in television has shifted considerably toward "serious journalism," and the contrast between television and the press has narrowed. But in 1966 it was still very great, and it was therefore natural for television to focus on the good moral tale of the peace offensive, while the elite papers gave their attention to the growing policy debate.

NOTES

1. Interview with Tom Wicker (*New York Times*), New York, September 11, 1984.
2. Leon V. Sigal, *Reporters and Officials: The Organization and Politics of Newsmaking.* Lexington, MA: D.C. Heath, 1973, ch. 6.
3. Robert Weissberg, *Public Opinion and Popular Government.* Englewood Cliffs, N.J.: Prentice-Hall, 1976, 234–237.
4. See Michael Schudson, *Discovering the News: A Social History of American Newspapers.* New York: Basic Books, 1978, 144–159.
5. Johan Galtung and Marie Ruge, "The Structure of Foreign News: The Presentation of The Congo, Cuba and Cypress Crises in Four Foreign Newspapers." *Journal of International Peace Research* 1 (1965).
6. Peter Grose, "Sabotage Raids on North Confirmed by Saigon Aide," *New York Times,* July 23, 1964, p. 1.
7. *Pentagon Papers,* Senator Gravel, ed. Boston: Beacon Press, 1971, Vol. IV, p. 33.
8. Quoted in Edward Jay Epstein, *News From Nowhere.* New York: Vintage, 1974, p. 64.
9. Paul Weaver, "Newspaper News and Television News," in Douglass Cater and Richard P. Adler, eds., *Television as a Social Force.* New York: Praeger, 1975; Michael J. Robinson and Margaret A. Sheehan, *Over the Wire and on TV: UPI and CBS in Campaign '80.* New York: Russell Sage Foundation, 1983; Daniel C. Hallin and Paolo Mancini, "Speaking of the President: Political Structure and Representational Form in U.S. and Italian TV News," *Theory and Society* 13:6 (November 1984).
10. NBC, January 3, 1966.
11. "U.S. Officers Killed in Blast During Truce," *New York Times,* January 22, 1966, p. 1.

DISCUSSION QUESTIONS

1. What evidence do you see in today's news that journalists rely extensively on official sources for facts and interpretations of political events? Do reporters have other sources readily available that they could call on? Consider how recent news accounts of a subject that interests you would differ if journalists relied less on official sources.
2. Hallin says, "The decision to weight equally conflicting accounts of political reality is no less a political act than the decision to report only one." Consider whether journalists, in trying to provide a balanced view of events, may not give more prominence to an opposing view than a truly "objective" observer would.
3. Is Hallin correct when he argues that television is less strictly objective than the press? Compare news reports of a recent event on television with the accounts in the newspaper. Can television provide equally compelling "visuals" of competing sides to a controversy?
4. If media, attempting to be objective, rely extensively on official sources for news and comments, can they successfully play an adversarial role in their dealings with government? Would they be less or more critical of government than you would otherwise expect?

2. MEDIA AND THE PUBLIC AGENDA

Despite our different experiences, different backgrounds, and different interests, it is surprising that we agree as much as we do about the major issues facing us. Southerners and northerners, farmers and merchants, immigrants and natives may disagree strongly about government policy on concerns that affect them, but they share a consensus about the issues government should address. Naturally, the consensus is not perfect, and sometimes we experience more conflict than agreement. Nevertheless, it is still meaningful to speak of the public agenda as the list of issues about which the public is concerned.

In this selection, Christopher Bosso uses coverage of the Ethiopian famine to examine the impact of the mass media on the process whereby an issue gets put on the public agenda. Not every story the media run will stimulate such a response from you and me that we consider the issue raised one of the important concerns of the day, but many will. Similarly, some issues the media cover over time may lose some of their urgency; we may become less concerned with them. There may be, in other words, a cycle of public attention to issues around us. How media coverage affects that cycle is not yet clear. To what extent does media coverage bring issues to public attention? Does this case study present an exception or not?

Setting the Agenda: Mass Media and the Discovery of Famine in Ethiopia

Christopher J. Bosso

Whether mass media "change" public opinion is still debated, but few argue that they do affect what it is Americans pay attention to.[1] And how an issue is presented—both in words and pictures—has everything to do with whether and how well the public responds....[2]

Issues vault most readily into mass consciousness when they are socially significant, apparently nontechnical, defined broadly, and above all, emotional.[3] There is, of course, a law of novelty governing our attention to any condition, no matter how emotive. That famine ravaged sub-Saharan Africa during the early 1980s was a "dog bites man" story as far as many media elites were concerned, not unlike their responses to another overloaded ferry boat sinking on the Ganges or more bombs devastating neighborhoods in Beirut. Bad things happen and people get hurt, but unless the victims are Americans, events in foreign lands merit little space in our news when they occur frequently.

Famine in Ethiopia is a case in point. It was not "new" news, for the roots of the 1984 disaster lay in conditions known years before the disaster hit the headlines. Ethiopia has experienced food shortages almost annually since the famine of 1973–74 caused an estimated 200,000 deaths and led to the overthrow of Emperor Haile Selassie.... And Ethiopia was not alone. Despite billions in Western aid, most sub-Saharan African nations remained dependent on annual infusions of foreign food. Drought, soil erosion, population growth, misguided development strategies, errant aid programs, war, and, of course, politics—both domestic and foreign—all played a part in making sub-Saharan Africa the beggar of the world....

Intensified appeals by both the Ethiopian government and international relief agencies through 1983 finally did prompt some media attention and subsequent official concern....

Elite concern did not, however, translate into widespread media attention, even as the famine worsened. Not that access to Ethiopia was cut off: British and other European news crews managed repeatedly to gain entry, but American networks largely avoided the region. And, insofar as they were concerned, the story had little real "news" value anyway. The three commercial networks had few personnel on the continent to begin with, and yet another famine story would have to compete with "hotter" topics like South African apartheid or Libya's war with Chad. Foreign news makes up the smallest part of the daily network news offering to begin with, and Africa historically gets the least attention of all, so the threshold for attention was very high indeed....[4]

The Ethiopian famine thus was not a sudden catastrophe, the sort of seismic event that invariably draws media attention. It was instead a condition that

SOURCE: From "Setting the Agenda: Mass Media and the Discovery of Famine in Ethiopia" by Christopher J. Bosso. In *Manipulating Public Opinion: Essays on Public Opinion as a Dependent Variable* by Michael Margolis and Gary A. Mauser (eds.). Copyright ©1989 by Wadsworth, Inc. Reprinted by permission of Brooks/Cole Publishing Company, Pacific Grove, CA 93950.

developed over several years, predicted well in advance by a wide array of international relief agencies, and fully understood by those in government. But, for a variety of reasons, mostly political, aid only trickled in. Official U.S. aid did increase in late 1983, and it appeared that the administration was willing to do more, but there remained sharp internal disagreements over assisting a communist nation. What is more, these conflicts attracted little public attention. That it would emerge sharply and with an element of shocked surprise proved bitter to those who had worked hard to meet the challenge much earlier. "That was it," said Rep. Harold Wolpe (D., Mich.), who led a congressional delegation to Ethiopia in August 1983. "The facts were there for anyone who wanted to see them two years ago. To say that we were taken by surprise is only to say that we didn't want to see before."[5]

"DISCOVERING" FAMINE

"As a result of some dramatic series of events," [Anthony] Downs argues, "or for other reasons, the public suddenly becomes both aware of and alarmed about the evils of a particular problem." What results upsets the "normal" rhythms of politics in America. "This alarmed discovery," he continues, "is invariably accompanied by euphoric enthusiasm about society's ability to 'solve this problem,' or 'do something effective' within a relatively short time. The combination of alarm and confidence results in part from the strong public pressure in America for political leaders to claim that every problem can be 'solved.'"[6]

Public "discovery" of the Ethiopian famine fit this pattern, particularly because it was the sort of problem that apparently could be attacked without reordering domestic priorities. The problem affected "others," and was presented in such a way that an "easy" solution was in sight. Americans, once they perceived that millions were starving in a faraway land, could mount a national crusade to speed aid to the unfortunate. Results would be immediate: starving people would get food. The Ethiopian famine thus presented a perfect challenge for a society to mobilize on behalf of some apparently unadulterated good. How Americans became mobilized is instructive.

On Tuesday, October 23, 1984, and for three successive nights afterward, NBC News aired stunning footage of starving Ethiopians massed together in immense government feeding stations. NBC anchor Tom Brokaw reported that some 6 million were endangered, while about 500,000 probably would die within a year. The graphic pictures had an immediate impact: UNICEF, the international childrens' [sic] relief agency, reported over 5,000 telephone calls during the next four days. The Save the Children Fund received over 12,000 calls in the same period, plus pledges of close to $75,000. Catholic Relief Services, whose earlier appeals produced relatively little, reported over $2 million in a single month. "The switchboards were all lit up here all day long," reported one CRS official, alluding to the day after the first NBC report.[7] That Americans reacted to the NBC footage with alarm and generosity indicates the power of television to raise awareness of a previously "hidden" issue.

But such film existed long before NBC brought it to its viewers, and the story had been reported by various media during the previous year. David Kline, an American free-lance journalist, shot film of the famine in October 1983 while on assignment for CBS, but that network rejected the material because, as he later explained, it was not "strong enough." Kline offered the film to both

AFTER THE DELUGE: THE FAMINE IN LIMBO

... The problem of famine in Africa thus was "settled" so far as the public, and many of its leaders, were concerned. Mass attention to the famine had subsided by the time the relief bill reached President Reagan's desk, and public gaze would not sharpen again, save for the momentary spasm of interest generated by the media-infused Live Aid Concert.

By mid-1985 the disaster had slipped from the front pages and some of the "normal politics of famine relief began to reemerge. . . ."

Despite the massive [relief] effort, some one million Ethiopians died during 1984–85, though the number no doubt would have been higher had the disaster not gained international attention. . . .

Whether Americans in fact became bored with the famine as soon as media coverage patterns suggest is difficult to divine. One local Boston television reporter, who spent a great deal of time on the issue, suggested that "the media got tired of it before the people did. . . ."[17]

Whatever the case, the famine receded completely from the national agenda by mid-1986, as Downs might have predicted, to the point that the administration once again was accused of intending to divert African relief funds to finance economic assistance to Central America. . . .

CONCLUSION: THE WORLDS OUTSIDE AND THE IMAGES IN OUR HEADS

... Issues compete for attention, so the choices made by those in mass media as to what constitutes "news" are critical to both policymakers and the mass public. This case essentially examined how a condition that existed for many years became a "problem" to Americans, even though the famine did not affect them directly. It also demonstrated the almost serendipitous nature of how we learn about some problems, a reality that may shake any faith we may have about our capacity to address grave conditions systematically.

Only the timing of media response was largely random. In a larger sense, this case also demonstrated how an issue can be kept out of the public gaze when its particulars do not constitute novelty or when the victims are not on the "right" side politically. Problems can be defined away through media indifference, or through the capacity of government elites to influence our perceptions. Fortune dictated that most Americans learned about the famine relatively unadulterated by government "spin," but that a Tom Brokaw has the capacity to raise national awareness of an issue certainly raises questions about the role media elites play in our political life. . . .

There is little doubt that geopolitical considerations fell swiftly before the tornado of public concern for the victims. *Public opinion* may not direct government action, and its substance indeed may be dependent on the actions and words of political and media elites, but concerted *public attention* to an issue certainly narrows the range of options a government can take. To do anything *but* send aid would have appeared immoral so long as the media highlighted the story and so long as the public paid attention. . . .

[B]ouncing from one temporarily newsworthy problem to another . . . also bears further study. Do we really talk of public opinion, or *spasms of public attention?* The former is diffuse and often inconsequential, the latter more focused and powerful, but fleeting. . . .

[P]erhaps it is time we begin to look more closely at the quality of the alternatives presented to [the public] either by governments or those controlling various media.

NOTES

1. Benjamin I. Page, Robert Y. Shapiro, and Glenn R. Dempsey, "What Moves Public Opinion?" *American Political Science Review* 81:23–43 (1987).
2. Doris A. Graber, 1987.
3. Cobb and Elder, 1972, pp. 112–24.
4. Doris A. Graber, *Mass Media and American Politics*, 2nd ed. Washington, D.C.: CQ Press, 1984, p. 311.
5. *Washington Post*, November 21, 1984: A10.
6. Anthony Downs, 1972, p. 39.
7. *Washington Post*, November 21, 1984: A10.
8. William Boot, "Ethiopia: Feasting on Famine," *Columbia Journalism Review* (March/April 1985), p. 47.
9. Boot, 1985, p. 47.
10. *Washington Post*, November 21, 1984: A10.
11. Boot, 1985, p. 47; *Washington Post*, November 13, 1984: B3.
12. *Washington Post*, November 6, 1984: A17.
13. *Boston Globe*, April 28, 1985: B32.
14. *Washington Post*, November 21, 1984: A10.
15. *Washington Post*, October 31, 1984: A13.
16. *Congressional Quarterly Weekly Report*, April 20, 1985: 753.
17. Personal interview, June 1986.

DISCUSSION QUESTIONS

1. Account for U.S. policy toward Somalia since 1992 along the lines of the argument Bosso makes here. Did media attention place Somalia on the national agenda? Why do you say so?
2. Secretary of State Warren Christopher was quoted in 1993 to the effect that media coverage cannot be the "lodestar" of U.S. foreign policy. Assess his position. Do you agree or disagree? Why?
3. Take another issue, such as gun control or abortion, and attempt to explain the cycles of public attention. To what extent does media coverage explain why we are sometimes more concerned with an issue than at other times?
4. Try to explain why some issues get coverage but do not seem to rise high on the public agenda.
5. A group called Project Censored each year compiles a list of the ten most underreported stories of the year. Check your library's periodical indices to find the most recent of its listings and try to explain why some of these stories, important as most of them are, never reached the public agenda.

3. TELEVISION AND PRINT MEDIA

Superficially, the news we get from television and from newspapers seems quite similar; the same major stories are covered from the same locations. However, these media treat the news differently, and we respond differently. Here, Neil Postman takes a provocative position on the contrast between print and electronic media. He argues essentially that television, far from being a valuable source of information, actually gets in our way as we try to make sense of the world. Postman argues that newspapers can present more complex ideas and abstract notions than television can. Further, he suggests, how we approach these two media also differs. Who ever heard of someone reading the paper while washing dishes, for example?

Television has made a significant impact on our view of the world. Much of what we know about other locales, whether abroad or in other sections of the United States, has become vivid for us through the images we have seen on television: Without having been there, we can picture Berlin without the Wall and we can imagine rush hour in Tokyo. But Postman points out that television and its images brings us information without context, essentially information devoid of meaning and relevance. Print media, by contrast, engages our minds and forces us to think about what we read. Our discussions about important issues, public discourse in our society, are unavoidably affected by media presentations of those issues. For a generation raised on television, Postman's arguments compel us to assess the impact of media on our way of viewing the world, an assessment many of us find troubling. Is there evidence to support Postman's position?

Amusing Ourselves to Death
Neil Postman

"MEDIA AS EPISTEMOLOGY"

It is my intention in this [selection] to show that a great media-metaphor shift has taken place in America, with the result that the content of much of our public discourse has become dangerous, nonsense. With this in view, my task ... is straightforward. I must, first, demonstrate how, under the governance of the printing press, discourse in America was different from what it is now—generally coherent, serious and rational; and then how, under the gover-

SOURCE: From *Amusing Ourselves to Death* by Neil Postman. Copyright ©1985 by Neil Postman. Used by permission of Viking Penguin, a division of Penguin Books USA, Inc.

nance of television, it has become shriveled and absurd.

... [W]hat a culture means by intelligence is derived from the character of its important forms of communication. In a purely oral culture, intelligence is often associated with aphoristic ingenuity, that is, the power to invent compact sayings of wide applicability. The wise Solomon, we are told in First Kings, knew three thousand proverbs. In a print culture, people with such a talent are thought to be quaint at best, more likely pompous bores. . . .

Although the general character of print-intelligence would be known to anyone who would be reading this book, you may arrive at a reasonably detailed definition of it by simply considering what is demanded of you *as you read this book.* You are required, first of all, to remain more or less immobile for a fairly long time. If you cannot do this (with this or any other book), our culture may label you as anything from hyperkinetic to undisciplined; in any case, as suffering from some sort of intellectual deficiency. The printing press makes rather stringent demands on our bodies as well as our minds. Controlling your body is, however, only a minimal requirement. You must also have learned to pay no attention to the shapes of the letters on the page. You must see through them, so to speak, so that you can go directly to the meanings of the words they form. If you are preoccupied with the shapes of the letters, you will be an intolerably inefficient reader, likely to be thought stupid. If you have learned how to get to meanings without aesthetic distraction, you are required to assume an attitude of detachment and objectivity. This includes your bringing to the task what Bertrand Russell called an "immunity to eloquence," meaning that you are able to distinguish between the sensuous pleasure, or charm, or ingratiating tone (if such there be) of the words, and the logic of their argument. But at the same time, you must be able to tell from the tone of the language what is the author's attitude toward the subject and toward the reader. You must, in other words, know the difference between a joke and an argument. And in judging the quality of an argument, you must be able to do several things at once, including delaying a verdict until the entire argument is finished, holding in mind questions until you have determined where, when or if the text answers them, and bringing to bear on the text all of your relevant experience as a counterargument to what is being proposed. You must also be able to withhold those parts of your knowledge and experience which, in fact, do not have a bearing on the argument. And in preparing yourself to do all of this, you must have divested yourself of the belief that words are magical and, above all, have learned to negotiate the world of abstractions, for there are very few phrases and sentences in this book that require you to call forth concrete images. In a print-culture, we are apt to say of people who are not intelligent that we must "draw them pictures" so that they may understand. Intelligence implies that one can dwell comfortably without pictures, in a field of concepts and generalizations.

To be able to do all of these things, and more, constitutes a primary definition of intelligence in a culture whose notions of truth are organized around the printed word. . . .

"THE TYPOGRAPHIC MIND"

... What are the implications for public discourse of a written, or typographic, metaphor? What is the character of its content? What does it demand of the public? What uses of the mind does it favor?

One must begin, I think, by pointing to the obvious fact that the written word, and an oratory based upon it, *has a content*: a semantic, paraphrasable, propositional content. This may sound odd, but since I shall be arguing soon enough that much of our discourse today has only a marginal propositional content, I must stress the point here. Whenever language is the principal medium of communication—especially language controlled by the rigors of print—an idea, a fact, a claim is the inevitable result. The idea may be banal, the fact irrelevant, the claim false, but there is no escape from meaning when language is the instrument guiding one's thought. Though one may accomplish it from time to time, it is very hard to say nothing when employing a written English sentence. What else is exposition good for? Words have very little to recommend them except as carriers of meaning. The shapes of written words are not especially interesting to look at. Even the sounds of sentences of spoken words are rarely engaging except when composed by those with extraordinary poetic gifts. If a sentence refuses to issue forth a fact, a request, a question, an assertion, an explanation, it is nonsense, a mere grammatical shell. As a consequence a language-centered discourse such as was characteristic of eighteenth- and nineteenth-century America tends to be both content-laden and serious, all the more so when it takes its form from print.

It is serious because meaning demands to be understood. A written sentence calls upon its author to say something, upon its reader to know the import of what is said. And when an author and reader are struggling with semantic meaning, they are engaged in the most serious challenge to the intellect. This is especially the case with the act of reading, for authors are not always trustworthy. They lie, they become confused, they overgeneralize, they abuse logic and, sometimes, common sense. The reader must come armed, in a serious state of intellectual readiness. This is not easy because he comes to the text alone. In reading, one's responses are isolated, one's intellect thrown back on its own resources. To be confronted by the cold abstractions of printed sentences is to look upon language bare, without the assistance of either beauty or community. Thus, reading is by its nature a serious business. It is also, of course, an essentially rational activity....

To understand the role that the printed word played in providing an earlier America with its assumptions about intelligence, truth and the nature of discourse, one must keep in view that the act of reading in the eighteenth and nineteenth centuries had an entirely different quality to it than the act of reading does today. For one thing, ... the printed word had a monopoly on both attention and intellect, there being no other means, besides the oral tradition, to have access to public knowledge. Public figures were known largely by their written words, for example, not by their looks or even their oratory. It is quite likely that most of the first fifteen presidents of the United States would not have been recognized had they passed the average citizen in the street. This would have been the case as well of the great lawyers, ministers and scientists of that era. To think about those men was to think about what they had written, to judge them by their public positions, their arguments, their knowledge as codified in the printed word. You may get some sense of how we are separated from this kind of consciousness by thinking about any of our recent presidents; or even preachers, lawyers and scientists who are or who have recently been public figures. Think of Richard Nixon or Jimmy Carter or Billy Graham, or even Albert Einstein, and what will come to your mind is an image, a picture of a face, most likely a face on a television screen (in Einstein's case, a photograph of a face). Of words, almost nothing will come to mind. This is the difference between thinking in a word-centered culture and thinking in an image-centered culture....

Almost anywhere one looks in the eighteenth and nineteenth centuries, then, one finds the resonances of the printed word and, in particular, its inextricable relationship to all forms of public expression. It may be true, as Charles Beard wrote, that the primary motivation of the writers of the United States Constitution was the protection of their economic interests. But it is also true that they assumed that participation in public life required the capacity to negotiate the printed word. To them, mature citizenship was not conceivable without sophisticated literacy, which is why the voting age in most states was set at twenty-one, and why Jefferson saw in universal education America's best hope. And that is also why, as Allan Nevins and Henry Steele Commager have pointed out, the voting restrictions against those who owned no property were frequently overlooked, but not one's inability to read.

It may be true, as Frederick Jackson Turner wrote, that the spirit that fired the American mind was the fact of an ever-expanding frontier. But it is also true, as Paul Anderson has written, that "it is no mere figure of speech to say that farm boys followed the plow with book in hand, be it Shakespeare, Emerson, or Thoreau."[1] For it was not only a frontier mentality that led Kansas to be the first state to permit women to vote in school elections, or Wyoming the first state to grant complete equality in the franchise. Women were probably more adept readers than men, and even in the frontier states the principal means of public discourse issued from the printed word. Those who could read had, inevitably, to become part of the conversation.

It may also be true, as Perry Miller has suggested, that the religious fervor of Americans provided much of their energy; or, as earlier historians told it, that America was created by an idea whose time had come. I quarrel with none of these explanations. I merely observe that the America they try to explain was dominated by a public discourse which took its form from the products of the printing press. For two centuries, America declared its intentions, expressed its ideology, designed its laws, sold its products, created its literature and addressed its deities with black squiggles on white paper. It did its talking in typography, and with that as the main feature of its symbolic environment rose to prominence in world civilization.

The name I give to that period of time during which the American mind submitted itself to the sovereignty of the printing press is the Age of Exposition. Exposition is a mode of thought, a method of learning, and a means of expression. Almost all of the characteristics we associate with mature discourse were amplified by typography, which has the strongest possible bias toward exposition: a sophisticated ability to think conceptually, deductively and sequentially; a high valuation of reason and order; an abhorrence of contradiction; a large capacity for detachment and objectivity; and a tolerance for delayed response. Toward the end of the nineteenth century, ... the Age of Exposition began to pass, and the early signs of its replacement could be discerned. Its replacement was to be the Age of Show Business.

"NOW ... THIS."

The American humorist H. Allen Smith once suggested that of all the worrisome words in the English language, the scariest is "'uh oh,' as when a physician looks at your X-rays, and with knitted brow says, 'Uh oh.'" I should like to suggest that the words which are the title of this [section] are as ominous as any, all the more so because they are spoken without knitted brow—indeed, with a kind of idiot's delight. The phrase, if that's what it may be called, adds to our grammar a new part of speech, a conjunction that does not connect anything to anything but does the opposite: separates everything from everything. As such, it serves as a compact metaphor for the discontinuities in so much that passes for public discourse in present-day America.

"Now . . . this" is commonly used on radio and television newscasts to indicate that what one has just heard or seen has no relevance to what one is about to hear or see, or possibly to anything one is ever likely to hear or see. The phrase is a means of acknowledging the fact that the world as mapped by the speeded-up electronic media has no order or meaning and is not to be taken seriously. There is no murder so brutal, no earthquake so devastating, no political blunder so costly—for that matter, no ball score so tantalizing or weather report so threatening—that it cannot be erased from our minds by a newscaster saying, "Now . . . this." The newscaster means that you have thought long enough on the previous matter (approximately forty-five seconds), that you must not be morbidly pre-occupied with it (let us say, for ninety seconds), and that you must now give your attention to another fragment of news or a commercial.

Television did not invent the "Now . . . this" world view. . . . But it is through television that it has been nurtured and brought to a perverse maturity. For on television, nearly every half hour is a discrete event, separated in content, context, and emotional texture from what precedes and follows it. In part because television sells its time in seconds and minutes, in part because television must use images rather than words, in part because its audience can move freely to and from the television set, programs are structured so that almost each eight-minute segment may stand as a complete event in itself. Viewers are rarely required to carry over any thought or feeling from one parcel of time to another.

Of course, in television's presentation of the "news of the day," we may see the "Now . . . this" mode of discourse in its boldest and most embarrassing form. For there, we are presented not only with fragmented news but news without context, without consequences, without value, and therefore without essential seriousness; that is to say, news as pure entertainment. . . .

All television news programs begin, end, and are somewhere in between punctuated with music. I have found very few Americans who regard this custom as peculiar, which fact I have taken as evidence for the dissolution of lines of demarcation between serious public discourse and entertainment. What has music to do with the news? Why is it there? It is there, I assume, for the same reason music is used in theater and films—to create a mood and provide a leitmotif for the entertainment. If there were no music—as is the case when any television program is interrupted for a news flash—viewers would expect something truly alarming, possibly life-altering. But as long as the music is there as a frame for the program, the viewer is comforted to believe that there is nothing to be greatly alarmed about; that, in fact, the events that are reported have as much relation to reality as do scenes in a play.

This perception of a news show as a stylized dramatic performance whose content has been staged largely to entertain is reinforced by several other features, including the fact that the average length of any story is forty-five seconds. While brevity does not always suggest triviality, in this case it clearly does. It is simply not possible to convey a sense of seriousness about any event if its implications are exhausted in less than one minute's time. In fact, it is quite obvious that TV news has no intention of suggesting that any story *has* any implications, for that would require viewers to continue to think about it when it is done and therefore obstruct their attending to the next story that waits panting in the wings. In any case, viewers are not provided with much opportunity to be distracted from the next story since in all likelihood it will consist of some film footage. Pictures have little difficulty in overwhelming words, and short-circuiting introspection. [Television producers] would be certain to give both prominence and precedence to any event for which there is some sort of visual documentation. A suspected killer being brought into a police station, the angry face of a cheated consumer, a barrel going over Niagara Falls (with a person alleged to be in it), the President disembarking from a helicopter on the White House lawn—these are always fascinating or amusing, and easily satisfy the requirements of an entertaining show. It is, of course, not necessary that the visuals actually document the point of a story. Neither is it necessary to explain why such images are intruding themselves on public consciousness. Film footage justifies itself, as every television producer well knows.

It is also of considerable help in maintaining a high level of unreality that the newscasters do not pause to grimace or shiver when they speak their prefaces or epilogs to the film clips. Indeed, many newscasters do not appear to grasp the meaning of what they are saying, and some hold to a fixed and ingratiating enthusiasm as they report on earthquakes, mass killings and other disasters. Viewers would be quite disconcerted by any show of concern or terror on the part of the newscasters. Viewers, after all, are partners with the newscasters in the "Now . . . this" culture, and they expect the newscaster to play out his or her role as a character who is marginally serious but who stays well clear of authentic understanding. The viewers, for their part, will not be caught contaminating their responses with a sense of reality, any more than an audience at a play would go scurrying to call home because a character on stage has said that a murderer is loose in the neighborhood.

The viewers also know that no matter how grave any fragment of news may appear (for example, on the day I write a Marine Corps general has declared that nuclear war between the United States and Russia is inevitable), it will shortly be followed by a series of commercials that will, in an instant, defuse the import of the news, in fact render it largely banal. This is a key element in the structure of a news program and all by itself refutes any claim that television news is designed as a serious form of public discourse. Imagine what you would think of me, and this book, if I were to pause here, tell you that I will return to my discussion in a moment, and then proceed to write a few words in behalf of United Airlines or the Chase Manhattan Bank. You would rightly think that I had no respect for you and, certainly, no respect for the subject. And if I did this not once but several times each chapter, you would think the whole enterprise unworthy of your attention. Why, then, do we not think a news story similarly unworthy? The reason, I believe, it that whereas we expect books and even other media (such as film) to maintain a consistency of tone and a continuity of content, we have no such expectation of television, and especially television news. We have become so accustomed to its discontinuities that we are no longer struck dumb, as any sane person would be, by a newscaster who having just reported that a nuclear war is inevitable goes on to say that he will be right back after this word from Burger

King; who says, in other words, "Now... this." One can hardly overestimate the damage that such juxtapositions do to our sense of the world as a serious place. The damage is especially massive to youthful viewers who depend so much on television for their clues as to how to respond to the world. In watching television news, they, more than any other segment of the audience, are drawn into an epistemology based on the assumption that all reporters of cruelty and death are greatly exaggerated and, in any case, not to be taken seriously or responded to sanely.

... The result of all this is that Americans are the best entertained and quite likely the least well-informed people in the Western world. I say this in the face of the popular conceit that television, as a window to the world, has made Americans exceedingly well informed. Much depends here, of course, on what is meant by being informed. I will pass over the now tiresome polls that tell us that, at any given moment, 70 percent of our citizens do not know who is the Secretary of State or the Chief Justice of the Supreme Court. Let us consider, instead, the case of Iran during the drama that was called the "Iran Hostage Crisis." I don't suppose there has been a story in years that received more continuous attention from television. We may assume, then, that Americans know most of what there is to know about this unhappy event. And now, I put these questions to you: Would it be an exaggeration to say that not one American in a hundred knows what language the Iranians speak? Or what the word "Ayatollah" means or implies? Or knows any details of the tenets of Iranian religious beliefs? Or the main outlines of their political history? Or knows who the Shah was, and where he came from?

Nonetheless, everyone had an opinion about this event, for in America everyone is entitled to an opinion, and it is certainly useful to have a few when a pollster shows up. But these are opinions of a quite different order from eighteenth- or nineteenth-century opinions. It is probably more accurate to call them emotions rather than opinions, which would account for the fact that they change from week to week, as the pollsters tell us. What is happening here is that television is altering the meaning of "being informed" by creating a species of information that might properly be called *disinformation.* I am using this word almost in the precise sense in which it is used by spies in the CIA or KGB. Disinformation does not mean false information. It means misleading information—misplaced, irrelevant, fragmented or superficial information—information that creates the illusion of knowing something but which in fact leads one away from knowing. In saying this, I do not mean to imply that television news deliberately aims to deprive Americans of a coherent, contextual understanding of their world. I mean to say that when news is packaged as entertainment, that is the inevitable result. And in saying that the television news show entertains but does not inform, I am saying something far more serious than that we are being deprived of authentic information. I am saying we are losing our sense of what it means to be well-informed. Ignorance is always correctable. But what shall we do if we take ignorance to be knowledge?

... My point is that we are by now so thoroughly adjusted to the "Now ... this" world of news—a world of fragments, where events stand alone, stripped of any connection to the past, or to the future, or to other events—that all assumptions of coherence have vanished. And so, perforce, has contradiction. In the context of *no context,* so to speak, it simply disappears. And in its absence, what possible interest could there be in a list of what the President says *now* and what he said *then?* It is merely a rehash of old news, and there is nothing interesting or entertaining in that. The only thing to be amused about is the bafflement of reporters at the public's indifference. There is an irony in the fact that the very group that has taken the world apart should, on trying to piece it together again, be surprised that no one notices much, or cares.

... I do not mean that the trivialization of public information is all accomplished *on* television. I mean that television is the paradigm for our conception of public information. As the printing press did in an earlier time, television has achieved the power to define the form in which news must come, and it has also defined how we shall respond to it. In presenting news to us packaged as vaudeville, television induces other media to do the same, so that the total information environment begins to mirror television.

... And so, we move rapidly into an information environment which may rightly be called trivial pursuit. As the game of that name uses facts as a source of amusement, so do our sources of news. It has been demonstrated many times that a culture can survive misinformation and false opinion. It has not yet been demonstrated whether a culture can survive if it takes the measure of the world in twenty-two minutes. Or if the value of its news is determined by the number of laughs it provides.

NOTE

1. Paul Anderson, *Platonism in the Midwest*. Philadelphia: Temple University Publications, 1963, p. 17.

DISCUSSION QUESTIONS

1. According to Postman, how is the Age of Exposition different from the Age of Show Business? Do you agree with his categorization of these periods?

2. Watch a network or local television news broadcast tonight; then consider how much of the format (the way the news is presented) reflects entertainment rather than news values. Is Postman correct about television news trivializing events?

3. Does Postman discount the impact of television images on our understanding of the world around us? How would you, as a member of the generation raised on television and first educated by "Sesame Street," answer him?

4. Compare how your local newspaper and local television station reported the same news; do the similarities and differences correspond to what Postman would lead you to expect? In what ways?

4. FRAMING THE NEWS

When journalists report the news, they unavoidably place it in a context. A vote on a bill before the House of Representatives may be presented as a measure of presidential support; a bureaucratic regulation may be seen as a sign of the growth of government; a state's revision of welfare policy may be put forward as an example for other states to consider. Context then gives us both a way to interpret an event, to find meaning in it, and a way to evaluate it, to come to a decision about it. Reporters generally have a great deal of leeway in their choice of contexts. Communications scholars refer to these choices as "framing" judgments. How a report is framed potentially influences how the public responds to it.

In the selection below, Robert Entman and Andrew Rojecki investigate how the *New York Times* and *Time* magazine framed their reports about the nuclear freeze movement in the early 1980s. This movement could have been seen as an outpouring of real concern about an important issue, or it could have been seen as a later manifestation of 1960s style protests. It could have been portrayed as serious with a realistic outlook on the question, or it could have been portrayed as either idealistic and out of touch or cynical, serving the interests of its leaders. The section reprinted here concerns how these media outlets framed the news about the nuclear freeze movement to make it seem less "mainstream" and less serious than it really was. Is it possible for media to be totally "objective"?

Freezing Out the Public

Robert M. Entman and Andrew Rojecki

We find several kinds of judgments apparently made by journalists that filter into the news and, in turn, likely affect the [anti-nuclear] movement's ability to build consensus and mobilize participation. These we call journalists' framing judgments, which journalists make in the course of selecting and conveying information about the movement. The judgments, we believe, are heavily influenced by elite sources and, it appears, by an underlying professional ideology ambivalent toward public participation: Although in theory supportive of mass involvement, the coverage suggests journalists harbor suspicions of mass movements once they organize to exert political power....

Our analysis of the U.S. anti-nuclear movement suggests seven evaluative dimensions of news messages that are likely to affect a movement's ability to garner public support and shape elites' calculations. These messages arise out of subjective framing judgments that journalists seem to make in the course of selecting and conveying information:

1. Rationality-emotionality: whether the movement is driven by intellectually sound policy ideas as opposed to emotionality.
2. Expertise: whether the movement has the technical capacity to analyze and recommend valid policy.
3. Public support: how many Americans agree with movement goals.

SOURCE: Excerpted from *Political Communication*, Vol. 10, No. 2 (April-June 1993), Robert M. Entman and Andrew Rojecki, Taylor & Francis, Washington, D.C. Reproduced with permission. All rights reserved.

4. Partisanship: whether movement participants seek to influence policy through the use of political strategy and power.
5. Unity: the degree of agreement among those pursuing the movement goal.
6. Extremism: whether participants deviate from the mainstream.
7. Power: whether the movement is likely to influence government policy.

The particular impact of these framing judgments arises from their unequal application. In Edelman's words, the media's framing means that "what is prominently displayed, what is repressed, and ... how observations are classified"[1] differs dramatically for the nuclear freeze movement as compared with government elites. Journalists consistently assessed the movement and mass opinion but were far less diligent and singular in their critiques of the Reagan administration officials and Congress members who made decisions about the movement's proposal. That is, the media in general belittled the public and its involvement, whereas critiques of elite opinion were rare, muted, and inconsistent in freeze coverage. The only dimension in which elites faced frequent negative judgments was unity. . . .

Throughout, we attempt to show both how the nuclear freeze movement was framed and how similar and plausible framing judgments about elites were generally not conveyed. In analyzing frames, it is as necessary to identify omissions in coverage as inclusions.[2] Describing voids in the news requires us to include critical observations about the Reagan administration; these should not be taken as a blanket endorsement of the freeze or condemnation of the administration. In retrospect, it seems reasonable to argue that the path to nuclear arms reduction that the government actually took turned out to work better than a freeze would have. Our purpose is not to praise *The Nuclear Freeze Movement* but to generate theoretical insight.

THE NUCLEAR FREEZE MOVEMENT

Turning now to the case, here is a word about the movement. It was started by Randall Forsberg, an M.I.T. Ph.D. in military policy and arms control, who believed it was possible to force debate on Congress and the executive if grass roots peace groups and, especially, the American middle class could be mobilized. In December, 1979, Forsberg succeeded in convincing a national convention of peace groups to unite around her draft proposal, an argument for a bilateral, technically verifiable freeze based on an analysis of American and Soviet weapons that, she argued, would leave both sides at net parity of strength. A national campaign was organized and Randy Kehler was appointed as its head. Other groups like Physicians for Social Responsibility, Federation of American Scientists, and Union of Concerned Scientists appeared later, including Ground Zero, a nonpartisan organization seeking to educate Americans on the effects of nuclear war, led by former National Security Council staffer Roger Molander.

The public peak of the movement was a massive rally in June, 1982, that brought 750,000 people to New York City to demonstrate on the eve of a United Nations session, apparently the largest political demonstration in U.S. history. A few months earlier, in March 1982, Senator Edward Kennedy (D. MA) and others had introduced freeze resolutions in Congress. During the congressional debate, the movement came under attack by the Reagan administration, which claimed that a freeze would lock in Soviet superiority and that the movement itself was supported by KGB funding.

... One of the freeze movement's distinguishing characteristics was its mainstream base of support. Freeze strategists made it a point to eschew any hint of radical symbolism or threat to the system's core values or legitimacy that the media could exaggerate. Public opinion in favor of the freeze remained high during and beyond this period. Indeed, Gallup polls showed freeze support increasing from 71% to 78% between 1983 and 1984, the very period during which the media implicitly declared the movement dead. This wide support does not belie the hypothesized dampening effect on the movement but rather suggests precisely how the media help to disconnect public opinion and participation from pressure on government and thereby to encourage a symbolic response. In fact, what makes this an interesting case theoretically is the contrast between it and the 1960s war movement. The freeze movement was moderate in tone and adult and middle class in leadership; equally important, overwhelming majorities of the public seemed to approve it in polls. Strictly on the basis of public support and moderation, we might expect coverage of the freeze to be more sympathetic than that of the 1960s peace movement, which in a variety of ways, Gitlin found, news frames tended to trivialize, discount, and marginalize. . . .[3]

The data for the study came from the NEXIS database of all *New York Times* and *Time* magazine stories between 1980 and 1983—the life span of the movement—in which the term *nuclear freeze* appeared in close juxtaposition to the word *movement*. Hereafter, to avoid confusion, we call the *Times* "NYT." Separate searches were also conducted for specific coverage of two key movement events: Ground Zero Week and the New York City demonstration, both held in the spring of 1982. Guided by the previous research of Gitlin on radical movements and of Bennett on the marginalization of public opinion,[4] we conducted a quantitative and qualitative analysis of the themes and frames used to describe the movement, systematically searching for uses of the seven framing judgments as well as decisions on who spoke for the movement and whether the aim was to convey its substantive reasoning. . . .

MARGINALIZING THE MOVEMENT

Ground Zero week and the New York City demonstration comprised the public zenith of the American freeze movement. During these events, public participation was at its most focused, providing the press with a variety of news pegs on which to hang their frames. As we shall see, however, the emphases are on the whimsical and bizarre, thus repressing the partisan or political elements and goals of the movement and diminishing its likely effectiveness.

New York Times

In NYT stories on Ground Zero, published the week of April 17, 1982, [Roger] Molander pushed the apolitical theme. He avoids a position on the freeze except to say that arms agreements with the Soviets are less important than trust between the two superpowers. The absence of a defined political strategy and goal makes Ground Zero an appealing diversion—even President Reagan supports it. The proclaimed mission of GZ is merely to make people aware of the destructiveness of nuclear weapons, which is hardly a matter for debate. Some of the GZ articles mention public empowerment but the overall thrust is to discourage participation. In an April 17 story, for example, Molander is quoted as saying that he has "confidence" in the public" (p. 8). Nevertheless, the antipartisan theme surfaces in a front-page GZ story (April 18), which notes that many freeze advocates favor directly political action but goes on that others "acknowledged the possibility that entering the political process as a lobbying group might fragment the movement, which has been growing rapidly" (p. 1).

Nearly one third of the front-page article on Ground Zero is a catalog of whimsical events of that week. These include a run-for-your-life race in which participants prove that people cannot outrun the blast wave of an exploding nuclear weapon, a bicycle fallout marathon, a hot-air balloon launch over Lawrence Livermore Laboratory, puppets-for-peace shows in Albuquerque, and a "swim-for-peace" by a seal to demonstrate that animals are no better equipped than humans to survive a nuclear war. Such coverage tends to trivialize organized mass application of political power to advance a defined policy objective.

The following week, the NYT covers New York City GZ events. Nearly half of this coverage also emphasizes the sideshow activities, against which is oddly juxtaposed mention of elite support for the movement. . . .

The focus on education is lauded by both publications, but their coverage of the freeze events serves ironically not to educate readers about the substantive case made but about the carnival-like atmosphere of the demonstrations. For example, in its front-page coverage of the June 12 freeze demonstration of 750,000—in an article nearly 1,700 words long—the NYT makes only two brief references to the speeches given at the rally in Central Park. The greater part of the article—replete with references to the 1960s—focuses on the logistics of moving the crowd and descriptions of the participants. By highlighting logistics and "color," the coverage disembodies the march from its political purpose, illustrating the antipartisan framing judgment and paralleling Gitlin's finding on the 1960s.[5] At the same time the coverage renders quite difficult achievement of the event's chief aim: conveying information about nuclear arms policy through media that might mobilize involvement of freeze supporters outside the movement. The antagonism toward partisan political activity by an organized mass movement also misleadingly implies that the Reagan administration's arms policies are uninfluenced by its own political calculations and partisan interests, thereby cloaking it in the legitimizing mantle of nonpartisanship.

Accompanying editorial commentary places the movement in a double bind: As it gains widespread support, it is charged with a variety of political sins that accompany popularity; yet had it not gained such support it would have remained politically impotent. In its editorial on the day of the march, the NYT acknowledges the widespread support of the American public for the freeze but says that "the very size and fervor of this movement makes it inarticulate" (June 13, 1982, p. 22). It cautions the public to come to terms with the intellectual issues surrounding arms control: "The nuclear nations still have much to learn from citizens who march and mobilize—if those citizens now master the arcane vocabulary and logic of stable deterrence. Anxiety is not enough" (June 13, 1982, p. 22).

This quote illustrates two imbalanced framing judgments that coverage frequently makes, asserting that the freeze analysis emerges from emotion not rationality and questioning the movement's expertise while making no such assessment of administration officials. The media focus on the fears of freeze participants rather than on the rationally defensible policy designed by well-credentialed experts that aim to reduce the danger.

By contrast, the highest levels of the Reagan administration were heavily populated with members of the Committee on the Present Danger (CPD), a sort of elite-level social movement. The Committee had been established in the mid-1970s by Norman Podhoretz, Paul Nitze, and Eugene Rostow, who recruited a number of conservative intellectuals to develop a counterweight to detente, which they considered dangerous to American interests. CPD publications and statements made alarming assertions about nuclear war and American vulnerability; the very name seemed designed to invoke and provoke anxiety. The CPD warned that the Soviets aimed to achieve nuclear superiority over the United States and believed they could vanquish the nation in a nuclear war. A CPD member himself, Ronald Reagan appointed over 50 CPD colleagues to key government positions.[6] The CPD's empirical claims on Soviet strength and intentions and U.S. weakness were seriously challenged by many defense analysts,[7] but media coverage of the freeze overlooks the anxious tone and the problematic quality of evidence animating CPD analyses, perhaps because of its elite status. President Reagan's (occasionally reported) ignorance of specific weapons systems and other policy details is not used in freeze movement stories to question whether he possesses sufficient expertise to serve as final arbiter of American policy.

... Characterizations of the public's but not the administration's rationality, treating only public views as significantly rooted in fearful emotion, delegitimizes the impact of the freeze movement or its proposal on Reagan and his officials. We counted all references to "fear," "worry," or "anxiety" (and cognates) linked to the public and those linked to elites. ... The bulk of the fear, anxiety, or worry is attributed to the public. The news repeatedly portrays the pro-freeze public as driven by these negative emotional reactions to nuclear horror.

Time

Time covers Ground Zero Week (April 17–24, 1982) in a short article. The writer refers to the sponsor, Roger Molander, as a man of reason and the article lauds him for his "deliberately low-key approach" (*Time*, May 3, 1982, p. 21). Nevertheless, the story describes mixed and somewhat disappointing results of GZ events (spotty turnout). Near the conclusion, the article reiterates Molander's opposition to a specific freeze proposal and mentions the administration's objections.

The magazine devotes coverage to the New York City freeze demonstration (June 13, 1982) before and after the event. The "before" story focuses on logistics and preparations and reiterates the frames developed over the previous 3 months. It uses the absence of the freeze opponent Molander—whom it had certified as a freeze leader despite his opposition—to conclude that the movement was in trouble.

Unlike the antiwar protesters of a decade ago, most of whom were young, white and middle-class, the freeze movement has attracted followers from across the socioeconomic spectrum. So far, this has been a source of vitality and political strength. But with upwards of 100 organizations either participating in this weekend's rally or lending their support, divisions have inevitably begun to appear.

Notably absent on June 12, for instance, will be representatives of the Washington, D.C.–based Ground

Zero, which has done much to stir national concern over nuclear arms. Explains Founder Roger Molander: "We are trying to maintain our character as an education organization, not a political organization or advocacy group" (*Time,* June 14, 1982, p. 14).

The story concludes that the rally "poses serious risks":

> If the demonstrators seem too radical, or even a little kooky, the antinuclear coalition could lose some of its broad-based support. Moreover, now that President Reagan has announced that a new round of strategic-arms talks with the Soviets will begin June 29, the movement could lose its momentum (p. 14).

Here, the frame, rooted in judgments of partisanship, rationality, unity, and extremism, is staked out to exclude those who are too radical or kooky, and once more assessments are imbalanced. Reagan's supporters demonstrably include radical conservatives well outside the mainstream[8]; such coalition partners are not used to delegitimize the Reagan position. Also, note that the freeze's political strength is here measured by its public support, without mention that polls show the administration's position to be weak by that standard.

One week later, when the afterdemonstration story appears, it is shorter and less prominent (p. 24 vs. p. 14). Recalling that this was the largest political demonstration in U.S. history, such placement illustrates how framing judgments of a movement's power and rationality can affect critical decisions on story play. The opening paragraph of the story condenses subsequent themes:

> There is something about emotionally charged political movements: until they mobilize enormous crowds of adherents in one place on one day, they do not feel quite bona fide. Last weekend in New York City, the diffuse U.S. antinuclear arms movement produced its first such mass spectacle when 15,000 protesters paraded past the nearly empty United Nations complex and then joined 350,000 more compatriots for a rally-cum-concert in Central Park. The Saturday demonstration, New York's largest ever, was well planned and peaceful (*Time,* June 21, 1982, p. 24).

The major theme emphasizes the movement's lack of power, an image of impotence reinforced by the description of an "emotionally charged" and "diffuse" event that was a "mass spectacle." The article describes the seemingly empty gesture of parading past a nearly vacant United Nations building, trivializes it as a "rally-cum-concert," and belittles its public support by reporting participation at less than half the police estimate, calling it New York's rather than the nation's largest-ever demonstration.

Two short paragraphs describe the speakers and speeches at the rally including William Sloan Coffin, Coretta King, Orson Welles, and Randall Forsberg (characterized as one of several speakers taking a "pointedly political tack," *Time,* June 21, 1982, p. 24). The article then describes some of the participants in the rally, part of what *Time* calls an "earnest horde." Like the NYT, the newsmagazine story focuses on the whimsical activities of unusual participants as well as the more serious minded who threaten to shut down the United Nations for a day.

Recall that the article of the previous week had set up a "kooky" test for the rally participants: if too many were perceived as being extreme or unusual, the movement might lose its momentum. The coverage then emphasizes just these features and neglects the substance of the movement and the demeanor of its majority. Additionally, the coverage includes repeated references to the New Left movement of the 1960s. In total, there are 72 invocations of Vietnam-era symbolic language in *Time*'s freeze coverage over the 3 years studied. These includes such explicit references as "1960s," "peaceniks," "Vietnam," and "protest" as well as implicit symbols such as "guitars," "concerts," and "dances." These descriptors implicitly equate this mainstream movement to one depicted as extreme, calling forth 1960s schematic understandings or stereotypes for the quite distinct freeze. Even if polls show the public mostly supports the freeze proposal despite such coverage, this treatment delegitimizes mass participation in a political movement that would pressure leaders to respond more than symbolically; in this way the coverage also discourages the institutionalization (long-term survival) of the freeze movement. Media coverage helps to isolate the freeze movement from its wide political base and from public opinion, misrepresenting the public to itself.

There is irony here: The movement reaches and overtly demonstrates its peak and by so doing apparently creates an elite backlash that leads to the movement's and the proposal's downfall. Echoing the theme of the NYT editorial discussed above, *Time*'s editors invoke the same double bind in which a broad base of support is paradoxically diagnosed as a liability, registering journalists' framing judgment on the movement's unity:

> The broad appeal of the antinuclear arms movement, which up to now had been its main strength, may have become its most serious weakness. With so many constituents to please, the movement seems uncertain about what to do next (*Time,* June 28, 1982, p. 37).

The same article supplies no supporting evidence for this negative perspective; no movement leaders are quoted. However, Roger Molander—again, a freeze opponent—is quoted. Described as "the single most visible and thoughtful leader in the nebulous movement," and the leader of "a scrupulously nonpartisan antinuclear education campaign" who understands that "it is hard for an impassioned mass movement to accommodate either slow practical progress or technical complexity," Molander is permitted a long quote in which he says that "thoughtful people" don't know the answer. In this way the Molander quote suggests that the movement and its public supporters are not thoughtful (perhaps not rational) and lack sufficient expertise legitimately to speak on this complex issue.

Picking up this theme of insufficient expertise, the article continues and develops what is to become the dominant theme—first articulated in the *Times* editorial—from the New York City demonstration on:

> Yet the very simplicity of the freeze proposal has helped attract so many millions of sympathizers. More precise or complicated nuclear arms control prescriptions—shelving plans for land-based cruise missiles in Europe, say—would not make inspirational rallying cries. And although the movement's freeze resolutions call for "bilateralism," the daunting difficulties implicit in U.S.–Soviet negotiations are rarely given more than glancing, wishful consideration (*Time,* June 21, 1982, p. 37).

The same *Time* (June 21, 1992, p. 37) article points out that although all the divergent groups in the movement are in favor of the freeze, beyond that goal there are disagreements. These stem from the dozens of "divergent factions" riding the "antinuclear bandwagon" who want to promote everything from government day-care funding to African development. Here we see, as for the antiwar coverage,[9] an assessment of unity and an emphasis on discord when covering the movement but not when reporting on government officials. The freeze movement is indeed a diverse and contentious coalition, but even within the Reagan administration there is considerable tension between those favoring serious negotiation and those opposing it,[10] although the latter remain in control. Moreover, the larger Reagan movement, like all presidential coalitions, is riven with conflicts between such factions as the social libertarians and social conservatives, the right-wing populists and the Wall Street traditionalists. Similarly, some members of the community of arms control experts favor the freeze or proposals close to it, whereas others do not; among both groups, unity on issues ranging from gun control to abortion could probably not be found. If groups had to demonstrate consensus across all of their members' policy preferences before becoming effective, no political coalitions or presidential campaigns would be possible.

Freeze adherents might have argued for a positive framing: that their ability to claim the allegiance of a large majority of citizens who are divided along other lines demonstrates the impressive power of the idea to fuse an unlikely coalition. Judging freeze proponents but not the Reagan administration, the CPD, or the arms control experts by an unrealistic standard of homogeneous unity further delegitimizes the movement.

Compounding this effect might be the implicit denunciation of "inspirational rallying cries." Freeze supporters might complain that when Reagan offers inspiring visions and slogans to rally his supporters, he is labeled "the Great Communicator." They might argue that it seems acceptable for elites to engage in emotional, symbolic, simplifying rhetoric but not for a mass-based movement. In this way, freeze members might say, media frames narrow the communicative options for building a grassroots public sphere, delimiting the techniques that movements can use to bring ordinary people into public space. Media practice seems to provide elites a much broader range of legitimate communicative options, with less danger of being downgraded for partisanship, emotionality, or insufficient expertise.

In one further imbalanced judgment, this and many other passages takes the movement to task for neglecting "daunting difficulties" in arms negotiations. However, a pro-freeze framing would note that the Reagan administration's negotiating positions during this era are themselves simplistic. This stance is indeed central to its overall arms control strategy—in itself intellectually defensible—which involves pushing a U.S. arms buildup while delaying progress in negotiation until American forces regain what administration officials regard as superiority.[11] The media hold the movement responsible for coming up with an integrated, comprehensive arms control proposal that would survive critical scrutiny and yet be acceptable to both sides. If freeze members were framing coverage, they might note that the U.S. government also fails to accomplish this mission. They might also argue that the daunting difficulties of such matters as abortion and civil rights have not prevented movements from speaking on their concerns without proposing ways to solve all the dilemmas surrounding their issues simultaneously. Movements rarely generate supporters by publicizing detailed position papers to which all members must fully and knowledgeably subscribe.

The final irony is that, as we have shown, the media afford the movement's spokespersons little opportunity to convey the specifics and rationales of Forsberg's detailed proposal, even if they had possessed all the answers. Nor did opinion polls provide the public with minutely detailed policy options; even if the public possessed highly sophisticated and differentiated opinions in support of the freeze, polls would not reveal them....

SUMMARY OF COVERAGE PATTERNS

Our analysis reveals some contrasts in coverage by the two outlets. Front-page coverage of the *New York Times* was largely an official record of elite views and reactions to a nearly invisible movement whose activities could only be discerned in less visible interior articles. Here the prose and angle highlighted the dramatic and eccentric elements in the movement, despite the movement's staid constituency and purpose. *Time*'s coverage focused more on movement participants, probably because its reporters had more time to assemble stories from a greater variety of sources. Nevertheless, the magazine's editors came to the same conclusions as those of the *New York Times,* that the nuclear weapons policies of the nation should not be dictated by the anxieties of an amorphous movement, one purportedly riven by discord....

CONCLUSION

When elites and a majority of the public support the president, we can expect journalism to be cautious in separating itself from the government line. However, the nuclear freeze presented a more auspicious context for autonomous journalism. Polls indicated the freeze proposal was supported by a large majority of Americans and at least some elites. Nevertheless, the framing judgments made and deployed in the text of the *New York Times* and *Time* magazine in freeze coverage reveal patterns that inhibited movement success. Neither the daily nor the magazine maligned the general goal of slowing the nuclear arms race, but they both consistently called into question the underpinnings of the mobilized mass pressure needed to induce genuine rather than symbolic government responsiveness.

If journalism can generate autonomy of official discourse, especially in the presence of a supportive audience, news coverage should have bolstered the freeze. Instead, news of the movement seemed to help the Reagan administration maintain political support despite opposing the freeze. Equally important, the coverage tended to delegitimize public participation in organized political movements. It is in such a context that symbolic politics can succeed and flourish.

NOTES

1. Murray Edelman, "Contestable Categories and Public Opinion," *Political Communication,* 10:152–153 (1993).
2. Edelman, "Contestable Categories."
3. Todd Gitlin, *The Whole World's Watching.* Berkeley, CA: University of California Press, 1980.
4. W. Lance Bennett, "Marginalizing the Majority: Conditioning Public Opinion to Accept Managerial Democracy." In Michael Margolis and Gary Mauser, eds., *Manipulating Public Opinion,* Pacific Grove, CA: Brooks/Cole, pp. 321–361.
5. Gitlin, *The Whole World's Watching.*

6. Robert Scheer, *With Enough Shovels,* New York: Random House, 1982, p. 39.
7. E.g., Richard Stubbing, *The Defense Game,* New York: Random House, 1986.
8. Garry Wills, *Reagan's America,* New York: Doubleday, pp. 287, 323.
9. Gitlin, *The Whole World's Watching.*
10. Strobe Talbott, *Deadly Gambits,* New York: Knopf, 1984.
11. Cf. Talbott, *Deadly Gambits,* pp. 247–248; Wills, *Reagan's America,* pp. 346, 353.

DISCUSSION QUESTIONS

1. Consider how a local controversy is framed in the media you pay attention to. Is one side to a dispute depicted differently than the other? You may want to read selection 22 in the light of this question.

2. If Entman and Rojecki's example is typical of media coverage, how can movement organizers generate publicity without being cast as unconventional, to put it mildly? Are their efforts doomed to failure?

3. Be skeptical here: How much of what Entman and Rojecki find may be due to the way that official news sources, of the kind Hallin discusses, depicted Nuclear Freeze proponents? Is it media or news sources doing the framing?

4. How aware do you think journalists are of the framing judgments they make? Do you think they make them without realizing it, or do you think they make them with some purpose in mind? Why do you say so?

CHAPTER 3
Media Effects on Attitudes and Opinions

We live in a media-rich environment, some might say, "media-saturated." We have televisions at home, some with satellite dishes in the backyard and others connected to cable, radios in our cars and hooked to our waistbands while we jog, magazines in our mailboxes, and newspapers on our doorstep. Wherever we turn, we can find some media outlet vying for our attention. Newspaper headlines virtually shout at us from streetcorner vending machines. Television programs are interrupted with short "teasers" of news and entertainment programs to follow. Radio announcers urge us to "stay tuned." Living even a day without contact with the media can hardly be imagined.

Not only is it difficult for us to avoid being exposed directly to the media in one form or another, much of what we hear from others reflects their exposure to media. We respond not so much to the events of the day as to the news of the day. What we judge as important, what we deem to be worth our efforts, what we consider relevant, all reflect, to some degree, our responses to media and media content. We wonder, therefore, whether media content affects our way of looking at the world, our political positions on the issues facing us, or our political activity—or all three.

Although we would not be surprised to find an effect of media on political culture, on the set of politically relevant attitudes, beliefs, and customs in society, we should be surprised to find a direct and strong short-term effect. Our basic political orientation is a result of a number of forces, including family influences, perspectives absorbed in school, and experiences we share. Media coverage of political news may help us form and reform our political attitudes, but the effect would be slow, at best. Further, since media content varies from outlet to outlet, and since we each pay attention to different television, radio stations, and newspapers, we may not share the same way of looking at the political world. The impact is then even less. Nevertheless, the media mirror our political culture and reinforce some aspects of it through their coverage of the world. James Carlson feels more strongly on this issue; he thinks media have a significant political socialization impact. His essay explores the effect of television crime shows on our underlying political orientations.

The impact on public opinion is also problematic. Although folklore is full of anecdotes that point to a direct and significant impact of media coverage on public opinion, the actual influences are more elusive. The media did not lose Vietnam—Dan Hallin's work demonstrates pretty clearly that reporters applying the techniques of objective journalism reflected official positions on the war more than that of demonstrators, who were seen as refugees from the Sphere of Deviance at best. Again, as readings in the previous chapter suggested, the media may affect which issues emerge onto the public agenda, but the process is unpredictable, to say the least.

Yet the perception persists that media affect public opinion. Robert Entman puts that perception to the test. He considers the conditions under which news and editorials may influence what you and I think about the issues of the day. And his conclusions, that we are more likely to be affected on issues that don't evoke basic attitudes we hold and that control over information is an important media asset, ring true. Moreover, his argument that elites respond to perceived public opinion suggests that the way media portray what the public thinks may be more important than what the public in fact thinks. Our responses to elite actions based on those perceptions will then, in turn, influence the way we think about the political issues around us.

Our awareness of what others think also influences our own positions on issues. When a really volatile issue arises, we hear about it from our colleagues and our acquaintances, we notice it in the media, and we begin to consider and reconsider how we ourselves feel on the matter. Recently, talk shows on radio, where guests defend their views on current issues and listeners call in to participate in the discussion, have proliferated. What effect do these shows have? Do they increase their listeners' political participation? Are callers and listeners different from the rest of us? Diana Owen considers this growing phenomenon, so important in the media of the 1990s, in the third selection in this chapter.

At the very least, media affect public opinion because they call issues to our attention ("Here, you should have an opinion about this!") and because they provide much of the information we base our opinions on. If media are not necessary to the formation of public opinion, they certainly seem intimately connected to it in our media-rich environment.

5. POLITICAL SOCIALIZATION THROUGH MEDIA

People who spend as much time as we do in front of television sets and reading newspapers are going to be affected in ways we are not always aware of. One of these ways is, hypothetically, an effect on our basic approach to politics and political life. If we frequently hear stories of corruption in politics, we may wind up thinking politics a less than honorable calling. More important, we may begin internalizing the standards media reports are using to evaluate political choices. We begin judging politics by criteria that we have adopted through our exposure to news reports. Because of the attention paid the president and the relatively sparse news coverage of Congress and state governments, we may begin thinking of the president as more important, compared to other institutions of government in the United States, than he is. Our view of the political system is shaped, unconsciously and probably unintentionally, through our exposure to the news.

James Carlson argues that our exposure to entertainment also forms our basic political orientations. Using "cultivation theory," he points out the tacit messages about politics in crime shows that reinforce some views about our society and undermine others. Implicit here is the notion that our basic orientations are more readily shaped when we are unaware that we are being affected. Explicit "indoctrination" makes us wary—we put our guard up. But messages that emerge as recurring themes in entertainment rarely bring out our defense mechanisms. Especially when we have little direct experience with the subject of the entertainment, those hidden messages may provide the underpinnings of our thinking about those matters. How frequent and widespread is crime, and, therefore, how big a political problem does it present? Our personal experiences rarely allow us to develop a reliable answer, but our impressions, formed by our exposure to the media, lead us to take positions on these questions, sometimes strongly held positions. Not all scholars agree about this impact, but the possibility should be taken seriously.

Television Entertainment and Political Socialization

James M. Carlson

People acquire their political values and attitudes through a process called political socialization. Those who have studied political socialization have given their attention to the substance of political orientations learned, the sources of what is learned, and the specific processes of learning. Here I will focus on the way mass media messages "encourage" political attitudes and values. I will explain why until recent years surprisingly little attention has been given the role of television and print media in political learning. I will argue that one of the reasons for neglect is that analysts have worked with a very narrow definition of what is "political" and that their definition has led them to ignore a most important source of political messages—television entertainment. Focusing on television crime shows as an example, I will argue that contrary to public belief entertainment programming is more likely to contribute to orientations that are supportive of the socio-political system than to deviance and aggressive behavior.

THE OBJECT OF POLITICAL SOCIALIZATION

It is useful to think of values or attitudes in terms of orientations towards politically relevant objects. The objects may be specific political figures such as the President of the United States, policies such as increased defense spending, or sets of ideas such as liberalism or capitalism. Orientations can be divided into two groups. Systemic orientations have to do with views concerning the legitimacy of the political system. They are relevant to the persistence of the political system itself. Allocative orientations have to do with views of "who should get what in society." Obviously, systemic orientations are the most critical to the stability and survival of the political system.

The most important systemic orientations have to do with diffuse support for the objects of the political system. Political scientist David Easton has described the objects as political au-

SOURCE: Original essay written especially for this volume.

thorities, the political regime, and the political community.[1] Political authorities refer to specific occupants of government positions such as the President, members of Congress, or police. The political regime refers to the "rules of the game" in the political system. Most analysts define orientations towards the regime in the American context in terms of support for democratic principles and feelings of political effectiveness. Support for the regime may also include positive orientations towards the legal system and support for basic American values such as materialism and individualism. Political community refers to the sense of nationhood or a commitment on the part of a group of people to be governed together. Orientations towards political community are usually defined in terms of patriotic symbols such as the American flag. However, that approach is too simple. The essence of community is individual trust in fellow citizens or generalized trust in people.

Allocative values, or views on who should get what from the political system, are usually defined in terms of partisan identification in the United States. Clearly, the liberal-conservative continuum also divides people in terms of allocative values. This is true in terms of material values such as wealth, as well as nonmaterial valued things such as freedom and equality. Allocative orientations can also be described in terms of specific public policies such as those that might reduce taxes or limit rights given to those who are accused of crimes.

AGENTS OF POLITICAL SOCIALIZATION

Studies of political socialization have been guided by the "primacy principle," that what is learned first is learned best, and the "structuring principle," that what is learned first structures later learning. Given the guidance of these two principles, it is not surprising that attention has focused primarily on the family and school as agents of the political system or teachers of political orientations. It is equally unsurprising that attention has focused primarily on what is learned in childhood. However, in recent years increased attention has been given to other agents such as peer groups, religious organizations, and the mass media. There has also been an increase in attention to adult political socialization.

The mass media as agents of political socialization were largely ignored because some early studies showed that media messages, especially from television, do little more than reinforce previously developed orientations. It was assumed that this was so because individuals only pay attention to media messages that support their point of view. The idea that mass media are irrelevant to political learning seemed to defy common sense, because the casual observer could see how pervasive television had become in American society.

A strong case can be made that television has a great opportunity to socialize simply because of the amount of exposure to its messages. The average household of three or more people spends sixty-one hours per week watching television. The average six-year-old watches for six or more hours per day.[2] By the time an individual has graduated from high school he or she will have spent 15,000 hours watching television compared to 11,000 hours in school.[3] It may be argued that by the time a person leaves school he or she will have spent more "contact hours" with television than with either family members or school teachers.

Some might argue that despite the great deal of exposure to television there are few politically relevant messages. Most scholars who have studied television and political socialization have emphasized news programming, finding few effects beyond increases in knowledge of politics and current events. Their emphasis has been misplaced for several reasons. First, over half of the American public does not watch television news at all. Few children watch either news programs or public affairs television. Second, if scholars believe that only the news contains political content, it is no wonder that few studies have found that news media contribute to political socialization. Those who pay close attention to the news are relatively highly educated people who have firmly established political views.

What is known is that both children and adults watch a great deal of entertainment television. But is there anything "political" about messages conveyed by entertainment? Communication specialist George Gerbner and his associates argue that:

Throughout history, once a ruling class has established its rule, the primary function of its cultural media has been the legitimation and maintenance of its authority. Folk tales and other traditional dramatic teaching stories always reinforced established authority, teaching that when society's rules are broken, retribution is visited upon violators. The importance of the existing order is always implicit in such stories.[4]

Today the medium that conveys "folk tales and other traditional dramatic teaching stories" is television. If one looks beyond messages about the institutions of American government and orientations directly relevant to citizen participatory roles, one finds that television entertainment is rife with teaching stories that are relevant to the maintenance of the political system. Scholars who have found a minimal role for television in the political system have based their conclusions on a definition of politics that is too narrow. They have forgotten the structuring principle that tells us that general politically relevant orientations structure the development of orientations that may be more directly relevant to contemporary institutions and processes.

Almost all types of television entertainment programming have something to teach about values. Family situation comedies teach about appropriate sex roles and individual achievement. Game shows teach about materialism and competition. Sports programs emphasize competition and the importance of rules of the game. Soap operas provide lessons about behavior that is acceptable and deviant. Perhaps the most system-supportive messages come from crime-detective shows, so that type of programming provides a good set of examples of how television entertainment can socialize.

HOW TELEVISION ENTERTAINMENT INFLUENCES POLITICAL VALUES

Before turning to a discussion of politically relevant messages found in crime shows, it is important to discuss the process of media effects. Early studies of effects proposed that the mass media were all-powerful and had a considerable effect on the shaping of values, opinions, and behavior. However, when these early assumptions were put to the test it was found that the mass media had minimal effects because people seemed to ignore messages that were inconsistent with their basic beliefs and opinions. What followed was a period of time where scholars believed that media had minimal effects on the views of people, but the common belief was that television especially played a powerful role in shaping how the world was viewed. In more recent years scholars have found that the effects of television are more subtle than previously believed.

I think that the best explanation of media effects flows from a process of inquiry called "cultivation analysis." The general idea of cultivation theory is that a single media message is unlikely to influence opinions and values, but a constant diet of messages that consistently encourage a particular point of view may over time have a considerable effect.[5] The most likely effects of media messages are on perceptions of social reality. Research has shown that when the world of television differs considerably from reality, heavy viewers have a view that is more consistent with that of television. Acceptance of television's portrayal of reality is associated with acceptance of values and opinions that are consistent with that reality.[6]

Those who believe that television cultivates a point of view over time begin their analysis by determining the differences between what is portrayed on television and what actually exists. Then they examine heavy viewers of television to see if they perceive a reality that closely resembles that which is portrayed in television programming. A final step is to determine whether television cultivates opinions and attitudes that are consistent with its own definition of reality.

Applying the approach to crime show programming I will describe the television world with respect to perceptions that may be relevant to support for political authorities, the regime, and the community. I will also describe the television point of view regarding support for these objects of the political system. Finally, I will cite some evidence that indicates that crime shows do in fact contribute to system-relevant viewpoints.

POLITICALLY RELEVANT MESSAGES IN CRIME SHOWS

Television crime shows have a great deal to say about the nature of community, characteristics of the regime like the need for legal compliance, and support for legal authorities like police and the judiciary. Television reality with regard to crime and criminal justice is quite different from the "real" world.

A great deal of concern has been expressed in recent years about the "excessive" violence in crime shows. The amount of violence in the television world is unrealistic. One study reported in 1978 that there were 5.9 violent episodes an hour on prime time television.[7] Fifty-four percent of all leading characters were involved in violent acts. Media critic Michael Parenti noted that in eighteen episodes of "Miami Vice" Crockett and Tubbs killed forty-three people, five times as many as were killed by the entire Miami Police Department in a year.[8]

A great deal of research has gone towards linking the viewing of violent television shows with aggressive and violent behavior. The results have been very mixed, and at best it is possible to conclude that in some circumstances heavy viewing of violence may be associated with aggression. I believe that the emphasis on deviant behavior has been misplaced. The violence on crime shows communicates two important messages. The first is that the world is a very frightening place where anyone could become a victim of violence at any time. The second is best articulated by George Gerbner:

> Violence plays a key role in television's portrayal of the social order. It is the simplest and the cheapest means to demonstrate who wins the game of life and the rules by which the game is played. It tells us who are the aggressors and who are the victims. It demonstrates who has power and who must acquiesce to power.... In the portrayal of violence there is a relationship between the roles of the violent and the victim. Both roles are there to be learned by the viewers. In generating among the many the fear of power of the few, television violence may achieve its greatest effect.[9]

So violence on television crime shows may serve the ends of conformity to societal norms, opposed to producing deviant behavior.

Television programs are also unrealistic with regard to police and police effectiveness. As an occupational group police are vastly over-represented on television. For the most part they are heroes who combat truly vicious criminals who seem to attack their victims at random. Some police may be unorthodox in their approaches to battling crime, but their lack of orthodoxy serves an important function. Usually television police fight two battles, one against the criminals and one against the bureaucracy and "legal technicalities" that hinder their attempts to make the streets safe for law-abiding citizens. The lack of orthodoxy suggests that conventional police who behave in a way that is consistent with norms and the law cannot get the job done. Implicitly, what is suggested is that breaking the rules is fine if the bad guy is brought to justice in the end. Ultimately, the criminal is brought to justice; police on television are highly successful. The message is that "crime does not pay."

Crime shows provide mixed messages with regard to the law. Certainly the stories presented encourage compliance with the law and support for the legal system. Violent ends for criminals make it clear that no good can come of violating the law. However, crime shows also seem to encourage an anti-civil libertarian crime control point of view. In their pursuit of criminals television police violate the rights of the accused. When criminals are captured they are given the Miranda warnings in a very disparaging sort of way. The message seems to be that constitutional due process guarantees are a major hindrance to law enforcement, and that violation of rights are worth it in the long run if truly nasty criminals are taken off the street.

So, what do crime shows have to do with the objects of the political system? It seems to me that they provide messages that are supportive of key political authorities, the police. Early studies of political socialization found that the first political authorities recognized by children were the President and police. Given their day-to-day contact with citizens, police would seem to be key political authorities. Messages regarding compliance with the law and support for the legal system are supportive of the political regime. In fact, the anti-civil libertarian messages likely encourage a point of view that values regime stability over rights of citizens. The tremendous amount of violence on television crime shows may make a negative contribution to a concept of political community. What is portrayed is a very mean world, where fellow citizens cannot be trusted. Ultimately because of fear of victimization, a sense of community may give way to acquiescence to legal authorities.

Crime shows may also have something to say about allocative values in society. Criminals are often portrayed as motivated by greed. They are often vaguely middle class, but in almost every instance criminality is attributed to individual deviance. Seldom is there a hint in crime shows that class structure of the distribution of wealth in society has anything to do with criminal behavior. The solution to the crime problem is always a conservative one—more police and fewer rights for the accused, not more job training programs and drug rehabilitation programs.

THE CULTIVATION OF POLITICALLY RELEVANT VALUES BY CRIME SHOWS

There is some evidence that the messages concerning authorities, the regime, and the political community have some influence on those who are heavy viewers of crime shows in particular and television in general. Most studies have found that after taking into account a number of important factors that may affect political values, television viewing has a small, but consistent effect on perceptions of reality and political values.

The strongest influence of television is on perceptions of the world of crime and law enforcement. Heavy viewers, both children and adults, tend to over-estimate the amount of crime in society, the number of people engaged in law enforcement, and the likelihood of criminal victimization.[11] They also tend to over-estimate the effectiveness of police in solving crimes.[12] Heavy viewers see police as especially competent and honest.

Perceptions of the reality regarding the criminal justice system have implications for knowledge, opinions, and values that are relevant to the larger political system. Those who are heavy viewers of crime dramas tend to have positive images of police, who are important authorities within the system. There is also some strong evidence that heavy viewers are more likely to support norms that are associated with the stability of the political regime. Crime shows seem to encourage a generalized support for the legal system and a belief in the importance of compliance with the law. They also encourage a "crime control" point of view, where there is a willingness to sacrifice the civil liberties of those accused of crimes in the interest of "law and order." Perhaps it is surprising that crime shows contribute little to knowledge of the legal system, but usually the story lines end with an arrest.[13]

Perhaps the greatest impact of crime shows is on perceptions of the nature of community. As I noted above, heavy viewers of crime shows and of television in general tend to see the world as a frightening place where victimization of crime is likely. The implication of this view is that many viewers have a perception of a "mean world" where people cannot be trusted.[14] Political community is based on a concept of mutual trust. If citizens are afraid to interact with other citizens and cannot develop feelings of mutual trust, then democratic politics becomes difficult.

Finally, there is some evidence that television viewing has broad implications for generalized support for the political system and for allocative values. Those who are heavy viewers of crime shows and demonstrate a high degree of support for the legal system and legal compliance are also supportive of the political system in general.[15] Heavy viewers of television are also likely to hold "mainstream" political views. George Gerbner and his associates have shown that television viewing is associated with the cultivation of a wide variety of political values. In almost every instance what is cultivated is a system supportive, moderately conservative, mainstream point of view.[16]

CONCLUSIONS

Television plays a role in the development of orientations that are relevant to the political system. The influence of television is much more subtle than many believe, but it is still an important agent of political socialization. It deserves greater attention than it has received until recent years because its influence is pervasive for both children and adults.

The type of television that is likely to be most influential is entertainment programs, because they are most likely to be viewed. Analysts have missed a great deal by not examining the political effects of entertainment more closely. Contrary to the concerns of many citizens and critics, television is more likely to encourage orientations that are supportive of the norms of the social and political system than deviance. This is hardly surprising once it is understood that those who control the electronic media have a large stake in the status quo.

NOTES

1. David Easton, *A Framework for Political Analysis* (Englewood Cliffs, N.J.: Prentice-Hall, 1965).
2. Michael Parenti, *Make Believe Media: The Politics of Entertainment* (New York: St. Martin's Press, 1992).
3. Doris Graber, *Mass Media and American Politics* (Washington, D.C.: CQ Press, 1989), 3rd ed., p. 184.
4. George Gerbner, Larry Gross, Michael Morgan, and Nancy Signorielli, "The 'Mainstreaming' of America: Violence Profile No. 11," *Journal of Communication* 30:12 (1980).
5. See Michael Morgan and Nancy Signorielli, eds., *Cultivation Analysis: New Directions in Media Effects Research* (Newbury Park, California: Sage Publications, 1990).
6. George Gerbner, Larry Gross, Michael Morgan, and Nancy Signorielli, "Political Correlates of Tele-

vision Viewing," *Public Opinion Quarterly* 48:283–300 (1984).
7. George Gerbner, Larry Gross, Marilyn Jackson-Beeck, Suzanne Jeffries-Fox, and Nancy Signorielli, "Cultural Indicators: Violence Profile No. 9," *Journal of Communication* 28:178 (1978).
8. Parenti, p. 121.
9. Gerbner, *et al.* (1980), p. 180.
10. Fred J. Greenstein, "The Benevolent Leader: Children's Images of Political Authorities," *American Political Science Review* 54:934–43 (1960).
11. Joseph Dominick, "Children's Viewing of Crime Shows and Attitudes on Law Enforcement," *Journalism Quarterly* 51:5–12 (1974).
12. James M. Carlson, *Prime Time Law Enforcement: Crime Show Viewing and Attitudes towards the Criminal Justice System* (New York: Praeger Publishers, 1985).
13. *Ibid.*
14. Gerbner, *et al.* (1980), p. 185.
15. Carlson, p. 203.
16. George Gerbner, Larry Gross, Michael Morgan, and Nancy Signorielli, "Charting the Mainstream: Television's Contribution to Political Orientations," *Journal of Communication* 32:100–127 (1982).

DISCUSSION QUESTIONS

1. Do you agree with Carlson when he suggests that television entertainment programs probably have a bigger impact on our basic political orientations than news broadcasts? What evidence would it take to convince you that he is correct? That he is wrong?

2. What are the underlying values implicit in your favorite television shows? How aware are viewers of these values, or do we consciously have to stop and think about it?

3. How would Carlson answer the contention that television entertainment reflects societal values rather than causes them? After all, can't we simply turn off shows that transmit values we don't like?

4. While I write this question, many people worry that shows such as *Beavis and Butthead* increase the chance impressionable children will reenact the stunts they see on television. What would you say to convince people that television shows have no such effect? What would you say to convince them otherwise?

5. Some people argue that the media's effect on political socialization is greater than it appears because of the indirect effect through other agents of political socialization, that the values we absorb from family, friends, and schools reflect media content as much as points of view. Others argue that family, friends, and schools help us interpret the world in familiar terms so that media have less of an impact than we might otherwise think. Which position do you hold? What evidence can you cite in support of your position?

6. PUBLIC OPINION AND THE MEDIA

Listening to people talk about the media, it is easy to get the impression that the press must have a strong influence on what the public thinks. Of course, you are smart enough not to be affected by media stories; you make up your own mind on today's issues. It's everybody else whose opinions are molded by the press. But conventional wisdom is not always right. Evidence in support of media's effect on public opinion is scant, to say the least. Much of it is anecdotal, and a lot is based on exceptional circumstances rather than on normal events. But, yet, many of us cannot avoid coming to the personal conclusion that media must have some demonstrable effect on public opinion.

Robert Entman provides some of the evidence we need. But his evidence supports a different conception of media effects: it isn't that media messages lead people to change their minds. It is more that media affect those who have no strong opinions on the issue in question. The effect depends on the schema or way of organizing information and preferences a person uses, so conservatives will be affected differently than liberals because some concerns are more central to conservatives than to liberals and some arguments are more convincing to liberals than to conservatives. The effect depends on an interaction between the messages in the media and the perspectives we bring to them.

How the Media Affect What People Think— and Think They Think

Robert M. Entman

... [T]his [section] shows that media messages significantly influence what the public and the elites think, by affecting what they perceive and think about.

... The central assumption of ... recent research on agenda setting has been that media do exert significant influence, but only in a narrow sphere. In this view, the news can affect what people think *about,* not what they think. The public's autonomy is not complete, but its susceptibility to media influence is limited to agendas.... [T]he media can overcome ... barriers in determining the issues people think about but not in shaping what they prefer to be done.

The problem with the agenda-setting position is that the distinction between "what to think" and "what to think about" is misleading. Nobody, no force, can ever successfully "tell people what to think." Short of sophisticated torture

SOURCE: Excerpted from *Democracy without Citizens: Media and the Decay of American Politics* by Robert M. Entman. Copyright © 1989 by Robert M. Entman. Reprinted by permission of Oxford University Press, Inc.

or "brainwashing," no form of communication can compel anything more than feigned obeisance. The way to control attitudes is to provide a partial selection of information for a person to think about, or process. The only means of influencing what people think is precisely to control what they think about.

However, no matter what the message, whether conveyed through media or in person, control over others' thinking can never be complete. Influence can be exerted though selection of information, but conclusions cannot be dictated. If the media (or anyone) can affect what people think about—the information they process—the media (or anyone) can affect their attitudes. This perspective yields an assumption of interdependence: public opinion grows out of an interaction between media messages and what audiences make of them.

. . . Identification as liberal, moderate, or conservative is a key component of the schema system that most people apply to political information. Ideological leanings affect responses to specific media reports; those who identify differently may read the same message differently. The interdependence model predicts that media influence varies according to the way each person processes specific news messages. Instead of treating ideology as a tool people use to filter out reports that conflict with their liberalism or conservatism, the model sees ideology as a schema that influences the use people make of media messages in more complicated ways.

The interaction between the attributes of the message and the schemas of the audience shapes the impact of the news. One component of this interaction is message salience. Stories that interest liberals may bore conservatives; items that intrigue ideologues on either side may not interest moderates, who have few strong preferences.

Another aspect of interaction is whether the message is relevant to peripheral or central attitudes. Centrality will differ for different groups, since liberals and conservatives appear to structure their ideas distinctively. Central to liberalism is attachment to ideals of change and equality; central to conservatism is attraction to capitalism.[1] The two groups probably process some media messages differently. This decidedly does not mean that liberals, say, screen out all material that challenges liberalism. Consider an editorial praising the ideal of capitalist markets and proposing to make the post office a private enterprise. While the message may conflict with some elements of liberal ideology, it does so only peripherally, since government ownership of public utilities is not fundamental to American liberalism. The message may not only bolster conservatism among conservatives but may weaken liberals' ties to liberalism, if only at the liberal margin.

Another point of interdependent interaction between media reports and the audiences' schema systems involves whether the media message comes from an editorial, with its overtly persuasive intent, or from a news story ostensibly designed merely to inform. Conservatives, for example, may be more likely to screen out liberal editorials than news slanted favorably to the left, since editorials are explicit while the slant of news is often subtle, and news stories appear to convey only factual information.

A final aspect of interdependence lies in how new or unfamiliar the reported topic is. All else being equal, the less familiar the object of the news, the less likely a person will respond by fitting the report into an established category and maintaining a set attitude. Where the subject of the news is unfamiliar to people across the ideological spectrum, all will be susceptible to media influence.

Four predictions emerge from this use of information processing theory to develop an interdependence model. . . .

Prediction 1. Editorials will affect those who identify with a particular ideology more than moderates. Those identifying themselves as liberals or conservatives are likely to find ideologically charged editorial messages salient. Those who eschew ideological commitments, the moderates, may not find ideological editorials relevant.

Prediction 2. Liberal editorials should exert a leftward push on those attitudes of conservatives not central to their ideology.

Prediction 3. Editorials have a stronger effect when coverage is of a new subject rather than a long-familiar one.

Prediction 4. News slant affects beliefs among liberals, moderates, and conservatives alike. Shaped by objectivity rules, news stories are designed to appear neutral to audiences. . . .[2] [S]lant nonetheless enters into "objective" reports. Because of the appearance of neutrality, people probably screen out these messages less than editorials.

. . . The data generally support my four predictions. The findings suggest that media messages can indeed move audiences in directions counter to their predominant dispositions. The influence of news stories and editorials that oppose existing dispositions or reinforce current beliefs varies depending upon the message, attitude, and schema involved. In particular, as Prediction 1 suggests, editorials have little impact on moderates, who may find them of little interest. But editorials do influence those who consider themselves liberals or conservatives. The influence does not hold across the board, however. As Prediction 2 hypothesizes, liberal editorials appear most influential in moving conservatives against their dispositions on matters not crucial to their identities as conservatives. But while the beliefs susceptible to influence may not be central to conservatives' ideological self-images, they may be significant to their political behavior. For example, the data show that conservatives who read liberal newspapers were significantly more likely than readers of conservative papers to vote for Jimmy Carter over Gerald Ford in 1976. . . .

The data also support Prediction 3, that attitudes toward the unfamiliar are more susceptible to media influence than those toward the familiar. The most important evidence is that opinions toward the previously-unknown former governor Jimmy Carter were affected by editorials among conservatives, and even among moderates, who were otherwise immune to the impact of editorials. Finally, Prediction 4 receives considerable buttressing from the statistical analysis: news slant, measured as diversity in perspectives, appears to influence people in all three ideological groups. Selectivity and inattention seem to apply less when people read the news than when they read editorials. For example, the more diverse the news perspectives in a paper, the more likely were its conservative readers to evaluate liberal and groups positively. Lacking strong selectivity tendencies, moderates were most susceptible to news slant. For them, reading more diverse newspapers was associated with more liberal responses on five of seven opinion indexes.

This finding highlights a barrier that objectivity erects against any ideal marketplace of ideas. Free of the requirements to conform to objectivity rules or to play by the other rules of the political market, editorialists can take explicit stands and argue for truth. According to a number of researchers, newspaper editorials and columns often provide information and analysis that overtly challenge the claims of presidents or other elites who may be taking advantage of reporters' objectivity to manage the news.[3] Editorials and opinion pieces, at least in the print media, may contain more of the data readers need to make autonomous judgments than do news reports, whose important and powerful political implications are often subtle and unplanned. Yet, though editorial pages may be more likely than news pages to offer complex truths, they are labeled as opinion and lack the legitimizing mantle of objectivity, and they appear far from the front page. As the findings suggest, most of the time they probably exert less direct influence than news slant over the thinking of most audience members.

Perhaps we should amend the old phrase to read "The media do not control what people prefer; they influence public opinion by providing much of the information people think about and by shaping how they think about it." Americans exercise their varied dispositions as they ponder political news, but the media's selection of data makes a significant contribution to the outcome of each person's thinking.

... These impacts should not be exaggerated. Scholars simply do not know very much about how and why ordinary or elite Americans develop their basic ideological orientations or their specific political attitudes. The forces that move actual and perceived public opinion remain complicated and mysterious, and the media fill in only part of the puzzle.

While this [section] makes a strong case for taking the media's role seriously, it does not assert that the media are the only important source of information or influence.

Still, in a democracy, the public must and should rely in some measure on the mass media. The autonomy model takes the assumption that audiences resist media influence so far that it implicitly denies the press can enhance democracy at all. To participate effectively in politics, the public must remain responsive to the changing conditions portrayed (however imperfectly) in the news. The implication is clear: democracy in the United States is significantly affected by the performance and power of journalism.

NOTES

1. P.J. Conover and S. Feldman. "The Origins and Meaning of Liberal/Conservative Self-identifications." *American Journal of Political Science* 25:617–645 (1981).
2. E.g., Michael Schudson, *Discovering the News: A Social History of American Newspapers,* New York: Basic Books (1978); Gaye Tuchman, *Making News: A Study in the Construction of Reality,* New York: Free Press (1978); H.L. Molotch and D. Boden, "Talking Social Structure: Discourse, Domination and the Watergate Hearings." *American Sociological Review* 50:273–288.
3. See, for example, Daniel C. Hallin, *The "Uncensored War": The Media and Vietnam.* New York: Oxford University Press (1986); Robert M. Entman, Affidavit in State of California v. Raymond and Peggy Buckey, unpublished; W.A. Dorman and M. Farhang, *The U.S. Press and Iran.* Berkeley: University of California Press (1987).

DISCUSSION QUESTIONS

1. Find a recent editorial in your local paper. How strong a position is a writer taking? Is the writer suggesting readers take a certain stance toward the issue in question, or is the writer arguing forcefully for one side or the other? Which would you be more likely to respond to?

2. One possible effect on public opinion that Entman does not discuss is the likelihood that media coverage of events will have a mobilizing effect—that people will feel stimulated to participate directly. Some have argued that media are more likely to have a demobilizing effect, encouraging passivity rather than activity. Have you seen evidence of either of these effects in your community or in the nation? What would it take for the media to have a mobilizing effect?

3. How strong an effect, all things considered, do media have on our opinions on matters of public concern? Are those who worry about media domination of public opinion correct or not? Why do you take that position?

7. POLITICAL PARTICIPATION THROUGH MEDIA

Of all the ways people can and do participate in politics, most require access to information. Whether it is information about opportunities to attend rallies, news about upcoming legislation affecting our lives, or opinions about the direction the nation is going, we most likely learn about it through the media, directly or indirectly. Sometimes media reports contain what we call "mobilizing information," that is, information that enables us to take effective action, such as pointing out where and when a crucial decision is going to be made. At other times, news accounts simply keep us abreast of events, so that we can respond or not.

But this picture of media effects on political participation portrays a one-way channel of communication. Diana Owen, in this selection, discusses a revitalized form of political participation through media, talk radio, that allows listeners to become contributors to an ongoing discussion of political issues. First prominent in the 1992 elections, talk radio attracts a larger and larger audience, many of whom hold strong and intense political opinions. Using data from a survey conducted in the spring of 1992 by the Times-Mirror Center for the People and the Press, which included questions about talk radio, Owen profiles the talk radio audience and examines how it responds to politics and 1992's presidential candidates.

Talk Radio

Diana Owen

Every hour of every day, millions of Americans across the country are tuned into talk radio programs. For many of these listeners, and especially for callers, talk radio has come to represent a form of community in a society increasingly characterized by loneliness and isolation. Unlike other mass media formats that encourage passive acceptance of institutionalized reports, talk radio thrives on the active expression of personal views. Talk radio may be "the last frontier" for mass political discourse.

After a long period of stagnation and decline, political talk radio has experienced an enormous surge of popularity during the last decade. Its audience has been growing steadily in number and diversity. Once predominantly the domain of the disillusioned and the discontented, the new breed of talk jockeys, listeners, and callers treat radio as a medium of mainstream political empowerment. Talk radio has made politics at the local, state, and national levels more accessible to the mass public. It has provided a forum for venting opinion, has stimulated political discussion, and has even sparked political action.[1]

Talk radio's new-found prominence on the political front was clearly evident during the 1992 presidential election. In a campaign where alternative media and "infotainment politics" became the norm, talk radio's collective voice resonated loudly among candidates, voters, and the mainstream press. No longer the stepchild of the more "powerful" political media, talk radio's call-in format was widely adapted for television. Recognizing the potential to reach, and perhaps to mobilize, a sizable segment of the voting public, presidential candidates courted appearances on talk radio programs and their television counterparts to an unprecedented degree. Ross Perot, in fact, made political history by kicking off his presidential campaign on CNN's *Larry King Live* by expressing his willingness to run if drafted by the American people.[2] Further, the popular hosts of politically-oriented talk radio programs, such as Rush Limbaugh, established themselves as multi-media celebrities, making their views known in print, on TV, and even on videocassette.[3]

TALK RADIO'S EMERGENCE AS A CULTURAL PHENOMENON

While the popularity of political talk radio during the 1992 campaign may have caught some observers by surprise, a glance at some basic statistics indicates that the infrastructure necessary to expedite this phenomenon was well in place. Americans own more radios—over 530 million—than televisions.[4] Ninety-nine percent of households have at least one radio, with the average being five. There are approximately 10,000 radio stations across the country, and every day 80 percent of the population listens to the radio at one time or another.[5] Between 6 a.m. and 6 p.m., Americans spend *49 percent* of their media time listening to the radio compared to 33 percent watching television, 12 percent reading the

SOURCE: From "Politics and the 'Last Frontier': The Talk Radio Audience and the 1992 Presidential Election," presented at the annual meeting of the Midwest Political Science Association, April 15–17, 1993.

newspaper, and 6 percent reading magazines.[6]

Call-in radio shows are the fastest growing segment of the market,[7] and they now account for nearly ten percent of all programming.[8] Every day, approximately 15 million Americans tune in to at least a portion of a talk radio program.[9] Advances in technology, economic incentives, and the changing demographic profile of the American public partially account for these trends. Satellite technology has made it practical and cost effective to develop network talk radio, where stations channel programs to their affiliates who share the expenses. This strategy has allowed AM radio, whose market base had been deteriorating, to overcome the stigma of being the "weaker frequency" and to develop a new identity predicated on the power of talk. Coinciding with the technological advances that have made talk formats an economical choice for radio stations, demographic trends also have helped the radio industry. As radio listeners age, they begin to favor talk to music.[10] As the baby boom generation ages, its "rock and roll" tastes have been undergoing a transformation. Raised on a heavy diet of political music, they now prefer their politics without accompanying melodies. Further, their penchant for car phones has contributed to the ever rising number of call-ins.[11]

Yet, the rapidly-engaging trend toward political talk radio may be more than simply the timely coincidence of technology and demographics. Talk radio is evolving into a widespread and deeply entrenched cultural form. According to Michael Harrison, editor and publisher of *Talkers,* a talk radio industry newspaper, "Information is replacing popular music as popular culture. Modern talk radio is a major pop culture phenomenon, and more and more people are switching to it from music."[12]

Talk radio attracts a dynamic and ever-increasing cadre of loyal listeners who tune in to offerings that have become more diverse, specialized, and engrossing over the past ten years. Americans have developed a passionate relationship with talk radio similar to their preoccupation with music, television programs, movies, and novels. Talk radio contains all of the elements of personal drama and entertainment that people have come to expect from popular culture. They know the "stars," they follow the "story lines," and they can even participate in the productions.

Talk radio is a perfect medium for the "popularization" of politics. Call-in radio programs convey the constantly unfolding drama of politics in a way that allows listeners to feel as if they are insiders. This opens up a new world to a citizenry that is largely disaffected from and distrustful of formal political institutions, including mainstream mass media.[13] Talk radio represents one of the few forums where ordinary Americans perceive that people like themselves have a say in the political process.[14]

Sparked by the freshly realized potential of the medium, the "new" talk radio audience is more diverse in composition and has more varied motivations for listening than any in the fifty year history of the format. Prior research on the radio audience, especially the small number of studies of talk radio conducted over the past two decades, provides us with a basis for comparison with the present. . . .

TALK RADIO AND THE MASS AUDIENCE

Radio research was once at the center of studies of mass communication. In the 1940s, myriad studies explored the wide and multifaceted dimension of the public's affinity for the world of radio. Detailed survey analyses of the relationship between listeners and all types of programs—political and nonpolitical—were conducted.... However, when television supplanted radio as the public's electronic medium of choice, radio research all but disappeared from the scene.

In the 1970s and 1980s, a handful of studies of the talk radio audience were conducted. This research focused predominantly on callers as opposed to listeners more generally. Taking its lead from the early uses and gratifications research, this work centers on the role that talk radio plays in the lives of its audience. These studies reach the overall conclusion that the primary function of talk radio is to provide an alternative connection to the political and social world for citizens who are largely alienated from traditional outlets for communication. Talk radio serves as an accessible and nonthreatening surrogate for direct interpersonal communication for people who are isolated, not mobile, single, unattached to formal organizations, and who are seeking companionship.[15]

... [C]hanges in the nature and scope of talk radio programming over the past several years have rendered these findings time bound. Talk radio still serves as a surrogate for community, but the neighbors are no longer predominantly bored, immobile, or highly alienated from society. Political talk radio, in particular, provides a forum for expression by those whose voices are already well represented, as well as for those whose access to the political realm is more limited. Thus, talk radio has the potential to further democratic goals and aims, particularly when specific formats, such as an "open mike," are used. Citizens become more personally engaged with political problems which can inspire action, especially on the local level.[16] In sum, talk radio provides a convenient, exciting, and entertaining means of passing the time and gaining information for both callers and listeners....

POLITICAL PROFILE OF THE TALK RADIO AUDIENCE

The political profile of the "new" talk radio audience is intriguing and somewhat paradoxical. While listeners are largely disaffected from formal institutions, they are not alienated from the political process. They still feel that their voice can and should be heard....

Evidence suggests that the talk radio audience shares some basic political orientations. Talk radio listeners are thought to be disproportionately conservative in their ideological identification....[17] Our data ... indicate ... that those who tune into talk radio are slightly more Republican and Independent in partisan identification than their nonlistening counterparts, although these differences are not statistically significant.

The broad demographic and political profiles [of talk show listeners] characterize a "new" talk radio audience that is moving upscale and leans toward the conservative end of the political spectrum. However, this group is still quite diverse, and basic demographic and ideological distinctions do not preclude listeners' generalized agreement on some political fundamentals. While specific talk jocks are associated with right or left wing politics, they are inclined to adopt populist positions, such as opposition to big companies and government bureaucracies.[18] These proclivities also are embraced by audience members positioned across the ideological spectrum....

THE TALK RADIO AUDIENCE AND THE 1992 PRESIDENTIAL CAMPAIGN

Classic voting behavior studies conducted in radio's heyday—prior to the television era—downplayed the power of mass media over political preferences in favor of personal influence. However, this research conceded that radio, especially when contrasted with newspapers, brought candidates and campaigns to life and provided a point of personal access to politics for listeners. If any mass medium was to have an impact on voters, radio was it.[19]

It appears, however, that radio in the age of "infotainment" politics has gained a level of respect that it never received in its glory days. Anecdotal evidence of radio's significance in the 1992 campaign abounds. Here are a few examples. Ross Perot's clever use of the medium is cited as a contributing factor to his surprising showing in November. There is conjecture that Rush Limbaugh's endorsement of Pat Buchanan before the New Hampshire primary contributed to President Bush's troubles in that state.[20] Some go so far as to attribute Jerry Brown's victory in the Connecticut primary to his courting of talk radio there. And Bill Clinton's ability to keep afloat during the New York primary is rumored to have been helped by talk radio appearances.[21]

The Times Mirror data shed a little bit of light on these presumptions. One impressive bit of evidence of talk radio's importance in the 1992 campaign is that voters perceived that they were gaining information from talk radio that they did not receive from other sources. Fifty-seven percent of listeners reported that they had learned something about the candidates from talk radio that they had not heard before. This constitutes twenty-five percent of all respondents to the Times Mirror survey.

Whether or not talk radio swayed candidate preference in the election is a more complicated matter that cannot be addressed directly [here]. Talk radio long has been the domain of Republicans and conservatives,[22] but these dynamics changed during the 1992 contest. First, Democratic candidates discovered radio. But perhaps more importantly, independent candidate Ross Perot took to the airwaves with an unorthodox political style that appealed to an audience that strives to distance itself from big government and formal institutions.

While we can't directly test whether talk radio influenced vote choice in 1992, especially since the survey was conducted in April [1992], we can explore how listeners' attitudes about candidates differed from those of nonlisteners. We expect that members of the talk radio audience will be more likely than nonmembers to favor Ross Perot and to consider voting for him in the November election. Further, we hypothesize that talk radio fans will follow Perot's candidacy more closely than will other voters.

The Times Mirror data support our hypothesis that the talk radio audience would be more attracted to an "outsider" candidate than would nonlisteners. The survey respondents were asked who they would vote for if the election were held today. Of Perot supporters in the sample, a majority—fifty-two percent—were talk radio listeners. Further, more respondents were asked if they would consider voting for Perot. Of those who reported that they would entertain this possibility, fifty-one percent were talk radio users. Among those who would not, only forty-four percent listened to talk radio. . . .

Our expectation that talk radio listeners were more attentive to Perot's candidacy than nonlisteners is one of the strongest findings of this study. The survey respondents were asked to assess how much they knew about Ross Perot's stands on issues and how much they had heard about his candidacy. . . . [S]ixty-four percent of respondents who reported that they knew a great deal about Perot's issue positions were talk radio users. Only thirty-four percent of those who stated that they knew nothing were listeners. The percentages are nearly identical for the question which measured how much respondents had heard about Perot.

The evidence to this point seems to indicate that talk radio listeners were drawn to Perot because of his eccentric manner and anti-institutional rhetoric. However, the talk radio audience tends to view politics and politicians with a jaundiced eye. Dissonance and controversy are integral to the format's popular appeal. Therefore, even candidates favored by talk radio listeners do not escape scrutiny. This is especially true when following a renegade candidate becomes a talk radio obsession as it became with Ross Perot. While members [of the] talk radio community may have been more attracted to Perot than were other citizens, they were not uncritical in their evaluations of him. It appears as though his candidacy was welcomed as an antiestablishment alternative, but also was greeted with a healthy degree of skepticism in the talk radio neighborhood. This division of sentiments is revealed as we probe further into the data.

Using the Times Mirror survey, we are able to gauge how voters evaluated the candidates' ability to handle particular presidential responsibilities. The survey participants were asked which candidate they felt would do the best job of dealing with the racial situation and with improving conditions for the middle class and the poor in the United States. . . . [T]alk radio devotees did not consider Ross Perot to be the most qualified to handle either of these problems. Bill Clinton fared best on both of these items. George Bush did considerably better than Ross Perot on the race question, although not on the economic conditions variable. However, of those who selected Ross Perot as the candidate most qualified to handle the racial situation in this country, fifty-nine percent were talk radio listeners. Similarly, among those who considered Perot to be best able to deal with the conditions facing the middle class and poor, fifty-three percent were talk radio users.

We have further evidence that the talk radio audience was divided about Perot's ability to perform as president. The respondents were questioned about whether they felt Perot would make mistakes in office. Of those who believed that he would make few blunders, fifty-three percent were talk radio listeners. However, among the respondents who felt that Perot would make many errors, fifty-two percent tuned into talk radio. These data also provide an ancillary insight into the talk radio audience. This group tends to assert more definite opinions than nonlisteners. While fifty-four percent of nonlisteners stated that they anticipated that Perot would make some mistakes, only forty-six percent of listeners took the middle ground.

CONCLUSION

Talk radio is an intriguing phenomenon which deserves to be reinstated on the agenda of mass communication scholars. It is well on its way to becoming an established fixture of the American political process as we move through the newly-emergent era of "infotainment" politics. Although talk radio cut its teeth on highly charged local issues in cities, such as New York, Chicago, and Boston, and this is where the majority of programs still place their emphasis,[23] political talk radio has become "nationalized." The amount of impassioned conversation generated by the Gulf War[24] and the 1992 presidential contest secured a prominent place on the national political agenda for talk radio. Thus, talk radio is a fertile field for the study of political engagement through mass media at all levels of government.

Talk radio has also earned its place as a bonafide cultural phenomenon. It is ironic that this "new" channel for expression—this "last frontier" for political discourse—has emerged from the reinvention of an old communication mechanism. While the audience of a previous era found personal solace in the localized talk radio ghetto, the "new" generation of talk radio devotees makes connections in a national community. Whereas the audience of an earlier age used talk radio as a mechanism for dealing with individual isolation, the "new" talk radio audience uses the medium to contend with social isolation, where interpersonal contacts may be many, but close relationships are few. The old talk radio produced close-knit families consisting of hosts, listeners, and callers. The "new" talk radio orchestrates large-scale political dramas designed to amuse, outrage, enlighten, and cajole a neighborhood of strangers.

This broad overview has revealed that the "new" audience for the reincarnated political talk format is culturally diverse and politically complex. The talk radio audience is not alienated from the political process as political observers have been quick to state. Quite the opposite is true. Listeners are efficacious and have a strong sense of civic commitment. They are supportive of the democratic system of government. Yet, they are disaffected from big, formal institutions, and they seek new means of accessing politics from within the confines of their milieu. Talk radio provides listeners with this outlet and draws them in the political process.

NOTES

1. Peter J. Boyer, "Bull Rush." *Vanity Fair,* 55:156–160 (May, 1992); Mike Hoyt, "Talk Radio Turning Up the Volume." *Columbia Journalism Review,* 31:44–50 (November–December 1992).
2. Diana Owen and Michael Robinson, "Media in Review: 1992 Heralds 'Electronic Populism.'" *The World & I.* 114–119 (February 1993).
3. Boyer, "Bull Rush."
4. Blayne Cutler, "High Frequency." *American Demographics,* 11–12 (March 1990).
5. James C. Roberts, "The Power of Talk Radio." *The American Enterprise,* 56–61 (May/June 1991).
6. Blayne Cutler, "Mature Audiences Only." *American Demographics.* 20–26 (October 1989).
7. Adult contemporary ("soft rock" and New Age/jazz) and country music are the two most popular radio formats. Talk radio is the third most popular format. See Cutler, "High Frequency."
8. Howard Fineman, "The Power of Talk." *Newsweek,* 24–28 (February 28, 1993).
9. Walter Goodman, "C-SPAN Dials Call-In Radio and Gets Quite an Earful." *New York Times,* November 22, 1990, section 2:25, 36.
10. Cutler, "Mature Audiences Only"; Fineman, "The Power of Talk."
11. For the most part, only one or two percent of listeners call into talk radio programs (Cf. Fineman, "The Power of Talk"). However, a CBS news poll, broadcast on the evening newscast on February 16, 1993, reported that 16 percent of listeners called into talk programs either on radio or television during the 1992 election. Calls from car phones constitute an increasing proportion of all calls. For some programs, three out of every five calls come from a car phone (cf. Goodman, "C-SPAN Dials Call-In Radio").
12. Quoted in Roberts, "The Power of Talk Radio," at 60.
13. Murray B. Levin. *Talk Radio and the American Dream.* Lexington, MA: Lexington Books, 1987; Peter Viles, "Talk Radio Riding High."

Broadcasting, 122:24 (June 14, 1992).
14. Hoyt, "Talk Radio Turning Up the Volume."
15. Joseph Turow, "Talk Show Radio as Interpersonal Communication." *Journal of Broadcasting,* 18:171–179 (1974); Jeffrey Bierig and John Dimmick, "The Late Night Radio Talk Show as Interpersonal Communication." *Journalism Quarterly,* 56:92–96 (1979); Harriet Tramer and Leo W. Jeffres, "Talk Radio—Forum and Companion." *Journal of Broadcasting,* 27:297–300 (1983).
16. John Crittenden, "Democratic Functions of the Open Mike Radio Forum." *Public Opinion Quarterly,* 35:200–210 (1971).
17. Roberts, "The Power of Talk Radio"; Fineman, "The Power of Talk."
18. *The Economist,* "Talk Radio: Lines Are Open." 34–35 (June 17, 1989); Roberts, "The Power of Talk Radio."
19. Paul F. Lazarsfeld, Bernard Berelson, and Hazel Gaudet, *The People's Choice,* 2nd edition. New York: Columbia University Press, 1948.
20. Boyer, "Bull Rush."
21. Hoyt, "Talk Radio Turning Up the Volume."
22. Fineman, "The Power of Talk."
23. Fineman, "The Power of Talk."
24. Mike Royko, "Oh, The Excitement of War-Talk Radio." *Chicago Tribune,* October 18, 1990, section 1:3.

DISCUSSION QUESTIONS

1. How would you characterize the political leanings of the people who call in to the radio talk shows in your locality? Are they generally more conservative or liberal than the rest of the people in your area?

2. How can talk radio programs influence politics and political decisions? Could a controversial talk radio program raise the salience of an issue so much that government has to deal with it? Do you know of an instance when that happened?

3. If you were campaigning for office, or if you were a public official who wanted to influence public opinion on an issue, could you take advantage of talk radio? How would you go about doing that?

4. How representative of the public as a whole do you think the callers to talk radio shows are? Do you think they reflect what noncallers are thinking, or do you think that the show's producers select callers who are more likely to take controversial positions (because it creates audience interest)?

CHAPTER 4
Campaigns, Elections, and Media

If one element in the contemporary political scene immediately brings the relationship of media to politics to mind, it is elections. Headlines reporting the latest gaffe by a presidential campaign and television ads criticizing unworthy opponents surround us between Labor Day and Election Day every two years. Over the last thirty years, parties and party workers contacting voters in campaigns have been displaced by candidates seeking to reach the electorate through the media instead. With the possible exception of candidates for minor local offices, office seekers design their campaigns to win as much favorable exposure for their candidacies in the media as possible. Whether presidential nominees or potential state legislators, campaigners worry about how well their efforts come across in the media.

At the presidential level, the emphasis on media is especially heavy; no other mechanism for reaching voters is as cost-effective, despite the heavy expense of television spots and press operations. The media effect on campaign actions, whether a stump speech at an airport or a motorcade on a downtown street, counts more heavily in campaign strategy than the number of people who witness the event in person. Even national nominating conventions, those spectacular gatherings of party faithful, are orchestrated for maximum media coverage and a favorable party image. The actual nomination of the party's candidate for president is now as much a media event as a party event. Larry David Smith and Dan Nimmo describe the impact of the changes in these conventions, suggesting that we should see them as the complex political phenomenon they are. They are neither meaningless anachronisms of the past nor events staged purely for the media coverage they generate.

During the campaign itself, the media play a critical role, even if they only want to report on campaign events. F. Christopher Arterton argues that the presence of media unavoidably and inevitably alters the nature of campaigning at the presidential level. Far from neutral outside observers who report what occurs during a campaign, journalists are integral elements in the campaign as perceived by the candidates and their staffs.

Events occur *because* reporters are there to report on them, and candidates adjust their actions accordingly. News people have an effect on campaigns, whether they wish to or not.

The tendency of campaign coverage to focus on appealing "sound bites," or short quotations from the candidates, during network news has also affected campaigns. Campaigners now worry as much about getting the right phrases excerpted on television as they do getting a favorable response from the crowds they see in person. Some would argue, indeed, that sound-bite campaigning reduces campaign discourse to sloganeering, at the expense of serious discussion of policy issues. Nevertheless, much as we may like it to be different, the sound-bite game is the one that's being played today; that is how presidential candidates are covered.

As a response to this (and other) patterns of campaign reporting, 1992 presidential candidates attempted to by-pass the traditional media to reach voters through somewhat less conventional means. Bill Clinton and Al Gore were most closely identified with these new techniques, although H. Ross Perot also used them extensively. Appearances on talk shows, MTV interviews, *Larry King Show* viewer call-ins, and 800 numbers became staples of presidential campaigning. The implications for future campaigns and elections are not yet clear.

If one problem in campaigning for president is a surfeit of press attention, candidates for Congress generally find it difficult to attract the coverage they would like. Of course, well-known incumbents need news coverage a lot less than their lesser-known challengers. And these challengers find it extraordinarily difficult to get mentioned in the news. My piece included here argues, following Alford, Henry, and Campbell,[1] that the congruence of congressional district lines and the reach of the major media serving that district generally makes it difficult for challengers to afford the kind of media exposure that will enable them to seem credible opponents to incumbents. The relative paucity of coverage of congressional campaigns reflects both incumbency advantage (without a strong challenge, the contest may not be newsworthy) and media market–district fit. As a result, you and I may not learn what we would like to know about the candidates for Congress running in our district.

The impact of media in local elections is less widely researched. We don't know as much about that as we do the effect of media in presidential elections, for instance. Not much evidence is yet available. We do know that the less information voters have, the more important each piece of information is. Therefore, we suspect that news coverage, scant as it frequently may be, is nonetheless significant. We know, too, that other media decisions carry some weight as well. Both the press and campaigners take

---

[1] James Campbell, John R. Alford, and Keith Henry, "Television Markets and Congressional Elections." *Legislative Studies Quarterly*. 9:665–78 (1984).

editorial endorsements seriously. The selection from *New York* magazine by Edwin Diamond describes some of the internal decision-making process that goes on at large newspapers before they make an endorsement. Internal media politics affects external campaign politics.

8. PARTIES, MEDIA, AND NATIONAL NOMINATING CONVENTIONS

The most visible activity of political parties in the United States consists of the quadrennial national nominating conventions, the spectacular gatherings of party delegates representing all fifty states, the territories, and even citizens living overseas. Here Democrats and Republicans formally nominate their presidential and vice presidential candidates and adopt their platforms—the statement of their principles and goals on which they can, for the moment, agree. Here delegates can mingle with party activists from other states and exchange ideas, argue issues, and make connections for the future. Here potential presidential candidates for the next go-round can begin to test their support and gauge the party faithful's responses to their chances. Here party leaders can begin to forge the direction of the party for the near future.

Much of this happens out of sight of the public. What you and I see on television, hear on the radio, or read about in newspapers and newsmagazines is much different. News about the conventions centers on the unexpected, on potential or real conflict, on personalities, and on speculation about the course of the presidential campaign to follow. Not surprisingly, argue Larry David Smith and Dan Nimmo, parties coordinate their conventions to present a favorable image to the public while still accomplishing their internal goals. The real decisions, they say, are made elsewhere—for instance, through the series of primary elections when many delegates are elected, pledged to a specific presidential candidate. What leaders do is to "orchestrate" the conventions so that a "cordial concurrence," a friendly ratification of previous decisions, can occur, a task greatly influenced by the nature of media covering the conventions. In the telepolitical age, Smith and Nimmo suggest, conventions are multifaceted and exciting events.

Cordial Concurrence: Orchestrating National Party Conventions in the Telepolitical Age

Larry David Smith and Dan Nimmo

Political, media, and reformist critics of contemporary convention orchestration differ in their complaints and in their proposed remedies. Uniting them, however, is a fervent nostalgia for an earlier time when televised conventions were full of fun, excitement, and doubt. If boarding a time machine they might well choose the 1952 Democratic National Convention in Chicago, where spontaneity reigned (three ballots to nominate the presidential candidate), network TV aired the drama on 18 million sets (all of them black and white), viewers watched the intimate picture in record numbers (60 million), and consumers endured scores of Westinghouse (CBS), Philco (NBC), and Admiral (ABC) household appliance commercials.

As Marty McFly discovered in the move, going *Back to the Future* can be shocking. What one thought once was, never was. In many respects the nostalgia surrounding the spontaneity of the 1952 DNC ignores the orchestrated cordial concurrence of the gathering. To be sure, the nomination fight was exciting and made for marvelous television. After a second ballot the outcome appeared in doubt. Tennessee Senator Estes Kefauver, who had campaigned and won in party primaries, led (362 1/2 votes). The reluctant candidate, Illinois governor Adlai Stevenson, having agreed after many weeks to be considered, was a close second (324 1/2). Senator Richard Russell of Georgia (294 votes) and Averell Harriman of New York (121 votes) still harbored hopes. All the contenders were well short of the 611 vote majority. Concurrence at all, let alone cordial, seemed unlikely—most certainly not on a third ballot. However, party leaders had already orchestrated two events that guaranteed Stevenson's victory. On a crucial earlier roll-call vote over seating a Virginia delegation that opposed a strong Democratic civil rights stand, the Illinois delegation threw its support behind the Virginia delegation 52 to 8. The vote came in spite of the pro–civil rights position of the Illinois delegation. "It suddenly dawned on us what was happening," said Stevenson's manager Jacob Arvey.[1] Kefauver and Harriman had struck a deal to pressure Southern delegations on civil rights to force a walkout. That would reduce the total convention vote, thus making it easier for Kefauver to win the party nomination. The convention seated Virginia with a 650 1/2 vote majority, dealing Kefauver a defeat.

Yet if the Kefauver-Harriman alliance held, the outcome of the presidential roll call was still in doubt. For two ballots it held. During the first of those two ballots President Harry Truman boarded a plane in Washington for Chicago. A TV network used a split-

SOURCE: From Larry David Smith and Dan Nimmo, *Cordial Concurrence: Orchestrating National Party Conventions in the Telepolitical Age,* copyright ©1991 by Larry David Smith and Dan Nimmo, p. 41, pp. 43–44, pp. 215–218, pp. 226–228. Praeger Publishers, an imprint of Greenwood Publishing Group, Inc, Westport, CT. Reprinted with permission.

screen picture to show the president's departure while simultaneously telecasting a vote in the Missouri delegation for Stevenson by Truman's alternate—a precisely orchestrated timing that served the interests of Stevenson, Truman, and the network.[2] Truman arrived in Chicago during the middle of the second ballot. Shortly afterward he had dinner at the Stockyard Inn near the convention hall. Present were several party leaders—impresarios including Arvey, Speaker of the House and convention chair Sam Rayburn, and others. During the dinner a representative from Averell Harriman arrived. Harriman would withdraw, thus breaking with Kefauver, and support Stevenson. The switch didn't just happen. Earlier in the dinner recess Truman sent an emissary to Harriman requesting a withdrawal in favor of Stevenson. "The obedient Harriman, without notifying Kefauver as per their agreement, sent his already prepared statement."[3]

As party leaders orchestrated the presidential roll-call drama, so too did they orchestrate TV network coverage. They had seen how the networks covered the GOP convention in Chicago two weeks earlier. Democratic impresarios capitalized on Republican mistakes and improved their own TV image. For one thing, the GOP barred all cameras from the party's national committee meeting; the chair of the DNC announced all party committee meetings would be open to the media; the Democrats, after all, were the "party of the people."[4] Party leaders and professional consultants worked to "make sure all Democratic Convention speeches would carry a uniform theme."[5] To improve the convention's telegenic features orchestrators located banners and signs with cameras, not delegates, in mind; painted floors, chairs, and benches gray to avoid a distracting glare on TV; synchronized musical numbers with the convention program; built a six-foot staircase to the podium so that speakers would appear to walk unrestrained and calmly to the microphones; opted against teleprompters for fear viewers at home could see them in use; and arranged for each TV network's studio to be high above and behind the convention rostrum, rather than removed from the hall. "And so ended," writes Reinsch, "the age of innocence in televised conventions."[6]

... Many an adult grown tired and weary, bored with the humdrum of daily life and disappointed at the narrowing opportunities that come with the "sunset" years, can recall memories of fleeting childhood, youth's innocence, and a time when "those were the days, my friend; we thought they'd never end." Collectively people do so in other ways. Watching a cherished film, say *Gone with the Wind,* elicits "they sure don't make 'em like they used to." And, why can't we return to "the golden days of television?" Or, "Where have you gone, Joe DiMaggio?" Where, indeed, are the shows of yesteryear? So, perhaps, critics of telepolitical conventions can be forgiven for dismissing the quadrennial conclaves as "dinosaurs." They ain't what they used to be, so dump 'em.

Reinsch is correct: the age of innocence is over. Why then remain innocent of how *lacking* in innocence party conventions have always been? More frequently than not convention concurrence, and its cordial tone, have been the norm of national party conventions from their conception in the 1830's. Single ballots and staged harmony did not arrive with the electronic era. Group-mediated, mass-mediated, and telepolitical conventions have always relied upon orchestral genius, not only for their success in selecting candidates capable of competing for the presidency but also for achieving a sense among party members, voters at large, and all Americans that *national parties exist*.

What has changed is that in preproduction, production, and postproduction phases conventions orchestration has become a sophisticated, specialized, bureaucratic activity that seeks to coordinate a plurality of institutional forces. Party bosses no longer play the orchestral role they once did; professional convention managers and consultants do. Talented artists no longer freely declaim their oratorical arias from center stage; technicians schedule their appearances, draft their speeches, critique their rehearsals, style their hair, and make up their faces. Party leaders no longer stage their "show of shows" in full knowledge that TV networks will cover them; the networks obey their own commercial instincts, orchestrate their own productions, and largely ignore the party's convention (except to blame the parties for low Nielsen ratings). About all that hasn't changed is that convention critics continue doing what H. L. Mencken did—"damning politicians up hill and down dale . . . as rogues, and vagabonds, frauds, and scoundrels."[7]

. . . With 1984 the age of telepolitical conventions arrived to stay, but for how long no one knows. . . .

In the telepolitical era the operation of communication technologies are no longer restricted to such organizations as TV networks, but are available to any organization, group, or faction with the knowledge and resources to use them. Unlike [in previous eras] the telepolitical convention not only caters to delegates and media needs but exploits satellite technology, professional television producers, computers, and other means to create, coordinate, and disseminate the show.

Today the orchestration of cordial concurrence takes on several new dimensions. In part telepolitical conventions are a synthesis of group and mass mobilization techniques. However, the intense focus of convention planners on preproduction operations is distinctive. For example, convention sites selected two or more years in advance, qualify only if [they are] capable of housing thousands of delegates, media, and party personnel; possess the transportation requirements of all these groups; are amenable to creating telegenic convention halls; and, most important, satisfy the political requirements of site-selection committees, party officials, and financial contributors. . . .

A key consideration . . . is the coordination of the convention hall's visual appearance and content. To achieve the best possible visuals, for example, both parties retained professional television producers in 1988. The Democrats hired Hollywood-based Smith-Hemion Productions (Gary Smith and Dwight Hemion) and the GOP turned to Washington-based Mark Goode Enterprises. When asked why his party turned to professional television producers for assistance, the Democrats' chief executive officer, Don Fowler, said: "What Smith-Hemion did was to take what was decided upon politically and help us to craft it into a good TV package. They did not tell us what to do . . . *[ellipsis in original]* they helped us shape [the show *{brackets in original}*] and make it look as good as it possibly could." In orchestrating the visual qualities of staging and content, the Democrats' Smith-Hemion initially hoped to provide an innovative, entertaining convention format of "Barbra Streisand and Barry Manilow and Bill Cosby and Aretha Franklin performing and introducing people and taking a very active role in the show.[8] As DNC communications director Mike McCurry pointed out, Smith-Hemion had to adjust its original concept after a meeting with network executives. Nonetheless, it did produce a "more visually attractive" convention through its set design and program direction.

... Another distinguishing aspect of the telepolitical convention is a pronounced emphasis on the production's thematic continuity. Today the political prima donna appears on a visually inspiring stage for a tightly scripted, prime-time aria and quickly exits once the roses (more accurately, balloons) are tossed on stage. Unlike the practices in group or mass mediation, however, these solos are products of message committees who work diligently to score continuity between standardized recitative performances. An example of the state of the art in thematic conventions was the Monday evening session of the 1984 Republican convention. The GOP presented a "ladies night" program that featured Margaret Heckler, Jeane Kirkpatrick, and Katherine Ortega (the keynoter) as principal speakers. All speakers pursued an "our house is your house" invitation for Democrats to join the Republican cause. The session was confined to two hours, used video introductions and brief speeches to maintain pace, and focused on a specific story line.

... Given what has remained the same over the years and what has changed in major ways, what can be summarized as the state of national party conventions in contemporary American telepolitics? Both critics and defenders of convention politics admit one convention accomplishment: it is the only gathering in one city, under one roof, at one time of representatives of local and state parties focusing upon party *qua* party matters as a national organization. That has always been the case, even in those years—as in 1948 with the Democrats—when party members bolted their convention. However, a telepolitical convention is a national gathering of more than elected and non-elected party representatives. It is also the only national televised conclave that bring diverse religious, racial, ethnic, and doctrinal party representatives into intense, intimate, and concentrated contact with candidates for office, and their organizations, at all levels; with elected and nonelected government officials of all levels; with professional political operatives and technicians; with working journalists of all types from every conceivable type of media in the nation and the world; with media moguls, executives, producers, directors, and technicians of all varieties and news organizations; and with critics, pressure-group spokespersons, protestors, entertainment celebrities, academicians, and a host of assorted political junkies, novices, groupies, and hangers-on.

A national party convention, in short, is a week-long hyped, publicized, televised spectacle that recognizes politics for what it is as currently practiced. . . . Teleconventions . . . showcase what is normally a concealed side of the contemporary conciliation of interests, the "public actions of free men" as orchestrated not spontaneous.

... National party conventions are, of course, both political and media events. They are, depending upon one's perspective, also news events, entertainment events, promotional events, business meetings, trade shows, rituals, celebrations, and commercial enterprises. [Our] perspective [is] . . . upon something else—namely, conventions as orchestrated events—the orchestration of cordial concurrence. . . . [T]hey have been such events from their beginnings in the early days of the Republic. They have remained so through their group-mediated and mass-mediated eras of development. They are even more so in the contemporary telepolitical age.

Today the term *national party conventions* is a misnomer.... [C]onventions involve the concurrence of far more numerous institutions than those that make up the membership of what people know as "the Democrats" or "the Republicans." To be sure, present are the party leaders, notables, celebrities, and rank and file. Present also are the candidates—winners and losers—and their entourages. So, too, are party technical consultants—for media, fund-raising, vote targeting, speechwriting, bite control, spin control, and damage control. With these campaign technicians are the professionals specializing in conventions, managers, entertainment directors, communication liaisons, publicity personnel, satellite network producers, even specialists in seat arrangements, balloon drops, demonstration choreographers, and "hand-painted sign" artists.

Joining this diversified company of party members, campaigners, and production personnel are representatives of nonparty institutions. From the host city are both government and private groups with a stake in the convention. There are also the superintendents and workers of the House and Senate galleries—for press, radio/TV, periodicals, and photographers. These professionals represent their own institutions, and thereby the federal government that pays their salaries, yet act as go-betweens for the political parties and the news media. And what a pluralist and diversified institutional complex are the news media! Represented are the print press—the dailies, weeklies, monthlies; newspapers, newsmagazines, and journals of opinion; publications of international, national, metropolitan, local, and countywide circulation. Omnipresent in the hall are the broadcast media—radio and TV; network, cable, and satellite; international, national, group, and local. A national political convention reminds one of the line from the film *Casablanca*, "Everybody comes to Rick's cafe"; everybody comes to the spectacle, not just the partisans.

There is a pronounced tendency among many who criticize and some who defend national political conventions to assume that the convention remains, or should be, party dominated—that for most citizens convention politics is, or should be, group mediated. Other critics and proponents alike argue that the political realities of party conventions are mass mediated through the filters of party and media consultants, the press, and broadcast journalists. Neither viewpoint fully captures the character of the secondhand realities of teleconvention politics. To borrow a phrase from Jesse Jackson's 1988 address before the DNC, "It's more profound than that." Telepolitical realities can be reduced neither to group nor mass mediation. They are the shifting political impressions derived from interinstitutional mediation, a mediation constructed from the orchestral acts of [a] vast array of institutional players.... [P]arty, governmental, media, and technical impresarios agree, disagree, argue, cajole, and negotiate to orchestrate the show and the spectacle that is a telepolitical convention. But it is more than a dinosaur being resurrected every four years; more than a party being refreshed for electoral battle; and more than an audience-driven vaudeville being staged. Politics is happening: the orchestration of shifting alliances of a plurality of powerful institutions, and the interinstitutional mediation for citizens of what is real and illusory in their political worlds. Abolish the convention and you remove not the relic of an extinct species, or even a showcase for the national parties or networks, or the legerdemain of technological wizards. Abolish conventions and you lose instead something of vaster consequence—the single, longest running production still in existence that, in a concentrated period on a single stage, showcases a microcosm of all that *is* American politics.

NOTES

1. J. B. Martin, *Adlai Stevenson of Illinois.* New York: Anchor Books, 1977, p. 594.
2. Martin, *Adlai Stevenson,* p. 597.
3. C. L. Fountenay, *Estes Kefauver: A Biography.* Knoxville, TN: University of Tennessee Press, 1980, p. 225.
4. J. Leonard Reinsch, *Getting Elected.* New York: Hippocrene Books, 1988, p. 64.
5. Reinsch, *Getting Elected,* p. 72.
6. Reinsch, *Getting Elected,* p. 77.
7. H.L. Mencken, *A Mencken Crestomathy.* New York: Alfred A. Knopf, 1956. p. 148.
8. E. Bark, "Business vs. Show Business: Networks Cool to Producers' Orchestration." *Dallas Morning News,* July 18, 1988, p. 2F.

DISCUSSION QUESTIONS

1. Why should an average voter pay attention to news about the parties' national nominating conventions? How accurate a picture of the events that take place at those conventions do the media provide?

2. Some delegates to the conventions bring portable television sets so that they can watch media coverage of the events they are attending. What purposes do platform activities serve, if even many of the delegates follow the convention through the media?

3. What changes do you expect to see in national nominating conventions the next time they meet? What changes would you propose to the parties?

4. Does media coverage of the conventions provide the information the public needs? What suggestions would you make to the media to improve convention reporting?

9. PRESIDENTIAL CAMPAIGNS AND THE PRESS

Campaigners try to reach voters, and journalists cover their efforts because they are newsworthy. Or so it seems. It seems as if candidates conduct campaigns to win office, and newspeople act as flies on the wall, observing candidate activities without affecting them themselves. F. Christopher Arterton argues that in presidential elections, at least, that conception of campaigns is misleading at best. In fact, he says, reporters occupy a central position in the campaign context, and, far from being inert elements in that context, they are instead catalysts for campaign activities, conduits for candidate communication with voters, and inescapable factors in campaign strategy.

Modern presidential campaigns use the media to reach voters. Of course, television advertisements are one way to do that, and candidates spend a lot of money airing campaign spots. Another way to reach voters is to generate news coverage. So candidates plan campaign activities to maximize the chances they will get prominent play on television newscasts and favorable treatment in the newspapers. To campaigners, then, journalists are not merely casual observers standing by in case something newsworthy happens. Journalists are in reality guardians of an important communications channel that candidates attempt to take advantage of to get the news coverage they need. And since reporters want good stories to file, the relationship works out well for both sides.

Especially during the primary season, expectations of success play a big role. Arterton argues that campaigners exert quite an effort influencing how journalists perceive primary outcomes. How should we judge the progress the campaign is making? What standards should we use to make such judgments? But influencing the choice of standards is not enough. If winning delegates is to be the standard, how many delegates is evidence of success? What benchmarks, in other words, should the media use to evaluate the candidates' efforts? Campaigners do not leave journalists to establish such standards and benchmarks in isolation but work hard to influence those judgments.

Media Politics: Do They Make a Difference?

F. Christopher Arterton

If the importance of campaigning through the news process has increased..., what have been the consequences of this change? Interactions with journalists take up a major part of campaigners' time. Not only does media campaigning provide them with the best channel for reaching voters, but journalists also become the prime conduit for exchanges with competitors. Charges and countercharges are made to the press corps as each candidate seeks to dominate the headlines to his or her advantage. The consequences of devoting so much time to the generation of news can be seen in organizational, substantive, and strategic campaign behavior.

CAMPAIGN ORGANIZATION EFFECTS

Relations with journalists have a major role in how campaigners allocate the organizational resources. The press of-

SOURCE: Reprinted with the permission of Lexington Books, an imprint of Macmillan, Inc., from *Media Politics: The News Strategies of Presidential Campaigns,* by F. Christopher Arterton. Copyright 1984 by D.C. Heath and Company.

fice of a major presidential campaign organization takes up only a small proportion of the financial and staff resources available. Time is a more important drain. Campaign managers frequently report spending much of each day responding to journalists' inquiries. Candidates also have intensive daily contacts with newsmen in press conferences and exclusive interviews.

The campaign's daily schedule is also organized by the quest for news coverage. If a candidate spends one hour in a city, he is likely to receive the same amount of news coverage of that visit as he would during a four-hour or eight-hour campaign stop in the same location. Thus, modern presidential candidates are kept continually on the move by their desire for local news coverage. The scheduler's goal is to set up appearances in three or four major news markets each day.

CAMPAIGN CONTENT EFFECTS

All campaigns develop themes that they would like communicated to the electorate through the news-reporting process, persuasive messages that the campaigners hope will energize political support and differentiate their candidate from his competitors. Accordingly, media politics have implications for the substantive content of modern election campaigns.

Journalists, of course, retain ultimate control over what is disseminated as the news of the day. In making this determination, they respond to more than simply the desires of one campaign. As campaign-generated events are transformed into news, furthermore, they undergo a journalistic process that incorporates other information, points of view, and, perhaps unintentionally, the reporters' implicit values. Political journalists face an inevitable dilemma: by reporting events as they occur—and thus not intruding into the electoral process—they may be surrendering the content of their stories to politicians (who would like nothing better than to dictate the news).

To project appealing messages to voters, campaigners must anticipate the transformation that their words and actions will undergo as they become reported news. A news strategy is, therefore, quite different from an advertising campaign in which the politician can control the content. Media politics demand that candidates and their operatives accommodate the values of journalists who will transmit their messages. Such accommodations distort—in some ways beneficially, in some ways adversely—the content of the campaign.

Journalists argue that campaign appeals are entirely the result of interactions between voters or party activists, on the one hand, and campaigners, on the other. Campaigners, however, react to news reports, regardless of what their polls tell them about voters' intentions. Candidates believe, for example, that if negative press commentary is not an electoral problem for today, news reporting will make it a problem for them tomorrow. They expend a great deal of effort, therefore, to head off negative news before it creates a major political problem. In the process, the news-reporting industry can intrude into the content of the campaign, an indirect form of agenda-setting.

Media politics can influence the content of campaigns in other subtle ways. Reporters often indicate that campaign speeches are appeals for voters, attempts to belittle the opposition, tries at putting the best face on a bad situation, or rebuttals to criticisms of public positions or candidacies. Such commentary alerts the audience that the speaker is trying to influence its thinking, in turn diminishing the impact of the campaigner's persuasive message. The message is implicit: Politicians are manipulative, journalists objective.

[One must] distinguish between a candidate's image among the public at large and the labels that are consistently used to describe the candidate in news reporting. The two are obviously related. However, one difference flows from journalists' understandable reluctance to make positive statements about politicians. Although laudatory comments in campaign reporting can be found—mostly in discussions of the political acumen of winners—they are less frequent than critical comments and images. Journalists' reputation for objectivity may be easier to maintain if affirmative evaluations are kept to a minimum. Negative statements are less likely to be construed as partisan, particularly when all politicians are criticized equally. To the extent that the public holds positive images of candidates, however, there may be a disjunction with information carried by the news media.

Some authors have viewed this critical function of news reporting as a needed corrective to the efforts of politicians and their public relations advisers to manipulate public sentiment.[1] However, if carried too far, persistently negative commentary may have an adverse impact on the electoral process....

POLITICAL STRATEGY EFFECTS

Strategic planning is a third area in which media politics influence modern presidential campaigns. In practice, editors and producers must make certain decisions that significantly shape the political race. For example, since serious candidates are newsworthy, those without prospects for winning are given less of the limited news space available to electoral politics. Criteria must be established that distinguish candidates with serious electoral prospects to communicate as much information about them as possible to voters.

Editors and producers also have to decide on an approximate starting point for the campaign. The assumption is that voters are less attentive to campaign news during the preliminary stages of the campaign. Once the race is in full swing, journalists must give greater space to those events which they perceived as pivotally important to the outcome. Such advanced planning greatly facilitates the commitment of media resources, particularly for the networks who must deploy cumbersome equipment and numerous people.

In each case, news industry decisions affect the volume of coverage available to the contenders. As a result, campaigners conform to these decisions in their strategic planning. Once journalists decide on a given criterion for discriminating serious campaigns from those without real prospects for victory (say, for example, the ability to qualify for federal matching funds), campaigners compete along those dimensions. The timing of major campaign events also mirrors the decisions of journalists about when the campaign will begin to receive voluminous news coverage. Campaigners know, for example, that a policy speech will more likely to be reported if scheduled during the so-called campaign season established by the media. These decisions create a cycle: as political events such as primary contests merit heavier news coverage, more competitors are drawn to them.

Media and campaign decisions are often intertwined. This cyclical process escalates the importance of some factors out of proportion to their political significance. In other words, the weighting given to certain achievements by the competitors or to certain events may be substantially different from pure political considerations once the news-

mobilize resources and their access to news coverage.

As presidential candidates succeed politically, they increasingly gain influence over the substance of horserace reporting for several reasons. Success in the primaries validates the scenarios, standards, and benchmarks promoted by winning campaigners. . . .

Successful presidential candidates have the means to orient reporters toward questions which suit their purposes. For example, to make Ohio seem like the critical primary [in 1976], the Carter campaign coordinated the behavior of other politicians in a manner that might lead reporters to the appropriate conclusions. Furthermore, the large press retinue traveling with Carter became a resource through which the campaign could orchestrate horserace reporting onto advantageous questions. Specifically, the staff kept attention focused on Carter's delegate count while [then-California Governor Jerry] Brown and other candidates argued that journalists should concentrate on the results of competitive primaries.

Thus, these recent experiences indicate that the political relationship between campaigners and journalists generally depends on the candidate's electoral success. . . .

The general election, lacking a sequential nature, is generally devoid of horserace reporting at the level of standards and benchmarks. When broad scenarios of electoral college strategies become quickly exhausted in terms of news value, campaign reporting tends to concentrate on policy questions or peripheral events that might shape the outcome. Coverage has generally been critical, often throwing candidates onto the defensive. In this atmosphere, campaigners reintroduce horserace questions to give journalists something to report upon other than a series of campaign gaffes. The televised presidential debates serve this purpose ideally; they have become transformed into pseudo-primaries.

In asserting that horserace reporting can influence voting, campaigners are really arguing that the impact of journalists lies in communicating perceived factual assertions, rather than opinions or attitudes. . . .

This perceived impact of factual assertions in the news is a variant of the agenda-setting power of mass media. In this case, however, the influence on voters is perceived as originating in the content of news reports as well as in coverage decisions that highlight certain candidates over others.

Media considerations and journalistic consensus play a major—if not primary—role in campaign decision making. . . . This influence seems strongest during the preprimary and early primary periods when the candidates have not yet developed strong political relationships with journalists. Campaigners reported that media considerations often resulted in major changes in their campaign plans. In retrospect, some campaigners complain about not being free to pursue the presidency without the judgments of journalists influencing their strategies and behaviors. In general, though, most take the view that those who live by the sword risk perishing that way as well.

NOTE

1. See, for example, Stanley Kelley, Jr., *Professional Public Relations and Political Power*. Baltimore, MD: Johns Hopkins University Press, 1956; Melvyn Bloom, *Public Relations and Presidential Campaigns: A Crisis in Democracy*. New York: Crowell, 1973; and James Perry, *Us and Them*. New York: Potter, 1973.

DISCUSSION QUESTIONS

1. How can reporters cover campaigns thoroughly and minimize their own impact on campaign events and strategies? Can you make some suggestions for reporters in this regard as they prepare for their next presidential campaign?
2. How well did journalists report the last presidential campaign in providing relevant information to the public? Did their reporting activities, in your estimation, affect the course of the campaign itself? Why or why not?
3. What would you say to reporters who say that the content of campaign coverage is determined most by the presidential campaign organizations themselves, pointing to the many staffers charged with press relations?
4. Do journalists' expectations about the progress of the presidential campaign have too much influence over the contest among the candidates? How can we minimize the effect of those expectations, especially during the primary season?

10. NEW TECHNIQUES IN 1992

The 1992 presidential election campaign was unique not only because of the strong showing of H. Ross Perot with his folksy and colorful language, his 30-minute "infomercials," and his challenge to Democratic and Republican dominance of the election. The campaign also marked the arrival of a series of relatively new technological developments at the presidential campaign level. Many of the devices used in 1992 were not exactly new, but they had rarely been used by presidential candidates—and never as much and as well. Bill Clinton played his saxophone on *The Arsenio Hall Show;* on the *Larry King Show,* Perot invited viewers to call him to urge him to run for president; Jerry Brown flashed an 800 number during televised primary debates whenever he could. And MTV reporters covered the presidential conventions.

Lee Wilkins and Philip Patterson explore the implications of these and other technological innovations in presidential campaigning. Clearly, the media are no longer monolithic, centralized in New York or Washington, providing candidates with no way to reach large numbers of voters except through them. Candidates are learning to target specific audiences, rather than trying to reach mass audiences through the media, much as they had frequently done through direct mail. And perhaps the candidates exercised more control over the messages voters ultimately received. Will we see a recurrence in 1996? The reviews for 1992 were encouraging!

Playing to a Friendly House: Narrowcasting and Politics

Lee Wilkins and Philip Patterson

As voters evaluate the November 1992 elections, President Clinton will have added two new images to America's political vocabulary: the bus and the dish. His campaign will be remembered as much for its podiums—MTV, Nickelodeon, a 48-passenger bus—as it will for its platform—a lengthy booklet few voters read.

But both his podiums and his platform represent a use of technology to achieve the same end: specific messages targeted to specific groups of voters, alike either by geography or demography. In both cases, Clinton was able to use technology to bypass the grip of traditional news media (wire services, news magazines, and television networks) in delivering his message. Other candidates employed the same tactics:

- Ross Perot began his Presidential odyssey on the CNN's *Larry King Show,* not one of the traditional television networks. He responded at length to voters in morning news and entertainment programs such as *Today* and *Good Morning America,* not in the *New York Times.*
- Both political parties credentialed representatives of MTV and The Comedy Channel to cover party proceedings. Traditional journalists scoffed, but the candidates didn't. Both Bill Clinton and Vice President Dan Quayle responded with lengthy interviews carrying messages targeted at younger voters.

SOURCE: Reprinted from *Nebraska Humanities,* Vol. III, No. 1, 1993, pp. 27–28, with permission of the Nebraska Humanities Council.

- And Dan Quayle's attack on Murphy Brown wasn't nearly as inept as it seemed. In giving a fictional character something important to say about a significant political issue, Quayle did openly what voters do in the privacy of the voting booth. He blurred the lines between "real politics" and popular culture.

What these instances and others reflect is a shift in political communication and what constitutes a political message.

NARROWCASTING: TALKING TO THE MASSES A FEW AT A TIME

The shift in how Americans are communicating has required a minor technological revolution: narrowcasting via cable television, zoned newspaper editions, magazines targeted at specialized audiences, and a variety of emerging mediums. Narrowcasting, whether by the satellite dish or the campaign bus, has allowed candidates and specific groups of voters to control their messages and to predict which audience will receive them.

Candidates understand that narrowcasting allows them to bypass the traditional journalist employing traditional definitions of news. While the technology of narrowcasting has much to recommend it from the candidate's perspective, its impact on the polis is equivocal.

Narrowcasting has a historical precedent in politics: the Chautauqua circuit. Before there was television, or even a mass distribution print press, candidates for national office used to travel the Chautauqua circuit, speaking to geographically- and politically-well-defined communities. The Chautauqua required an orator of some strength and it gave the country one of its truly great presidents, Abraham Lincoln, as well as some of its better-known also-rans like William Jennings Bryan. Franklin Roosevelt's fireside chats, beamed as they were to homes that could afford radio, and Harry Truman's whistlestop campaign, are more contemporary versions of the same idea.

But what the technology of narrowcasting makes possible is to allow the candidates to reach those they might not otherwise be able to reach with highly specific messages. The young people who watch MTV wanted to know how the candidates stood on issues of interest to them. The candidates responded with messages that were tailored to that portion of the electorate. The nation's more than 10,000 magazines provide the print equivalent of narrowcasting. Get your message about the environment into a publication such as *Trout Unlimited* and a candidate knows a great deal about what to say, who is likely to receive the message, and how that message is likely to be understood.

With more than 110 television channels and more than 10,000 magazines to chose [sic] from, narrowcasting is an effective way to get the attention of voters and contributors. For instance Clinton—ignored by the national news media during Perot's flirtation with the political process—played the sax on the *Arsenio Hall Show* just to corral some time to talk politics.

President George Bush waited for the broadcasters to leave the Republican National Convention to narrowcast to a convention of the religious right, telling them that Clinton had drafted a platform without "God." The President was confident his message would be well-received by his target audience while sustaining relatively little attention from the national press corps. He was following a well-validated political dictum: motivate your own supporters, then work on the undecided or weakly committed voter.

THE MESSAGE IS MORE THAN JUST THE MEDIUM

While the technology of narrowcasting changed how candidates communicate with voters, it also influenced the message itself. By selecting specific channels and target audiences, the candidates are attempting to wrest political reporting from traditional journalists who have reduced an opportunity for national political discourse to a "horse race." Research has documented that contemporary journalism portrays electoral politics as a series of events, photo opportunities, and dueling 10-second televised sound bites.

This peculiar journalistic framing of elections, which is the result of an unreflective adherence to a [sic] ethic of objectivity, has three significant results. First, in the name of balance, the process legitimizes two candidates (and no more than two) for almost all partisan political offices. In fact, it was this understanding of the legitimizing impact of traditional journalism that led to the formation of EMILY's list, a political action committee that funnels money only to women candidates early in their campaigns to help develop organizations and media strategies that allow women to be perceived as legitimate political contenders by both journalists and voters.

Second, a strict adherence to an ethical standard of objectivity often results in a bipolar discussion of complex issues while ignoring other more complicated—and time-consuming—visions. In 1992, the Clinton campaign discovered that the nine-second sound bite (the length of time the candidate is actually pictured saying his own words on the network news) that had dominated the 1988 television coverage of the Presidential campaign had shrunk to less than seven seconds during the early primaries. Rather than subject the candidate and his ideas to such journalistic silliness, the Clinton campaign opted for the alternative media of narrowcasting to allow the candidate the time to get his message out.

But third, and most seriously, the simplistic and reductionistic application of a [sic] ethic of objectivity to highly charged and complicated political issues has allowed readers and viewers to turn off the mainstream media. Instead, viewers and readers have turned to channels of communication they believe more accurately reflect their individual points of view.

Pessimists have argued that this message-centered narrowcasting allows the candidates to fragment political dialogue to the point of cacophony. In such a wall of sound, voters are more likely to listen only to the most narrowly-defined segments of the electorate. Narrowcasting's detractors fear that in such splintered discourse, no one will speak for the republic.

THE ETHICS OF INVOLVEMENT

This is not to say, however, that the public has no appetite for political discourse. Readers and viewers are more interested in and energized by stories that deal with issues rather than image.

In January of 1992, in an attempt to puncture reader dismissal of traditional political coverage, the *Charlotte Observer* polled its readers about which political issues were most important to them. The readers disregarded character in favor of the environment, the economy, and education. The paper then recruited a local ABC television affiliate to help focus coverage on those issues.

What the *Observer* did, through asking its readers what they wanted to hear about politics, was to uncover the common political discourse. Furthermore, that common political discourse substituted one ethical standard, strict objectivity, for another: involvement. Within these broad guidelines, the newspaper devoted substantial space and resources to issues and analysis of interest to the community. Character, which received a secondary emphasis, was still covered in depth. Advertising claims were treated as news.

In short, the *Observer* challenged traditional notions of the division between journalists and their readers, between advertising and news, and between detached objectivity and news coverage which purposefully seeks to involve the reader in the democratic process. The *Observer* began to "narrowcast" with the goal of rebuilding a cohesive political community.

"What is needed, and desperately, is a resurgence of the language of common citizenship," according to *Washington Post* political writer E. J. Dionne. In *Why Americans Hate Politics,* he blames both the left and the right for the current bankruptcy of American political discourse.

It is too early to know whether the *Observer*'s experiment, Clinton's appearance on *Arsenio Hall,* and Perot's use of sophisticated technology have succeeded in rediscovering a language of common citizenship. But, the experiments provide traditional journalism with a profound set of incentives to reevaluate its own ethics. If traditional and objective news coverage distances voters from their political community, then alternative media could become the mainstream source of political information. For traditional journalists to reclaim a stake in the process, they must discover a new balance between strict objectivity and partisan involvement, one that emphasizes a continuation of democratic government as much as an honest critique of the process.

DISCUSSION QUESTIONS

1. Does the strategy adopted by 1992 presidential candidates to reach targeted audiences through narrowcasting make sense to you? Why or why not?

2. What changes in technology and the public's television viewing habits make narrowcasting a viable campaign option for the future? Are campaigners going to market their candidates through the media as carefully as manufacturers market soap?

3. Many cable television systems now enable advertisers to select quite narrowly defined geographic areas for their messages. Have you noticed whether candidates in your state and locality are using narrowcasting and cable advertising to reach specific groups of voters?

4. What strategy would you adopt, if you were a national news reporter, to reexert your influence over the way presidential campaigns are reported? Are you doomed to be eclipsed by the newer technology and techniques?

11. CONGRESSIONAL CAMPAIGN COVERAGE

The great attention presidential contenders receive from the media and from the public as a whole far surpasses the relatively meager news coverage congressional campaigners manage to attract. As a consequence, the informational context for voters and the campaign strategies for the candidates differ tremendously from those in campaigns for the nation's highest office. House challengers, especially, suffer from the dearth of news coverage, and, since they rarely have the extensive financial resources to purchase widespread exposure through television spots, challengers find themselves at a severe disadvantage compared to incumbents. Stimulating media coverage becomes a difficult task for them, much different than the task faced by presidential candidates who struggle to portray the right image for the ever-present media.

In this selection, I develop the notion that the configuration of congressional districts not only affects what you and I are likely to learn about congressional campaigns but also structures the opportunities candidates have to reach us with their campaign messages. As a result, a race for the House of Representatives is generally a low-visibility election, with incumbency advantages magnified. In open seat races, the contest may be newsworthy enough to attract a lot of news coverage, but most incumbent-challenger contests don't come close to meeting reporters' newsworthiness criteria, a situation incumbents don't mind in the least.

Do Challengers Even Have a Chance? Media Coverage of Congressional Elections

J. P. Vermeer

Consider the dilemma a candidate hoping to unseat a congressional incumbent faces, if the district in question happens to fall in a large metropolitan area. Many do, as a matter of fact: the Los Angeles area, the San Francisco Bay area, Chicago and its suburbs, the New York City tri-state area, and Dallas-Fort Worth all contain numerous congressional districts, some as many as twelve to sixteen. The media that serve those large urban areas cover the entire metropolis. But one congressional district extends over only a small portion of that area.

Challengers trying to unseat incumbents generally face an uphill battle. The incumbent is usually well-known and well-liked. The incumbent is usually well-financed. And incumbents almost never lose when they seek reelection. Challengers, on the other hand, are rarely well-known, and most voters don't know enough about them to decide whether they like them or not. They also find it difficult to raise the amount of money (spending half a million dollars in a congressional campaign is no longer unusual) they need to make a credible showing. Who would donate lots of money to someone who seems likely to lose?

To win, a challenger needs to become better known. That's where the dilemma comes in. The best way to become better known is through media coverage. But in metropolitan areas, media coverage is hard to come by, especially for challengers. For one thing, there are lots of challengers and incumbents and campaigns for the media to cover. They are unlikely to devote much of their resources to any but the most exciting, newsworthy campaigns. But those campaigns are usually ones where there is no incumbent or where the challenger is already well-known. That's no help to an unknown challenger who needs publicity.

For another, if the media in metropolitan areas cover a congressional candidate, most of their audience will have only a passing interest in the news story. After all, most will live in another congressional district and cannot vote for or against the candidate covered in the news story. Since media are in business to deliver an audience to advertisers, whether readers of newspapers or viewers of television news, they want to emphasize stories of interest to as many viewers as possible. And a story about a challenger in northeastern Orange

SOURCE: Original essay written especially for this volume.

County in the Los Angeles area is of little interest to readers in the San Fernando Valley. Why would the *Los Angeles Times* devote much space to such a news item? And why should they display the story prominently enough so that readers who do live in the candidate's district would be likely to notice it?

Candidates for Congress, then, cannot rely on free news coverage to build their name recognition among voters. They will have to use other means to reach the electorate. Chief among these are the paid media: advertising on television and radio and in newspapers. But here the candidate is no better off. Rates for advertising are based on the size of the audience, and audiences for media in metropolitan areas can be huge. But only a small proportion of them can vote for the candidate, because only a small percentage live in the candidate's district. A candidate has to pay high costs to reach potential voters, a cost that is more difficult to meet because challengers cannot raise funds easily in the first place. But there is little alternative. If that weren't bad enough, with so many candidates in metropolitan areas having to adopt the same strategy out of necessity, any one candidate's campaign ads risk being overwhelmed by the flood of ads for other candidates. Now it's not only a question of paying for a larger audience than one needs but also a question of standing out from the crowd, of being distinctive, of coming up with media messages that catch voters' attention. Challengers in congressional elections in metropolitan areas face a daunting task in reaching enough voters so that they have a chance of winning. Is it any wonder that so many incumbents win?

I am talking about what political scientists refer to as media market-district "fit."[1] Some districts "fit" the local media market very nicely. For instance, Peter Hoagland's district in Nebraska coincides nicely with the reach of Omaha radio and television stations and the dominant circulation area of the *Omaha World-Herald*. That kind of fit is relatively rare. Another possibility is that a member of Congress may represent an area that encompasses a number of media markets, perhaps some in part and others completely. One example is the Sixth District of Kentucky, which includes Frankfort, the state capital, and Lexington, both important cities with important media outlets. But segments of the district are within easy reach of the Cincinnati and the Louisville media markets, both of which also encompass other congressional districts.

Perhaps one of the most important things to know about media coverage of congressional elections is the "fit" between the district and the media market. The closer the fit, the easier it is for congressional candidates to use the media to reach voters in the district. For most candidates, the fit ranges from poor to abysmal. How effectively candidates can use mass media in their election campaigns depends in part, then, on how well media markets and congressional districts correspond. The problem is the challenger's, because incumbents don't need media coverage to the extent challengers do. Why is that? It is simply because incumbents tend to be well-known already. If voters show up at the polls uninformed about a congressional contest, they are much more likely to recognize the incumbent's name on the ballot than the challenger's. They are much more likely to have favorable feelings toward the incumbent than toward the challenger.[2] The result is usually a vote for the incumbent. So, to overcome those advantages, the challenger needs media coverage more than the incumbent does.

In fact, even in media markets where challengers can more effectively generate news coverage, incumbents still enjoy marked advantages. Those advantages are largely the result of journalistic routines, the judgments about newsworthiness and the decisions about coverage that reporters normally make all the time. One advantage is that incumbents are inherently more newsworthy than challengers. After all, they hold significant office. They can take official actions, such as announcing grants and introducing bills, that depict them working for the district. They are better-known, and journalists tend to report on people the public is already aware of. Rare is the challenger who can generate enough press coverage to balance the attention incumbents receive in the media.

Another edge, although more subtle, is that every story about the challenger is likely to mention the incumbent prominently. In most such stories, the challenger is identified in terms of the incumbent (*e.g.*, "Susan Schroeder, the Democratic challenger to long-time congressional incumbent Joe Parsons, today said . . .) instead of on the basis of his or her own characteristics, while stories about the incumbent much less frequently mention the challenger.[3] Now, there are some advantages to the challenger in being referred to in this way, chiefly that it provides a context in which voters may remember him or her, but the disadvantage should be clear, also. The story about the challenger reminds people of their positive feeling about the incumbent. So challengers are not perceived in their own right as much as alternatives to incumbents, incumbents voters tend to be satisfied with.

Finally, incumbents can influence the news coverage challengers receive. A number of members of Congress, faced with a potentially strong challenger, downplay the election contest on purpose. They stay in Washington longer than they would otherwise, instead of coming home to campaign, they delay or even eliminate television advertisements on their behalf, and they avoid the usual series of announcements of endorsements and campaign committee appointments. The result these incumbents hope for is that the media decide the race is not very exciting and that the challenger does not present a real threat. The race is therefore not newsworthy. The media's resources are devoted elsewhere. Stories that otherwise might be written or aired about the campaign are passed over. And the challenger has even a greater difficulty in generating the news coverage that is essential to breaking into the public's consciousness. To the incumbent's advantage.

As far as the press is concerned, most congressional elections are low-information, low-interest contests. Media have little incentive to devote much of their resources to reporting the activities, appearances, and announcements of candidates for Congress. After all, virtually every state will have another electoral contest occurring at the same time, whether it is a presidential race, a race for the U.S. Senate, or a gubernatorial campaign. Media personnel do not have to worry about media market-district fit in covering these races. Both candidates in these contests are generally well-known (although not always), and public awareness of and interest in the election is usually quite a bit higher. So it is rational for the media simply to spend its resources covering the presidential race, the Senate race, or the gubernatorial race—whatever the dominant game is at the time—and leave congressional contests as an afterthought.

Open-seat elections are another matter altogether. When no incumbent is running for reelection, a congressional contest is likely to be a great deal more competitive. Potential candidates who have been waiting in the wings for the incumbent to retire, run for another office, or die emerge for their chance at the seat. State legislators, big city mayors, other state office-holders, and local celebrities of one kind or another see an open seat as an opportunity of a lifetime.[4] They fear that if they wait, someone else will win the seat and hold it for ten or more terms. And twenty years is a long time to wait for another chance at the office without having to face an incumbent. The kinds of candidates who seek the seat, then, are stronger and frequently better-known and more experienced than the typical challenger running against an incumbent.

These races are more exciting, largely because the candidates manage to raise substantial sums of money and therefore have the resources to buy extensive television time and to mount aggressive campaigns. The media expect a vigorous contest and devote proportionately more of their own resources to coverage. So press releases get used more. Reporters seek out stories on their own initiative. Candidate statements and personal appearances get covered. Editorials are written. And public awareness of both candidates increases. The resulting campaign coverage does not resemble coverage of incumbent-challenger contests at all, even in metropolitan districts.

Open-seat contests embody greater conflict, a prime attraction for journalists. It allows them also to write the kind of stories they specialize in for covering campaigns: the horse-race story. Horse-race stories emphasize who is winning, who is losing, what the public is thinking now, what an event means for the ultimate outcome of the election, and what people in the know are predicting. The stories do not report statements, positions on issues, or discussions of what the candidates are likely to do if elected. Open-seat races give reporters plenty of chances to write horse-race stories, because the race is usually in doubt. And the closeness of the race, compared to incumbent-challenger campaigns, gives rise to conflict between the sides that attract reader attention and meet press criteria for newsworthiness. As one consequence, we all as media consumers learn more about an open-seat campaign than we do about incumbents' reelection efforts.

As in other campaigns, candidates have to work to get their names known, their supporters energized, and their voters to the polls. They have to talk about the issues, explain why they are better than their opponents, and criticize their opponents' record. They have to reach voters with their campaign messages. And of the many means available to do these things, the media are among the most significant.

The recent spate of radio talk shows giving callers a chance to vent their spleen at developments that bother them works at least a little to challengers' advantage. To the extent that talk shows hosts and their guests rail at politicians in Washington, argue for term limits, and hint at behind-the-scenes machinations to the detriment of the public interest, incumbents may be seen less favorably and challengers as a more attractive alternative. Challengers may be able to take advantage of this highly political anti-political rhetoric by demonstrating how their opponents typify the "mess in Washington" and how they themselves are untainted. They still need, however, to get the public's ear to make these points, and although talk shows may make some elements of the electorate more receptive to challenger appeals, the problem of reaching the voters still remains.

As should be clear by now, however, incumbents do a lot better in using the media in congressional elections than challengers do. Despite the best efforts of challengers, generally underfunded and not well-known, incumbents enjoy tremendous advantages in getting their campaign messages across to the voters through the media. More importantly, incumbents need to communicate their messages much less urgently than challengers do. And the structure of the media environment and the impact of journalistic routines work together to magnify the incumbents' advantages in congressional elections. If you add to the picture the fact that members of Congress running for reelection rarely have severe difficulty raising campaign funds, is it any wonder that such a high percentage of incumbents get returned to office?

Indeed, it is more of a wonder that any get defeated at all. And the way media cover congressional campaigns is one of the most important reasons.

NOTES

1. See, for instance, James Campbell, John R. Alford, and Keith Henry, "Television Markets and Congressional Elections." *Legislative Studies Quarterly*. 9:665–78 (1984); and Timothy S. Prinz, "From Home Style to Video Style? Mass Media and Members' Attention to the District." Paper presented at the annual meeting of the Midwest Political Science Association, Chicago, Illinois, 1991.
2. Barbara Hinckley, *Congressional Elections*. Washington, D.C.: CQ Press, 1981, pp. 25–28.
3. Jan P. Vermeer, "Congressional Campaign Coverage in Rural Districts," in Jan P. Vermeer, ed., *Campaigns in the News: Mass Media and Congressional Elections*. Westport, CT: Greenwood Press, 1987, p. 86.
4. See, for instance, Gary C. Jacobson, *The Politics of Congressional Elections*. Boston: Little, Brown and Co., 1983, p. 38.

DISCUSSION QUESTIONS

1. Describe your home congressional district in terms of its fit with the media market serving it. Is it one of many congressional districts in the same market, does it have one market serving it, or do several media markets serve it?

2. Why are incumbents more newsworthy than challengers? How do incumbents take advantage of that?

3. What can challengers do to attract more media coverage? Would you suggest that they run a campaign critical of the incumbents?

4. What can you suggest to reporters to equalize the coverage challengers and incumbents get? Would "equal coverage" help challengers enough to make a difference?

12. ENDORSEMENTS IN LOCAL POLITICS

The outcome of city elections makes quite a difference to local newspapers and their publishers. Much of the news these papers will be covering in the succeeding years will be generated by the actions of a mayor, for instance. Most of the issues with which the editorial boards and the publisher are concerned will be dealt with by the public officials elevated to office by the electorate. And because a great deal of public business is discussed behind the scenes by those actively involved, publishers of local papers (usually people who are part of the city's inner circle) care a great deal who wields the formal political power.

That doesn't mean that decisions about endorsements are easy for newspapers to make. They know that their endorsement is an important signal not only to voters but to the political elites whose future decisions will determine the course of the city. Sometimes the decision is easy, but sometimes an endorsement decision splits an editorial board down the middle. Edwin Diamond here describes the process in New York City's four main newspapers after a particularly divisive mayoral campaign in the Big Apple in 1989. Newspaper politics can be as turbulent as any.

The Papers Vote: Endorsement Politics
Edwin Diamond

Of all the television images, the final two were the most arresting. On primary eve, a Koch and a Dinkins commercial appeared back-to-back on Channel 7—right before the late-night news. Koch's spot showed endorsements from the *Times* and the *Post;* Dinkin's showed the New York *Newsday* editorial. In their final appeals, the two candidates let other people speak for them—and in dull, non-telegenic print at that. According to the accepted wisdom, in a municipal contest where no candidate inspires high hopes, editorials may influence enough of the undecided or unenthusiastic to determine the results. But then, there's never been a pattern of endorsements as bizarre as this one. Koch won over two of the four dailies, but the *News*—the one paper whose endorsement might have helped Koch—supported Richard Ravitch, who at the time had around 5 percent in the polls. The way each paper handled its endorsements revealed more about the papers than about the primary. At the *News,* in fact, the Ravitch editorial cost the paper its editor, F. Gilman Spencer, who quit two days after the primary.

The process was least tortured at the *Post,* the first of the four dailies to endorse—and the paper with the fewest doubts about its choice. Owner Peter Kalikow, who bought the *Post* in 1988, kept the paper true to its past endorsements of Koch. Editorial-page editor

SOURCE: Copyright ©1992 K-III Magazine Corporation. All rights reserved. Reprinted with permission of *New York* Magazine.

Eric Breindel wrote not one but *two* pieces supporting Koch. Dinkins, in the *Post*'s view, was left of center, pro-labor, pro-big government, and pro-higher taxes. "It just wasn't a close call for us," said Breindel.

At *Newsday,* the endorsement process was more complicated. There are really two *Newsdays* and two *Newsday* editorial staffs: the Long Island edition, under the editorial-page leadership of Jim Klurfeld, and the New York edition, under Tom Plate, who reports to Klurfeld. The two staffs confer regularly, usually by phone—"missing the body language and eye contact," according to one insider. In addition, Steven Isenberg, associate publisher, and Robert M. Johnson, president and publisher of both editions, sit in on major decisions. Isenberg and Johnson agreed on the Dinkins endorsement. When there are differences of opinion, says Isenberg, "the last word belongs to Bob."

At the *Times,* an endorsement of Koch never seemed in doubt. Editorial-page editor Jack Rosenthal reports to the publisher, Arthur O. Sulzberger. And while the *Times*'s eighteen-person editorial board goes through what Rosenthal calls a "collegial process," the final decisions are made by the publisher. "The paper has a long-standing relationship with Koch," a *Times* political reporter says. "If there was any way we could see to endorse him, I knew we would."

But the way the *Times* made its Koch endorsement called as much attention to the "process" as the result. The editorial's headline, THE CASE FOR KOCH—AND HIS DUTY—, made a case for genetic engineering. According to the *Times,* Dinkins is "a measured man, highly likeable, dignified, decent." Koch, while provocative, "has proved his ability to run the city." Each man, said the *Times,* offered what the other most lacked. "The ideal outcome would be both." And so it went as the *Times* added up the pluses and minuses. The end product was so evenhanded that Dinkins supporters carved a primary day flier out of it (" '. . . The city might be well served by a Mayor Dinkins' ").

Yet readers with long memories should have been prepared for the *Times*'s exquisitely balanced editorial. In last year's presidential election, Sulzberger judged the board's favorite, Michael Dukakis, underwhelming. The resulting editorial, "Two Good Men," came out for the Democrat, but readers couldn't be sure until the last paragraph. "You always have to do a balancing," says Rosenthal. "In politics, it's not often easy."

At the *News,* the selection proved so difficult that the paper lost its balance and its editor, falling publicly on its face. Part of the *News*'s trouble is organizational. It's the sole city daily, for example, where the editor of the news pages—Gil Spencer—participates in endorsement decisions along with the publisher, James Hoge, and the editorial-page editor, Michael Pakenham. At the other papers, a well-defined wall separates—in theory—the news pages and the editorial pages. The *News*'s endorsement process this time was further complicated by the paper's history. Though it supported Koch in his three previous mayoral campaigns, the *News* has been increasingly critical of the mayor in the past three years. Its tough anti-Koch stance, in fact, went across the board: in its news coverage, supervised by Spencer, of civic corruption; in the opinion pieces of political writer Jack Newfield; in the rotating columns of the *News*'s four city columnists—and on the editorial page itself.

The biggest complication came when it was time to make the endorsement.

Pakenham had met with the *News*'s six-person editorial board and achieved what one participant called a "consensus" for Dinkins in the Democratic race. The endorsement never materialized. First it was delayed by what another participant calls "bad timing": Hoge and Spencer were unavailable because of a combination of vacations, personal reasons, and professional obligations. But when the three men finally got together in late August, it turned out that they weren't together. Hoge wanted Koch; Spencer and Pakenham wanted Dinkins, but Hoge won. "The publisher has the last word," says Pakenham. "There's no pretense that this is a democratic process, and I don't know a paper where it's different."

Daily papers may not be democracies, but the *News* has loosened the old imperial rules considerably under Hoge. Jack Newfield came to the paper last year after two decades on the barricades at *The Village Voice*. He made what he calls his "pre-endorsement" of Dinkins in his column of August 28. The *News*'s four city columnists—Gail Collins, Bob Herbert, Juan Gonzalez, and Mike McAlary—are a rainbow coalition of younger writers brought in specifically to enliven the news pages. While Hoge, Spencer, and Pakenham debated, rumors about their differences circulated through the newsroom. "The immediate reaction was 'mutter, mutter, mutter,' " says Collins. The mutterers acknowledged that, as Collins says, "the editorial page reflects management views. But to go for Koch, after how hard we'd been on him—it seemed worth fighting."

The newsroom couldn't develop a consensus on how to stop a Koch endorsement. Newfield was a proponent of taking out an advertisement in the paper refuting any Koch endorsement. Collins proposed that the four city columnists write and sign a joint dissent—"I was the most 'left-wing' on that," she says now. All such collective action became moot when, on September 7, the *News* came out for Ravitch.

"The decision was made by 3 people," Pakenham says, "not 30 or 300." Still, the dissenters could claim a kind of victory. As Collins put it, "The Ravitch endorsement may look foolish, but I'll take silly to craven any day." The 64-year-old Spencer, however, ultimately voted with his feet. His replacement was the *News*'s managing editor, Jim Willse, 45, who had avoided the whole endorsement fracas.

In a perfect world, of course, each paper would promote the public weal (and every candidate would be an exemplary leader). In the real New York, with its competitive market pressures, newspapers have to worry about their own interests as well. In the primary, each paper was true to itself and its readership. The *Times* is the paper of the established order. The *Post* has long been the paper of a largely Jewish middle class and has grown more conservative along with its constituency. New York *Newsday* has positioned itself as the paper of the nineties, with a developing readership in Queens and long-range plans to reach into Brooklyn and Manhattan. Its morning-after coverage of the primary results stressed its own self-image: The headline over twin stories on Dinkins and Koch read: FUTURE OUTSHINES GLOW OF PAST. Finally, the *News*'s focus in the city is split, just as its top editors were. Once the paper of the white ethnic working classes, the *News* now seeks to hold its traditional base and attract more black and Hispanic readers— that is, the city past and future.

Next month, the "process" begins again as editorial pages look for balance, publishers exercise their checks— and consumers read between the lines.

DISCUSSION QUESTIONS

1. Diamond's discussion makes it seem as if newspaper endorsements matter to the outcome of local elections. How important a factor is the local newspaper's endorsement in your area? Do you get the impression that the endorsed candidate receives more favorable coverage, or did the paper stay impartial, despite its editorial stance?

2. Why is it so difficult for editorial staffs on some newspapers to agree on the paper's endorsement?

3. Candidates worry about newspaper endorsements. Why do candidates think they are important? Are they more likely to seem important in low-information elections, where voters do not know as much about the candidates?

4. If you were a candidate for local office, how would you go about influencing a newspaper's endorsement?

CHAPTER 5
Media and the Institutions of Government

It would be ludicrous to expect government policymakers not to be keenly aware of the work of the press. Whether legislator or executive, whether elected official or appointed, whether a representative or a judge, government leaders find themselves working with the media, working despite the media, or using the media to achieve their own goals. Or all the above.

Some public officials work in a veritable fish bowl of media attention. Presidents, for instance, have their entire days scrutinized by the White House press corps, watching their comings and goings, buttonholing visitors, and shouting questions whenever they can, all in the hope of divining the course of decision making in the Oval Office. Presidents find it useful to limit the press's access in part to give the president some elbow room, so to speak, some freedom of action. At the same time, presidents' need for favorable coverage of their activities lead them to develop extensive public relations enterprises in the White House to influence the picture of the administration we in the rest of the country see. Reaching the public through the media not only becomes an inevitable by-product of media attempts to cover the president, it is a strategy presidents use to manipulate the media, and bypass them if necessary, to ensure that the administration's version of events is the one the public responds to.

Others can work more privately. Members of Congress seek publicity at home, in their districts, to maintain a favorable public image and high name recognition. In Washington, however, they have only recently begun to incorporate media strategies into their attempts at achieving their legislative goals. Timothy Cook describes the conflict between show horses and work horses and argues that making news is now an integral part of law making for our legislators in Congress. Generating news coverage is then not an end in itself, nor merely a means for reaching for higher office. It is a way to get the attention of fellow law makers. It is a way to get one member's concern on the agenda of the House of Representatives as a whole.

That doesn't mean, however, that representatives have "gone public" in the way Samuel Kernell describes for presidents. Presidential needs are different; presidents' main concern is to put their preferred spin on the stories that emerge out of the White House. How successful their efforts are may determine their standing in public opinion polls, their victories in Congress, and even their chances for reelection. Sidney Blumenthal portrays President Clinton's media operations, pointing out how the new administration's staffers utilize modern technology to bypass the White House press corps and reach local media directly. Such media access can allow a president both to inform and to manipulate the public.

Not every part of government wants publicity. The Supreme Court, for instance, only wants its decisions covered and then on its own terms, or so it seems. Richard Davis suggests that changing times may lead the Court to adapt itself to a more active media environment, possibly at the cost of losing its image of being above politics. Stephen Hess points out that openness to the press varies even among government agencies in Washington. Some agencies encourage media coverage and provide every help they can to the working press, hoping to influence the tenor of their reports. Others, however, would just as soon work without attracting media notice, concerned that news coverage would hurt more than it would help. The State Department, especially, sees the news as a hindrance to the effective implementation of U.S. foreign policy.

Whether in a fish bowl or in the shadows, government policymakers live and work with the realization that their actions may attract media attention. Whether it is the type of coverage they prefer, and whether it portrays them and their actions in a favorable light, is not often clear. Nevertheless, the news we receive from Washington results as much from the actions by members of government to stimulate or to discourage press coverage as it does from the newsworthy events that may occur. You may wish to consider carefully what kind of evidence would lead you to accept the arguments made by the authors of the selections included in these chapters. Certainly, a healthy skepticism about their positions would not be out of place.

13. LEGISLATORS AND THE NEWS MEDIA

You may occasionally see a news item about your member of the House of Representatives in the local media; chances are that the story originated in the member's own office, perhaps sent out as a news release by a press secretary, or perhaps from a telephone interview set up by a staffer. That kind of coverage tends to be positive, very helpful to reelection. But reelection is not a member's only goal. A representative also wants to be an effective legislator and to exert power within the legislative chamber. Tra-

ditionally, publicity had been seen, by legislators and political scientists alike, as detrimental to attempts to achieve real influence in the chamber. Working quietly and diligently behind the scenes, attending to the details of complex legislation through the committee process, and hammering out compromises in quiet consultations with other legislators led to success. Publicity was counterproductive; it made one seem to be grabbing credit and attention when both ought to be shared.

Timothy Cook argues persuasively that in the contemporary House of Representatives there is no dichotomy between legislation and publicity. Instead, he suggests, making news may be an indispensable and at least very helpful strategy in making laws. Members' offices are now structured to maximize the news coverage, both national and local, for the representative. More important, Cook suggests that the effect of media content on political activists may be more important than the impact on the public. And because political elites pay close attention to media content, members find publicity helpful in achieving their policy goals, because it draws the attention of legislative leaders to the member's proposals.

Making Laws and Making News
Timothy E. Cook

March 19, 1979, was like many other work days in the U.S. House of Representatives. Speaker Thomas P. (Tip) O'Neill, Jr., called the House to order at noon. After the chaplain's prayer and a smattering of one-minute speeches, a relatively minor bill, the Strategic and Critical Materials Stockpiling Act, was sent to the floor and introduced by Charles Bennett of Florida. The act passed with a minimum of debate and a voice vote. Several communications were reported to the Speaker, followed by debates on the international shipment of lottery materials and on establishing a new Select Committee

SOURCE: Reprinted from Timothy E. Cook, *Making Laws and Making News: Media Strategies in the U.S. House of Representatives,* pp. 1–10, pp. 167–171. Copyright 1989 by the Brookings Institution.

on Committees. After three one-minute speeches and three short special orders, the House adjourned at 2:21 p.m. All in all, a quiet day.

In one important respect, however, the legislative day was unlike any previous one: for the first time, floor proceedings were televised and broadcast across the country through C-SPAN, the Cable Satellite Public Affairs Network, to 350 affiliated cable systems. A transformation begun in the early 1970s had finally been completed; in less than a decade the House had changed from an institution that virtually prevented television from covering any part of the legislative process to one that almost welcomed its presence.

The House of the late 1960s was what one scholar termed "a large impersonal... machine for processing bills."[1] Its unspoken norms and folkways favored behind-the-scenes specialization and legislative labor, and the rules discouraging reporters' access to crucial behind-closed-doors decisions supported those norms. But by the end of the 1970s, at any of its legislative stages the House could bar scrutiny from reporters only with difficulty, and both print and electronic journalism were paying closer attention to it. The legislative process since then has occurred not so much in the light of sunshine laws but under the media's spotlight. Switching on the television cameras on March 19, however, may have been a landmark not in what it did but what it symbolized, the advent of a media-conscious institution.

That consciousness was very much a product of the mid-1970s, which remain a watershed in recent American history for all political institutions. After the Watergate scandal, the forced resignation of President Nixon in the summer of 1974, and the Democratic landslide in that fall's election, reform-minded politicians came to Washington to clean it up. In the process they may have created arrangements that made the policy process, never known for its coherence or completeness, even more dispersed and fluid. As more groups took advantage of the new permeability of the political process and entered the fray, coalition building moved away from assured management toward artful construction, issue by issue. The process of governance became more cumbersome, volatile, and unpredictable. All these changes should have encouraged, or at least facilitated, a more media-conscious membership, and indeed, changes within the House itself increased the importance of the media.

- The personal staffs of members expanded tremendously, and most legislators now employ full-time press secretaries, a post that was a rarity in 1970.
- The so-called Subcommittee Bill of Rights in 1973 mandated that committees set up subcommittees according to established jurisdictions, and the House Democratic Caucus in 1975 prevented members from chairing more than one subcommittee, effectively providing more bases for hearings and other events designed to win publicity.
- Junior members were no longer expected to serve an apprenticeship in which they might be seen but not heard. By the end of the decade virtually any member was expected to have a chance to sit on a desirable committee and to address his or her concerns.
- Sunshine reforms opened up committee and subcommittee hearings and deliberations to outside security. Closing committee hearings to keep out the press became the exception to the rule.
- The number of reporters credentialed to cover Congress grew dramatically, providing legislators more potential points of access to print and electronic media.
- Television began to dominate many congressional campaigns. By the end of the 1970s, over half of House campaign budgets went for media and advertising. A new generation was elected that was, of necessity, comfortable with the new technology.
- Members of the House and reporters for national news outlets had begun to discover each other, especially because the extraordinarily positive coverage of the House Judiciary Committee hearings in 1974 on the impeachment of President Nixon showed representatives what could be done with media attention and

showed reporters that the House could be newsworthy.

As a result of all this, one would expect changes in the House and how it deals with publicity—as Michael Robinson phrased his "First Law of Videopolitics": "Television alters the behavior of institutions in direct proportion to the amount of coverage provided or allowed; the greater the coverage, the more conspicuous the changes."[2] But has the ubiquity of the media really changed the most essential functions of the House? Has the new importance of making news transformed the process or the outcomes of making laws?

Many would reply that it has. Senators charged that the House's new visibility was enhancing the legislative power of the "other chamber" to their detriment. At least, that was the argument successfully advanced by senators who wished to follow the House's lead in televising floor proceedings. In 1985 Robert Byrd, then Senate minority leader, complained, "The Senate is fast becoming the invisible half of Congress. We cannot hold our own with the White House and the House of Representatives when it comes to news coverage of the important issues of the day."[3] Others alleged that the chamber had become a group of unruly individuals more concerned with self-publicizing than with legislative labor.

This interpretation was not only widely held but plausible, and it continues to have proponents. Nevertheless, I consider it mistaken. But neither do I find the counterargument—that the media's impact on legislating in the House has been vastly exaggerated because the news reflects rather than creates internal influence—fully satisfying. Newsmaking is neither incompatible with nor superfluous to the legislative process. Instead, perhaps making news has become a valuable component of making laws.

OBSERVATION: PUBLICITY DRIVES OUT LEGISLATING

The news media are accustomed to being blamed for (or credited with) many political developments. Television, especially, has been accused of contributing to the drop in the public's confidence in political institutions, the decline of political partisanship, the rise of image-oriented and candidate-centered campaigns, the drift toward a government more dominated by the president, and the general fragmentation of the American political system. Critics have also contended that the media aided the dispersion of power within the White House and made congressional leadership and collective decisionmaking even more awkward and difficult than it already was. Making laws and making news, they have argued, are not compatible tasks.

Claims of such a dichotomy are nothing new. They hearken back to the oft-cited distinction between industrious work horses and self-promoting show horses, the two hypothesized types of members of Congress. There was renewed concern, however, that show horses were becoming dominant. In an influential 1984 article in *Atlantic Monthly,* Gregg Easterbrook declared, "The yearning for a Washington badge of recognition and the additional perquisites that would make Capitol Hill life what [the new legislators] imagined it to be can set in almost immediately.... Fame may be an elusive goal, but publicity is not."[4] Publicity was said to undermine the coherence of the legislative process. Hedrick Smith argued, "Television helped break up the policy monopolies of established committees and throw open the power game. Overshadowing the grinding 'inside' spadework of bill drafting in committee, television offered shortcuts and a showcase . . . a marketplace for all 435 members of the House and one hundred senators to become policy entrepreneurs. That is one major reason why Congress seems so unruly today."[5] Or in the words of a political scientist who wrote on the nationalization of American politics, "The corrosive influence of television does not end when the elections are over. The Senate is now notorious for being less a legislative body than a publicity mill for many members, and the same trends are spreading, inexorably, to the House."[6]

The most sophisticated version of this observation has contended that the fragmentation of power within Congress is directly connected with the growth of the Washington media, the ascendancy of television as a major news source, and its gradual incursion into the workings of the institution. The media have supposedly helped create an "open Congress," in which members need not play by inside rules to advance the issues that concern them or to advance their careers. Mavericks are no longer tacitly disciplined and team players are no longer quietly rewarded; mavericks receive welcome attention, while the others are lost in the shadows. Members who seek publicity also have available to them increased staff and technological support, and legislative coalition building has taken a back seat to public relations. The media have, it is said, contributed another centrifugal force, dispersing power and hindering leadership and collective decisionmaking.

There is certainly evidence favoring this point of view. Many members have achieved publicity without leadership or committee positions. Members have devoted more resources to publicizing themselves and have become more sophisticated in pursuit of the now-willing Washington reporters. Yet, while credible, this conventional wisdom from the early 1980s has not gone unchallenged.

RESPONSE: PUBLICITY IS IRRELEVANT TO LEGISLATING

In *The Ultimate Insiders* Stephen Hess began by attacking the Achilles' heel of the argument, showing that most members of Congress are invisible to the national press. Those covered most heavily are "the *Ultimate Insiders*, the ones who call the committee meetings or direct the floor action, or would do so if their party were in the majority."[7] Zealously seeking publicity pays little dividend if the publicity-seeker is not in a category that reporters find newsworthy—presidential candidate, party leader, committee chair, sponsor of a key proposal, and so forth. The show horse–work horse dichotomy makes no sense as long as those receiving most of the attention are also those contributing most to legislative labors. The power of the media has been exaggerated, Hess concluded; instead of determining power on Capitol Hill, the press reflects it. Making news is then superfluous, even irrelevant, to making laws.

This perspective has also had proponents beyond the ranks of political scientists. A 1987 article on power in Congress argued, "Reporters will want to talk to [a committee chair or party leader] regardless of how articulate he is or how well he looks before a camera. What he has to say is important because of who he is, not how he says it."[8] An op-ed piece in the *New York Times* during the 1988 campaign also considered that reporters reflect power, but interpreted the situation as less benign: "[Journalists] have frequently ended up pulling their punches for fear of appearing biased.... Too often, the press has functioned as merely a stenographer to power."[9]

But the response is not without its own problems. Though a handful of senators are accorded the lion's share of national media attention, such dominance cannot suggest that other members have not altered their behavior. Hess granted this point, though he argued that it would be irrational for senators to pursue national publicity, given the media's lack of interest. Yet legislators could be more inclined to seek publicity diligently without succeeding every time. In fact, if backbench legislators are actively pursuing publicity, leaders might be maintaining their place in the spotlight only by aggressively wooing reporters, in which case the primacy of leaders in the news is even more to be expected.

More important, Hess argued that the Capitol Hill press corps is "almost totally reactive."[10] Yet in a collegial institution in which the chain of command is attenuated, knowing who or what to react to is far from obvious. Because current journalist practice requires stories featuring individual authorities, covering Congress has been called "the search for the ultimate spokesman."[11] Elsewhere in Washington, such a search is more straight-forward. Throughout the executive branch, press officers are designated to speak for the agency, the department, or the president. Reporters' tasks are simplified: they need only turn to the appropriate spokesperson when a given topic becomes newsworthy. With Congress, the solution is less simple. After all, neither chamber has anyone who can speak on behalf of all or even most of its members.

The national media do disproportionately favor leaders, committee chairs, and senior members as being in a position to know. But holding such a position is no guarantee of news coverage. After all, even if much of legislators' visibility can be explained by institutional power, there remains at least as much that is unexplained. Either additional reasons have yet to be discovered, or much of the coverage of members of Congress remains unpatterned and unpredictable. Reporters, even when conscientiously attempting to depict congressional power accurately, inevitably exercise choice in deciding whom to cover in Congress. Merely reflecting congressional power without contributing to it may be the goal of reporters, but it is a well-nigh impossible task.

A THIRD POSSIBILITY: MAKING NEWS LEADS TO MAKING LAWS

To comprehend the relationship of making news to making laws, one must understand that reporters and politicians are constantly negotiating and renegotiating the process by which news is made. Instead of a Congress that plays by reporters' rules or reporters that defer to Congress's decisions about what is important, the interactions between legislators and reporters are shifting and flexible. Making news can become a constructive component of the legislative process. By anticipating what a reporter will find newsworthy, House members can use the media to address an issue, move a proposal along, and enhance their career ambitions. Indeed, given the contemporary confusion in American politics, a media strategy may be a necessary part of many legislative strategies. Such a process is most accessible to those who wield the most power; but backbenchers, too, can become an authoritative source on a particular issue and thereby court publicity and accomplish legislative goals.

To understand how this process works, one must recognize that newsworthiness is inherently an elusive quality. If reporters are asked for the difference between news and non-news, they are likely to provide anecdotes or examples, not a hard-and-fast dividing line. Yet the demand for fresh news is incessant. To standardize an inherently unpredictable process, reporters routinely turn to people in positions of authority within an institution, thus not only ensuring a steady flow of copy but also helping guard against charges of bias or incompleteness by covering politicians whom peers, superiors, and audiences generally agree upon as newsworthy.

Such connections work to officials' advantage. Their involvement makes something newsworthy enough to get in the paper or on the air and creates events that can serve as occasions to write stories. Because reporters must worry about alienating their main sources, they come to report the world in ways fundamentally similar to the perspectives of those they are covering: they become "unwilling adjuncts to City Hall."[12]

Yet the reporters do not merely reflect a reality constructed by others. News inevitably constructs and reconstructs a public reality from privately experienced events. And journalists' selections and emphases do diverge from those that their authoritative sources would make. American journalism is based on the tenet that news must be both important and interesting. Reporters' judgments on what is important and interesting must anticipate not merely the political sources but the judgment of the news organization for which they work. Collusion is unlikely because reporters and politicians do not share identical definitions of what news is and how it should be covered. The media thus acts as powerful gatekeepers to the political arena.

Instead of determining or reflecting power on Capitol Hill, reporters and sources *negotiate* power, constantly bargaining with each other over the rules of their interactions and the shape of the final product. Each tries to manage the other—the sources to place the most favorable light on their activity and the journalists to extract the information they seek with minimal difficulty. Sometimes the relationship may be adversarial. More typically, however, politicians need publicity and journalists need copy, and the two sides can and do perform valuable services for each other.

Despite some disagreements with journalists, House members may, through effective media strategies, be able to manage the news from Capitol Hill. Journalists may go along to ensure the routine production of news. Frequent interaction leads to an unspoken set of ground rules. The forces encouraging collaboration instead of conflict tend to be greatest in dealing with those legislators who are important and hence regular, prized newsmakers. The adversarial model does not work most strongly at the highest levels of the political hierarchy, then; it may actually be most applicable toward those who *least* frequently make the news.

At the same time, there is enough flexibility in covering a collegial body that observations cannot stop there. As more members are perceived to be important newsmakers, they may be able to use media strategies to raise issues to prominence and advance their careers. Moreover, the ones reporters consider more interesting may be able to win coverage if leaders cannot provide news that conforms to the media's demands.

So concerns that backbenchers can grab headlines are not unfounded....

[T]he media in general and the national media in particular have become more important for members of the House as the dispersion of power has made legislating more difficult. Legislators can use the media in various ways in addition to pursuing the publicity necessary for getting reelected. But this is not to say that the House is overrun by a new breed of legislators interested in publicity for its own sake. Making laws and making news are not contradictory. Nor are they synonymous. Instead, they are different but complementary parts of the same process.

The outside strategy allowed by media publicity offers the potential to manage an increasingly unmanageable work load in a balkanized and balky political system. In the lingo of Washington the retail method of persuasion has been supplemented if not supplanted by the wholesale style. After all, the number of interest groups has dramatically increased, the legislative agenda is crowded, and the dispersion of power to more individuals makes one-on-one lobbying increasingly difficult. As presidents and interest groups find persuasion through media more useful to get things done in Washington, the same should be expected on Capitol Hill. After all, the media provide an important means to help set the Washington agenda, winnow down the alternative courses of action, keep pressure on politicians, and thus get something done in Congress.

MEDIA POWER AND CONGRESSIONAL POWER

The House of Representatives has long witnessed the chaotic comings and goings of its 435 members—from offices to committee rooms to the floor and back again while lobbyists and constituents try to get in a word or two on the run. But increasingly relations with the news media seem to take up legislators' time and effort. Dressed in telegenic blue shirts and red neckties, they stand before television cameras in the swamp, the section of the Capitol lawn set aside for interviews. Inside the Capitol, too, floor debates are often aimed at the discreetly placed cameras that broadcast the proceedings to members' offices, the press galleries, and homes across the country. Staffers and interns dash from one gallery to the next with stacks of press releases to be distributed. Reporters crowd outside hearing rooms to receive a committee report or corner a witness. In short, much of the hubbub of Capitol Hill today is contributed by the press and their would-be subjects. Making laws is far from the only business of the House. It has been supplemented by making news.

Making news was not always so important. Reporters have been present on Capitol Hill for nearly two centuries, but rarely before has seeking publicity been such a significant part of every House member's job. For most of the twentieth century the way to get things done and to advance a career in Washington was to play an inside game, building relationships with colleagues, deferring to senior members, and bargaining, while slowly building up the legislative longevity necessary to achieve a position of power. Legislators paid little attention to reporters except those from the press back home, and they severely restricted the access of radio and television to the House. The House was governed by party leaders and committee chairs who preferred to stay out of the spotlight whenever possible.

Now all that has changed. The media are useful to members for publicity to help them get reelected, of course, but increasingly also in policymaking, wielding influence in Congress and in Washington, and pursuing their personal ambitions. Making news has frequently become integral to the legislative process. Reporters for all kinds of news outlets can now be present at any stage of the legislative process and can be instrumental in shaping the results. Sophisticated House press operations try to create national constituencies for issues on which members can serve as authoritative sources and build reputations. At the very least, legislators who wish to be considered influential experts have to ensure that their media image fits their chosen self-portrait, so few of them, inside or outside leadership circles, can pass up opportunities to be newsworthy. Making news, in short, has become a crucial component of making laws.

... The conditions that made it not only possible but necessary to use the media to get legislative business accomplished ... show few signs of abating. The expansion of congressional staffs in the 1970s will not be reversed; and each new Congress will see members naming more full-time press secretaries. Likewise, the number of Washington reporters should continue to grow steadily. News organizations may be tightening their belts, but the rise of newspaper chains, the abundance of stringers, and the creation of groups such as Conus that contract out television news services mean that virtually any news outlet can have a relatively inexpensive link to Washington. Such easy hookups allow members to add their comments to stories that are bouncing among various newsbeats in the capital. Above all, the news media help House members set the legislative agenda, define the alternatives, influence public moods, and affect outcomes at a time when the political process is confused and unpredictable.

Yet if legislators need reporters, reporters also need legislators to create the events or provide the observation that can become the basis of a story. Even though the needs of the two are rarely identical, they can work in a symbiosis. House members, even at high levels of power, cannot automatically make news. Instead, they must ensure that their information and stories meet journalistic standards of timeliness, pertinence, and interest. Reporters' dependence on authoritative sources to suggest news means that journalism tends to reflect the perspectives of the more powerful. But such power is not absolute, because while politicians control definitions of importance, journalists still decide what is interesting. So House members and reporters negotiate and renegotiate newsworthiness. The questions should not then be what the news media have done *to* the House, or what the House has done *to* the news media, but what these two institutions have done *with* one another. What is the effect of this negotiation on policymaking and on representative democracy? The answers must be speculative, but they are well worth contemplating.

POLICYMAKING PROCESS AND THE MEDIA

The power of the press often buttresses established power and procedures in the House. Hill traditions of pursuing expertise and influence dovetail with reporters' search for sources who are in a position to know. Reporters accord a reassuring coherence to the legislative process by focusing on "particularly and peculiarly congressional actions," stressing the gradual, orderly nature of the way bills are passed rather than the chaos or stasis that characterizes much of congressional life.

But the priorities of journalists and politicians are not always so synchronized. Reporters have less leeway in whom to report about or when to report it than in the issues that will receive coverage. Some of the coverage of Congress is a by-product of the coverage of issues. Issues most likely to make news are easily described, have clearly characterized sides, affect a large part of the audience, and come with straightforward remedies. Journalists tend to pass up matters that are complex, unfamiliar, specialized, or not apparently easily addressed.

If members want news coverage, they must choose clear-cut issues or try to present the complex as simple. But such choices invite distortion or omission of complicating factors. The alternative ways to achieve tax reform in the Ninety-ninth Congress, for instance, were displaced by an either-or question: "Are you for tax reform or against it?" Likewise, the inadequacies of the patchwork system of unemployment compensation went unreported when journalists converged on the single problem of hundreds of thousands of unemployed in danger of being precipitously dropped from the rolls when the Federal Supplemental Compensation program expired.

Setting the agenda is only the first step in the journey of legislation; press attention affects later stages, too. Bargaining among members, once the hallmark of a legislative institution, becomes more difficult when reporters are watching—not so much because members act differently in public than in private but because reporters' dislike for noncommittal stances tends to discourage the fluidity and maneuverability necessary to resolve differences on the fine points and to enact legislation.

Legislators who wish to get something done must be both outside and inside players. Press coverage can enhance their reputations and direct colleagues' attention toward them as people to listen to. Inside strategies can lead to the influential post that can be used to gain the media's attention. Using them [inside and outside strategies] together can be synergistic, accomplishing more than using either one on its own. But... changing from one approach to another is not always easy to handle.

To the extent that the press spotlights problems and helps set the legislative agenda, an additional complication arises: the clock of Congress will resemble that of the news. The media have a limited attention span. They discover problems suddenly, but their interest rapidly wanes, whether or not the problems have been solved. As entrepreneurial politicians take advantage of the brief window of opportunity to get something done, agenda items can rise and fall in importance with dizzying rapidity. In such a fast-forward context legislators feel pressured to respond and may grab the first alternative presented to them, often in spite of the details, while hoping that the other chamber will take care of the problem. Cooling-off periods in committee or in conference may be necessary, as with the anti-drug abuse bill in the One-hundredth Congress, when the legislative process overheats.

Yet for all these drawbacks, the conjunction of media strategies and legislative strategies can aid policymaking, particularly in surmounting entrenched interests and facilitating large-scale legislative initiatives. The news suggests problems or alternatives that Congress has bypassed. It helps inform and mobilize public opinion. At the very least it forces legislators to look beyond the interests of organized groups with the most immediate stakes and perhaps toward the larger public interest. When members would prefer to do nothing, publicity can increase the risks of inaction. In short, members in the spotlight are pressured to deal with problems in a way that corresponds to their readings of public opinion.

NOTES

1. Nelson W. Polsby, "Policy Analysis and Congress." *Public Policy,* 18:64 (1969).
2. Michael J. Robinson, "A Twentieth-Century Medium in a Nineteenth Century Legislature: The Effects of Television on the American Congress," in Norman J. Ornstein, ed., *Congress in Change: Evolution and Reform* (Praeger, 1975), p. 241.
3. Steve Blakely, "Prospects Seen Brightening for Senate TV," *Congressional Quarterly Weekly Report,* September 21, 1985, p. 1877.
4. Gregg Easterbrook, "What's Wrong with Congress?" *Atlantic Monthly,* December 1984, p. 59.
5. Hedrick Smith, *The Power Game: How Washington Works.* Random House, 1988, p. 39.
6. William M. Lunch, *The Nationalization of American Politics.* University of California Press, 1987, p. 22.
7. Stephen Hess, *The Ultimate Insiders: U.S. Senators in the National Media.* Brookings, 1986, p. 7.
8. Nadine Cohodas, "Press Coverage: It's What You Do That Counts." *Congressional Quarterly Weekly Report,* January 3, 1987, p. 29.
9. Mark Hertsgaard, "Electoral Journalism: Not Yellow, But Yellow-Bellied," *New York Times,* September 21, 1988, p. A23.
10. Hess, *Ultimate Insiders,* p. 110.
11. Susan H. Miller, "News Coverage of Congress: The Search for the Ultimate Spokesman," *Journalism Quarterly,* 54:459–65 (1977).
12. Walter Gieber and Walter Johnson, "The City Hall 'Beat': A Study of Reporter and Source Roles," *Journalism Quarterly,* 38:289 (1961).

DISCUSSION QUESTIONS

1. What would you say are the major roadblocks that stand in the way of members of Congress obtaining news coverage for their policy objectives? What conditions would make it easier for senators and representatives to receive the kind of coverage that would help them push their legislative projects through to completion?

2. Many members of Congress speak quite critically of their colleagues and Congress as a whole when they are back home in their districts. Would you expect them to be as critical in the national press when they are trying to influence the course of legislation through the chamber?

3. If you were a member of Congress, would you be more interested in the national news coverage you generate or in the local news coverage you might get? Why do you say so? Could you manage to get both?

4. Whom do you think members of Congress are trying to influence when they attempt to stimulate news coverage for their favorite legislative objectives? How do you anticipate these people will respond to such publicity?

14. PRESIDENTS AND PUBLICITY

Just as members of Congress find it useful to stimulate publicity, so do presidents. In the last decades, the development of the mass media and the growth of the Washington press corps have provided presidents with ample opportunity to shape public perceptions of themselves and their programs. The high visibility of the presidency results not only from the public's innate interest in the activities and escapades of presidents and their families but also from the ease with which journalists can cover the White House. Besides, the president is a highly visible spokesperson for the executive branch, the federal government, and the United States as a whole. Media interests coincide with presidential interests.

To some extent. Presidents want to generate favorable publicity, and media want to report significant news. So presidents have adopted sophisticated media strategies to generate the exposure they want while minimizing the coverage of the issues they would rather keep quiet. And the news media put up with most of the manipulation of their reporting decisions in order to get the hard news that satisfies their audience. Samuel Kernell calls this strategy "going public" and argues that presidents use it as a device to bypass political elites in Washington and stimulate a favorable climate of public opinion among the citizens which legislators and other policymakers find hard to ignore. The game in Washington is no longer a bargaining game among political elites; the presence of the media and the way presidents use them have changed the nature of presidential politics.

Going Public: New Strategies of Presidential Leadership

Samuel Kernell

Let me briefly define going public.... Going public is a class of activities in which presidents engage as they promote themselves and their policies before the American public. Some examples of going public are a televised press conference, a special, prime time address to the nation, a speech before a business convention on the West Coast, a visit to a day care center, and a White House ceremony to decorate a local hero that is broadcast via satellite to the home town television station. What these various activities have in common is that they are intended principally to place the president and his message before the American people in a way that enhances his chances of success in Washington. Going public draws heavily upon techniques developed over the years in election campaigning; but in

SOURCE: Reprinted from Samuel Kernell, *Going Public: New Strategies of Presidential Leadership,* 2nd ed., copyright 1993 by permission of Congressional Quarterly Press.

going public, the ultimate object of the president's designs is not the American voter, but fellow politicians in Washington.

... The present day susceptibility of relations within Washington to public opinion manifests itself in a variety of ways. The influence of single-issue constituencies has been abetted by the discovery that by defeating one targeted incumbent a clear message will be sent to others. Issues also blow into Washington more quickly and in less-filtered form. During the 97th Congress, for example, President Reagan's supply-side program, with its unprecedented deficits, was being enacted while a majority in each house appeared ready to endorse a constitutional amendment requiring a balanced budget. And off to the side, a large bipartisan huddle was forming to carry forward the recently arrived "flat tax" rate reform.

In a recent appraisal of coalition politics within Congress during the past 30 years, Barbara Sinclair makes the same connection between internal organization and the effect of external forces: "Instead of a policy process dominated by powerful, conservative committee chairmen, one in which crucial decisions were made in secret and thus were relatively insulated from public influence, we now see a process characterized by extreme individualism, one in which open, public decision making often hinders compromise."[1] When asked by a reporter about changes in Congress, Reagan lobbyist Kenneth Duberstein echoed this conclusion and gave it recent origin: "It's not been like Lyndon Johnson's time, being able to work with 15 or 20 Congressmen and Senators to get something done. For most issues you have to lobby all 435 Congressmen and almost all 100 Senators."[2] As a result, "how Congress performs its legislative role," continues Sinclair, "depends much more upon the character of the environmental forces impinging upon its members than upon its internal organization."[3]

... To see how strategic prescriptions of going public differ from those of bargaining, consider the hypothetical case of a president requiring additional votes if he is to prevail in Congress. If a large number of votes is needed, the most obvious and direct course is to go on prime time television to solicit the public's active support. Employed at the right moment by a popular president, the effect may be dramatic. With this tactic, however, comes considerable costs and risks. A real debit of lost public support may occur when a president takes a forthright position. There is also the possibility that the public will not respond, which damages the president's future credibility. Given this, a president understandably finds the *threat* to go public frequently more attractive than the *act*. To the degree such a threat is credible, the anticipated responses of some representatives and senators may suffice to achieve victory.

A more focused application of popular pressure becomes available as an election nears. Fence-sitting representatives and senators may be plied with promises of reelection support or threats of presidential opposition. This may be done privately and selectively, or it may be tendered openly to all who may vote on the president's program. Then there is the election itself. By campaigning, the president who goes public can seek to alter the partisan composition of Congress and thereby gain influence over that institution's decisions in the future.

All of these methods for generating publicity notwithstanding, going public offers fewer and simpler stratagems than does ... bargaining, which above all else involves choice: choice among alternative coalitions, choice of specific partners, and choice of the goods and services to be bartered.... Going public promises a straightforward presidency—its options fewer, its strategy simpler, and consequently, its practitioner's behavior more predictable.

Thus there is a rationale for modern presidents to go public in the emerging character of Washington politics. As Washington comes to depend on looser, more individualistic political relations, presidents searching for strategies that work will increasingly go public.

... The fact that marginal shifts of preferences [among policy options], whether in Washington or in the rest of the country, often have major political consequences is what makes going public a viable strategy. The president makes an appeal; most citizens do not respond, but some do. A few of this latter group express their support actively. Most of the politicians who oppose the president's position will resist constituent pressure. A few whose positions are less fixed or who are electorally vulnerable will be persuaded that the president's course offers the least resistance. Frequently, this is all that is required for the president to appear to have worked his magic.

Moreover, the president possesses unusual institutional assets that may enhance his influence over public opinion well beyond that provided by his current popularity. The presidency's singular visibility allows its occupant to command the nation's attention; the office's broad constitutional mandate bestows upon him the authority to speak on any policy matter; and his acknowledged institutional expertise requires that his argument be weighed and, even if opposed, dealt with. In foreign policy, particularly, these resources will stand him in good stead.

No president will ever persuade all of his admirers to support his cause.... But with the office's exceptional public standing, the incumbent president can also appeal to his detractors. His failure to persuade some of his admirers may be partly compensated by citizens who, while disapproving his current performance, nonetheless defer to his judgment.

... The relative ease of public relations is no trivial matter. Without making any special claims for its efficacy, modern presidents may be tempted to resort to public relations for the simple reason that it is manageable.... Presidents Nixon, Carter, and Reagan were preoccupied in their prime time addresses with the Vietnam War, historically high inflation, and double-digit unemployment, respectively. None of these was in any way a trivial issue that rhetoric could gloss over. In going to the airwaves, these presidents sought the public's patience. However much they hoped to gain politically in their televised addresses, their activities had the piquant quality of being doable.

Convenience alone is insufficient to explain the dedicated way in which presidents and many of their staff pursue public and press relations. Presidents do it because they believe it wins the public's sympathy. One need not make presidents into Frank Capra's arrogant manipulators of public opinion in *Meet John Doe* to have them believe that they can talk their way into the hearts of the citizenry. Well before they had the wherewithal to do so, presidents must have felt this way....

The desire to explain one's actions and to respond to criticism springs from human nature. Probably every occupant of the White House has at some point blamed press treatment for his troubles in the country. Probably each has also depreciated the public's current disfavor by stressing the proverbial "burdens of office" and "complexity of problems," neither of which the average citizen can appreciate. In the face of tough problems and a "bad press," presidents want to tell their side of the story. Books and articles on the subject with such sinister titles as *The Selling of the President* and *On Bended Knee* miss the point.[4]

However phrased, the public's lack of expertise offers a comforting rationalization to a president who must otherwise confront the stark reality that he has failed. As self-serving as these sentiments are, one may assume they are sincere. The first line between "bad news" and a "bad press" gives presidents ample opportunity to think this way. That these feelings are genuine helps to explain why modern presidents are quick to go public to defend their actions. Rationalizations that offered presidents of an earlier era a measure of solace today prescribe a course of action.

... Thus far ... I have treated going public to counter failing popular support as a form of therapy and the product of an interaction between human nature and advanced technology. There is, however, another reason, special to the modern setting, that presidents will be especially inclined to resort to public relations to offset a decline in the polls. What fellow Washingtonians say publicly about the president's performance will, in fact, significantly influence the way people in the country judge him. What makes this explanation peculiar to the modern era is the extraordinary volume of messages transmitted from Washington to the country.... Because present-day Washington is less insulated from outside pressures, politicians are both more sensitive to public opinion and more inclined to try to shape it as a way of controlling their own destiny and of influencing that of other politicians. One member of Congress, Sen. Jesse Helms, recently went so far as to try to gain control of a major network for the stated purpose of altering its putative political slant in reporting public affairs.

An important result of the increased two-way communication is that the ordinary citizen has gained more information about the president and more varied opinions about his performance. Veteran Washington correspondent James Deakin concurs:

The relationship between the president of the United States and the nation's news media is a subject of endless fascination. It exerts an irresistible attraction for presidents, members of the White House staff, reporters, editors and broadcasters, politicians, bureaucrats, political scientists, historians and an increasing number of ordinary citizens. For a long time, it was a local cottage industry in Washington, of no great interest to the rest of the country. Now it is a vast national enterprise whose tentacles spread into every village and shire.

How is the president getting along with the news media? Are they treating him well or badly? Is he a master of communications or an ineffective performer on the tube? Is he accessible to reporters and candid with them? Or is he secretive, misleading the press ... ? Why doesn't he have more press conferences? Why have his press conferences become such increasingly meaningless spectacles? Why does he manipulate the press so brazenly to achieve his purposes? Why doesn't he use the press more effectively to achieve his purpose? Why is the press so subservient to the president? Why is the press so hostile to the president? The relationship between the president and the news media is a long-running soap. Drama. Suspense. Conflict. And a large, rapt audience.[5]

... Does this mean that the traditional observation that the president's standing in Washington bore little relation to his status in the country was wrong? Not at all. Washington has changed. What was true for Presidents Truman and Eisenhower may not be for Presidents Reagan and Bush. If the public now pays closer attention to politics in Washington than before, it is not because citizens today are somehow cognitively processing political information differently. Nor has there been a national epidemic of "Potomac fever." Rather, the reason is simply that citizens are exposed to more, and to more critical, information about the president than ever before. This is the argument. . . .

The record of White House coverage in the press during the past 30 years confirms the kind of change detected by Deakin and hypothesized here. One commonly employed indicator of the growing preponderance of presidential news is obtained by comparing it with news about Congress. Such comparisons are available for news coverage extending back to the mid-nineteenth century when, by one account, presidents received less press attention than congressional committees. During the twentieth century, the share of White House news has increased steadily to the point that today it attracts substantially more news stories than Congress.

. . . [The] susceptibility of modern politicians to the president's public appeals is bringing the president's reputation in Washington and his prestige in the country into an alignment that did not exist in Truman's and Eisenhower's time. Another reason for this convergence is that events in Washington, which in an earlier era would have only pricked the attention of the small segment of the public who are politically attentive, today frequently hold the entire country in rapture. Peace and prosperity may remain the primary concern of citizens as they judge the president, but president watchers both in Washington and throughout the country are sharing and comparing data as never before. The modern president who fails to rebut unfriendly remarks of Washington elites or to blunt criticism from the press may soon begin hearing echoes of these complaints emanating from the country.

The general strategy of going public . . . applies also to modern presidents who go public to help themselves. Technology makes it possible for them to satisfy the natural urge to answer their critics. Outsiders in the White House, who achieved their positions by repeatedly winning presidential primaries, have a special faith in rhetoric. Channels of competing and at times unfavorable news from Washington have opened up as the president's adversaries also go public. And a less deferential news media more willingly transmit, if not actually stimulate, unfavorable stories about the White House. All this suggests that when a president goes public to counter his decline in the polls, he may be acting on more than rationalization. Indeed, he may be acting rationally.

NOTES

1. Barbara Sinclair, "Coping with Uncertainty: Building Coalitions in the House and the Senate," in *The New Congress,* ed. Thomas E. Mann and Norman J. Ornstein, Washington, D.C.: American Enterprise Institute, 1981, p. 220.
2. Steven R. Weisman, "No. 1, the President is Very Result Oriented," *New York Times,* November 12, 1983, p. 10.
3. Sinclair, "Coping with Uncertainty," p. 220.
4. Joe McGinnis, *The Selling of the President.* New York: Trident Press,

1969; Mark Hertsgaard, *On Bended Knee.* New York: Farrar Straus Giroux, 1988.

5. James Deakin, *Straight Stuff.* New York: William Morrow, 1984, p. 44.

DISCUSSION QUESTIONS

1. Do you think the ability of the president to "go public" in Kernell's sense is essentially a product of advanced technology? What other elements (besides the technical capability of doing so) must be present for a president to go public effectively?
2. Try to identify the conditions that limit the president's success in going public. You may wonder about frequency, the issue, and the timing (among other factors).
3. Consider the president's last six months or so; do you think that he has "gone public" a great deal, occasionally, or seldom? Why do you say so? What factors would influence a president's choice to go public?
4. If you were a congressional leader working with the White House on a controversial piece of legislation, would you welcome or would you dislike a presidential decision to influence public opinion? Why?
5. Is "going public" a technique open to other leaders? Do H. Ross Perot's efforts to influence public decisions fall into this category? What differences and similarities do you see?

15. CLINTON AND THE MEDIA

Although presidents think communicating with the public is essential, they do not necessarily think that working with the national news media is the best way to do so. It is certainly convenient to use the White House press corps as a channel to the public, but correspondents based in Washington have their own ideas about what to report and how to report it. They may focus their attention more on shifts in influence within the White House, on the ebb and flow of power between the president and congressional leaders, and on relatively minor changes in policy proposals rather than on presidential goals and initiatives as a whole. The upshot for many presidents is that the convenience of using the White House press corps is overshadowed by the disadvantages of giving the press corps's journalists a chance to filter the message, or, indeed, report a different one.

Modern technology has made it feasible for presidents to bypass the White House press, if they choose. The opportunity to target specific news outlets in the nation with electronic hookups and other means allows a president the opportunity to deal with journalists around the country who are less concerned with the intrigues of Washington politics and, perhaps, more interested in the substance of presidential policy. President Reagan began bypassing the White House media to a limited extent. In this complimentary piece, Sidney Blumenthal details the efforts the Clinton administration has been making to make local and regional media outlets a significant part of its communications strategy. You may want to consider how the Washington press corps has responded and whether President Clinton has been successful in bypassing them as his term progresses.

Letter from Washington: The Syndicated Presidency

Sidney Blumenthal

Communications wonks are taking the White House press office into the future and Bill Clinton direct to the people, leaving the Big Media out of the picture.

Every spring thousands gather in Washington for a seasonal rite. It is not the Cherry Blossom Festival at the Tidal Basin; it is the celebration of, by, and for the national media at three drafty ballroom dinners. Virtually all of the personages of the press, from network anchormen to provincial bureau chiefs, assemble, in black tie (the Radio & Television Correspondents' Association and the White House Correspondents' Association) or white (the Gridiron), for off-the-record festivities. Sprinkled among the tables as guests are notables of the Administration, Congress, and the Supreme Court, who are entertained by comedy and drag acts, and then light remarks by the President of the United States.

By March 18th, when Bill Clinton spoke at the Radio & Television Correspondents' dinner, the new President had held twenty-five sesions of one

SOURCE: Reprinted by permission; ©1993 Sidney Blumenthal. Originally in *The New Yorker.* All Rights Reserved.

kind or another with representatives of the provincial media but he had not held a single press conference with those seated before him. They were his hosts, but he would not play host to them, with a full-dress press conference in the East Room, until March 23rd. The President was hardly embarrassed or apologetic. "You know why I can stiff you on the press conferences?" he asked. "Because Larry King liberated me by giving me to the American people directly."

"We're not pleased. It's really true," said Karen Hosler, a Washington correspondent for the Baltimore *Sun,* who is the president of the White House Correspondents' Association. Her complaints sound like the grieving of a union shop steward. "It is interesting the way they have really shut out the rank-and-file reporters who, day in and day out, go into the White House to cover the news. He's not given any interviews to anyone we would consider a White House reporter. He's given them to MTV; he's done things out in the field. Even that material is not available to the White House press corps." Clinton's elusiveness prompts Hosler to express nostalgia for the early months of the previous Administration, when President Bush invited the press to movie screenings in the White House, invited them to bounce on the bed in the Lincoln Bedroom, and parried their questions at a series of news conferences designed to display his un-Reaganlike familiarity with the existence of government. Bush loved going to dinner at the home of an important bureau chief and hoisting his host's child for the home-movie camera. It was all part of the game in which all the players accepted their traditional roles. For some in the press, this highly choreographed relationship was deeply personal. "George Bush was a nice man who always treated us with respect as human beings," said Hosler. "How can you dislike someone like that?"

"Larry King" has become Clinton's metaphor for the diminishing influence of the Big Media. And this sentiment is not fuelled simply by pique at the press for its invasive forays into the so-called character issue during the Democratic primaries. Clinton seeks accurate, immediate, politically sensitive transmission of his policies. For that reason, he has embraced the very technology that the media had believed was their monopoly: the electronic filigree, space satellites, and computer networks that are the pen and pencil of the modern press are also available to the White House. Clinton's campaign organizers mastered these instruments, and now in power the same individuals are not about to relinquish them. The narrowcasting that began when the candidate appeared with shades and sax on "Arsenio Hall" has been honed. Its purpose is no longer to elect Clinton, of course, or even merely to sustain his popularity. Policy and politics have merged: the Clinton Administration is an accelerating political machine, geared to the passage of programs. Constituencies and legislators are targeted with precision, in media market after media market.

Clinton's perpetual motion, his permanent campaign, is dictated, above all, by the system of checks and balances, which demands that he mobilize public pressures on legislators if he wishes to achieve anything. (Nowhere in the Federalist Papers is there a prophetic hint of the permanent campaign, but it is a natural by-product of Madisonianism.) Every one of the President's appearances in local media demonstrates his driven strategy: from Milwaukee to Shreveport, from North Dakota to Nebraska, he has been making appeals to pull opposing or fence-sitting senators his way. The national press, and especially the network news, is too blunt, too unfocussed, too superficial. It is inadequate at both ends of the spectrum: not only is it unable to provide intense immediacy to specific groups and places but its compulsive reduction of reality to sound-bite dimensions makes it incapable of carrying broad, sustained explanation. Though Clinton was to hold his first press conference less than a week after his pointed remark at the Radio & Television dinner, it was hardly an acknowledgment that the old forms of the media were back in place. When Ronald Reagan was elected President, CNN and C-SPAN were just getting off the ground. The networks did not offer footage of national and international events tailored to an affiliate's market; there was no independent company like Conus Communications to provide this service. Big Media, as they related to national politics, were a fairly settled oligopoly: there were two or three news magazines (*Time, Newsweek,* occasionally *US News*); two or three newspapers (the *Times,* the *Post,* the *Wall Street Journal,* occasionally the fading *Star*); the wires; and the three networks. Big Media, however, are no more likely to make a triumphant return than are the big bands.

From the first floor of the Old Executive Office Building one can observe television reporters doing their stand-ups on the White House lawn all day long. Behind them lies the downstairs West Wing entrance to the pressroom, hermetically sealed from the rest of the White House, unless special permission has been granted. This is the view from the office of Jeff Eller, the White House director of media affairs. He wears no tie, and the collar of his lightly starched shirt is unbuttoned. On his clear desk (there's not even a scrap of hard copy on it) is a Macintosh PowerBook, much prized by the White House. ("When we took office, I walked into the Oval Office—it's supposed to be the nerve center of the United States—and we found Jimmy Carter's telephone system," an amazed Clinton told employees at Silicon Graphics, in California, on February 22nd. "Then we went down into the basement, where we found Lyndon Johnson's switchboard. True story—where there were four operators working from early morning till late at night—literally, when a phone call would come ... they would pick up a little cord and push it into a little hole. That's today, right?") On a table next to Eller's desk are a Microsoft baseball cap and a large pitcher of iced tea. He chomps on a cigar, which he is prohibited by new White House rules from lighting. On his door he has posted a sign: "When entering this room, DO NOT SAY: 'We've never done it that way before.' "

Eller has just returned from a meeting in the West Wing, at which it was decided that Clinton must communicate his military-conversion program to those states hardest hit by base closings. In his office, Eller has convened his staff to arrange Presidential press conferences with Florida, California, and Connecticut media—events invisible to the national press. Eller, at thirty-seven, is the elder statesman; most members of his staff are twenty-something. No one wears a tie or a suit, but everyone wears beepers. Some have buzz-cut spiked haircuts. Doors are open all the time. Everyone works fourteen-hour days, and on breaks some relax by reading the magazine *Wired*.

The staff attempts to tap every media outlet except the Washington correspondents. Eller has divided the country into four quadrants. Within each region, local radio stations, television stations, and newspapers are called daily to see if they'd be interested in an interview with an Administration figure. (There is a thick loose-leaf media book for every state. "These are my bibles," said Kim Hopper, who handles the Western region.) The previous day, Leon Panetta, the budget director, had done an interview on the Dakota Radio Network, which consists of thirty-eight stations, and Tipper Gore had been interviewed by eight small Florida papers. Cabinet members are expected to be on call. On the fourth floor of the Old Executive Office Building, a television studio is in regular use. Aides estimate that they help stage at least one major media event a day, sometimes more. On March 24th, for example, the event was helping eleven visiting Democratic governors get interview after interview to voice their support for the investment part of Clinton's economic plan.

Press briefings and documents are constantly and instantly transmitted into cyberspace on computer networks like CompuServe and American Online. Presidential schedules, sometimes weeks in advance, are sent out on another computer network, US Newswire. (Exclusive press interviews, national or local, are not listed on the public schedule. Nor are transcripts of them released to other members of the media before the news is broadcast or printed. Press conferences of all kinds are included in the *Weekly Compilation of Presidential Documents.* And all White House releases are being archived, for the first time, in computer files, available to anyone on computer networks. On American Online "clinton pz" is the E-mail address for the White House.) Eller dreams of a C-SPAN-like channel to broadcast White House events around the clock: BC-TV, he calls it. He can't figure out how to finance it, however, or be sure that there would be enough public functions to broadcast.

Now he's concerned about Clinton's three press conferences with local media on base closings. "Here's who needs to be there," he tells his staff. "All television stations in Miami, the three network affiliates, the two big Hispanic stations. We need the defense writer for the Miami *Herald,* and make a call to the A.P. to see if they want to send anybody. We will invite INZ and IOD radio. We want to do a statewide California press conference. We need to issue an invitation to all television stations in San Jose, San Diego, L.A., San Francisco. In addition, the San Diego paper (there's only one, right?), and the L.A. *Times,* L.A. *Daily News,* San Jose *Mercury,* the *Chronicle,* the *Examiner,* and I'm not opposed to one person from the A.P. from California. We should extend the invitation to KGO radio. But the deal is they will sit as a group with the President."

"Will the Sacramento *Bee* be involved?" an aide asks.

"Good idea, invite the *Bee.* Invite Sacramento TV, too. And the third group is Connecticut. Same thing." Everyone rushes out of the room.

On March 13th, in the Roosevelt Room, often used as a workspace in the White House inner sanctum, thirteen members of the southern Florida press corps met the President, who was informally attired in a sweater, creating a further intimacy. For the reporters, the encounter was unique and perhaps thrilling. From the point of view of the regular White House correspondents, Clinton was not making real news, which must be *national* news. For Clinton, though, this was a chance to get extended exposure in those places most affected by his policies. He made an opening statement, enumerating a seven-point program dealing with the region. The questions that followed were all about southern Florida—Homestead Air Force base, specific economic-conversion plans, Haitian refugees, and, of course, Cuba. These were not questions that the White House correspondents would be likely to ask: they were too detailed and narrow. But they were not "softballs." They were carefully and sometimes sharply posed. ("Mr. President, in South Florida, there is a feeling among some people, a sense of betrayal....") For a President unacquainted with the arcane details of domestic policies, these would have been difficult pitches. Reagan or Bush, in such a setting, might have floundered. But Clinton has a depth of empirical knowledge that he displays at length. "We just have blind faith in the guy," said Eller.

Eller is the ideal man for his job, because he was once one of those he's now targeting. After attending Purdue for two and a half years without graduating, he worked in radio news in Crawfordsville, became a television reporter in Terre Haute, was elevated to a radio-news director's job, in Chattanooga, and then worked for five years at a Nashville TV station as an assignment editor and reporter. Eller left journalism for politics to work as a press secretary for a congressman, Bill Boner, who was about to be investigated for bribery.

(The Justice Department dropped the case, and Boner eventually left the House to become Mayor of Nashville.) "These kids come in and say, 'I'm having a bad day,' and I say, 'You know what a bad day is? A bad day is having two U.S. marshals hand you a subpoena for a federal grand jury in the basement of the Longworth Building—that's a bad day.' But it taught me a lot about crisis management. I don't think I'm that tough, but, you know, there ain't a whole lot of things that come up that really cause me to get real white. So I couldn't have had better training, although I wouldn't wish it on anybody." Handling disaster was Eller's credential, recommending him to the Democratic Congressional Campaign Committee, and it sent him to the most unstable districts. Eller is a unique version of the politico as wonk, able to traverse the two hemispheres of the Clintonian brain.

Eller's first job for Clinton was directing the Florida campaign in the primary, where Paul Tsongas was undone. There Eller invented "talking points"—daily faxes to activists and officials to keep them coordinated with the campaign's themes. It was a simple idea, an "old technology," said Eller, yet an innovation adapted for the campaign which had the effect of allowing Clinton's key supporters to feel connected. "He's the one who understood all the technology to keep all the states on the same message," Ruth Hunter, the deputy campaign manager in California, said of Eller. He also pulled network feeds from satellites during the day, before the stories were broadcast, and doing that allowed the campaign to ride the media waves. Whenever Bush appeared in an important media market, Eller saturated it the day after with interviews with Clinton by satellite. Eller was also responsible for maintaining the high velocity of response to any negative attack—responding within the same news cycle, so that the charge would not stand without its rebuttal.

Eller has carried the momentum of the campaign into the White House, adapting and extending the technology: a countervailing power to the Big Media, without any ideological imputation. "We'd like to give the public a broader view, and put information into the hands of affiliate TV and let it decide what's relevant," he said. "You're giving more editorial empowerment to local TV as opposed to a desk assistant who's never been out of Manhattan. You're changing filters."

Other Presidents have also attempted to go around, manipulate, or control the national press. But what Clinton is doing, motivated principally by his own political agenda and his facility with technology, is new. It was not really possible until the world of three-network media became anachronistic.

"The press is the enemy," Richard Nixon said many times. The media embodied the "establishment," which he loathed and believed was out to destroy him. To counter it, he created the "communications office," which enabled him, and Presidents after him, to reach beyond the West Wing pressroom. He supplemented his aboveground activity with darker methods: false front groups, false letter-writing campaigns to support the President, false leaks—a Potemkin Village populism.

Three-network television had established a new political ecosystem, in which the tactile pols like Hubert Humphrey began to die out. The Reagan Presidency may be best remembered as a succession of tableaux vivants, staged by the directors and producers of his White House. "I never thought of going around the Washington press corps," Michael Deaver, Reagan's chief impresario, said. The press, as Deaver saw it, was indispensable—performing the functions of key grip, camera operator, sound recorder, gaffer, and best boy. "We planned several weeks in advance what our story was going to be every day. The media were like starlings on a line."

George Bush disdained Reagan's skill at communication, regarding it as a form of legerdemain. Bush had a hierarchical view tempered only by his self-identification as a Washington player, the political sportsman. For him, the key relationships were offstage, which is why his ultimate form of communication was the thank-you note.

Bush hired a producer from ABC's "Nightline," Dorrance Smith, to develop innovative communications, yet Bush remained the incorrigible incumbent of Washington court politics. "We tried to do as many local stations as we had time for," said Smith. "The difference is that we didn't do that at the expense of the Washington press corps." Bush wanted to play the game as he understood it, a game of the status quo. "A lot of the stuff Eller is talking about, but by no means all of it, was suggested," said Tony Snow, who was for a while Bush's chief speechwriter. "No one wanted to do it. No one cared—nobody on the senior staff, no chief of staff. For the most part, for senior Bush officials the world had not changed since 1988. They only had to re-create it and they would win. They were wrong." Bush's final slogan was a pathetic attack on those he had so assiduously courted: "Annoy the liberal media. Reelect Bush."

Bill Clinton is like the old-style politician who is the student of human nature and focusses on the voter in front of him. The premium is on the personal encounter. But, unlike the old-style pol, Clinton can perform this seduction before cameras. Unlike Reagan, whose ideal situations involved packaged sound-bites, Clinton is the improvisor. He loves being unprotected before audiences, with no scrim. It is the sign that he is open to them; in revealing *his* feelings he showcases the voter's, attempting to create an intimate bond. ("I feel your pain.") Clinton offers a benediction in the sacred language of therapy: our fireside chat. He is the chairman of the Inner Children's Defense Fund. Reagan, who was hard-of-hearing, could read off the teleprompter with perfect inflection; Clinton riffs off teleprompters, and turns politics into a listening contest. He tosses scripts aside: the new narrative is episodic; the new temperament is interactive, a work in progress, going beyond technocratic tinkering to reinvent government.

Clinton's political advisers all understand these elements. Stanley Greenberg, his pollster, said, "There is a powerful impression that Clinton listens to people. It is perhaps the strongest element of his character at the moment. It's seen to be his genuine character. Empathy and caring are essential to his identity. The technology of the White House is catching up to who he is."

George Stephanopoulos, the communications director, said, "The means is an end as well. The technique says something about the kind of President Clinton wants to be and the kind of government he wants to run—a government in touch, a value in and of itself."

The Washington press corps will hardly disappear, but its old forms are in relative decline. Its fall may be attributed partly to its hubris. In the 1988 campaign, press stories actually drove Gary Hart and Joe Biden from the Presidential primaries. "Somebody had to prune the field," Paul Taylor, of the Washington *Post*—who had asked Hart at a press conference whether he'd committed adultery—wrote in his 1990 book, "See How They Run." "It simply wasn't practical for voters to make choices among a dozen or more contenders.... The assignment fell to the press—there was no one else."

After Clinton's victory, the national press began to suffer, at least a bit, the painful process known in the business world as disintermediation; that is, eliminating the middleman. What the President seeks is unmediated communication.

The future struggles for control may not be just between the national press and the President, but among various levels of the media themselves. Paul Friedman, executive vice-president of ABC News, told one newspaper reporter that he had asked affiliates "not to let themselves be used by the White House communications office and to reject their offers." "I don't blame them for doing what they're doing," he said later. "What seems to be different is the degree to which this is being done."

Tracy Bryan, a reporter with KCRA, in Sacramento, who was part of the contingent invited to interview the President about base closings, said, "I would not have been happy if I were a national-press-corps member and the local yokels got access. But I like it that Clinton goes to the people and opens himself up. I see both sides."

The situation is not static. It is conceivable that the media universe of today will seem as antiquated in a few years as the one of the early nineteen-eighties seems now. "We'll have five hundred channels and interactive channels, and we'll have both by the next election," said Mandy Grunwald, Clinton's director of advertising during the campaign and a political consultant who often advises him in the White House. "What makes it hard and fun is that it's addition, not a zero-sum game."

Clinton's media operations do not exist in a vacuum, like much of Reagan's, which used the press to project rehearsed images. Clinton exposes himself as no President before him has, and he does so in the service of his policies. Stephanopoulos says, "In the end, we'll be judged by what we do, not how we do it." But the Presidency is the nation's most personal office, and the sense of Clinton's emerging program is inextricable from the emerging sense of his personality.

DISCUSSION QUESTIONS

1. Blumenthal seems to admire the Clinton press operation. How do you think of it? Why?

2. Some would argue that bypassing the White House press corps also allows a president to avoid taking public positions on many of the major issues of the day. Others would argue that the White House press corps is not likely to focus on major issues but on relatively minor "political" concerns. Where do you stand? How would you argue for your position?

3. Critics are quick to charge "media manipulation" when a president or another political leader arranges press relationships to their advantage. There may be, however, a great deal of truth to the charge. What do you think: Is the Clinton press arrangement an attempt to manipulate media coverage and content? If so, what's wrong with that? If not, why not?

16. COVERING THE COURT

The least-reported-on branch of government in Washington is clearly the judiciary. Even the Supreme Court, which makes many significant and even earth-shaking decisions, rarely generates much coverage. When civil rights, criminal justice, abortion, or free speech decisions are handed down, the news media file their share of stories. But these stories deal with the outcome of the judicial process and the responses of others to them. They rarely say very much about the interplay of forces that led the Court to its decisions in the first place. Nor do stories report what members of the Court think of the decision's ramifications. The Justices speak through their official opinions and rarely in other ways.

According to Richard Davis, the Court may be on the verge of changing its perspective on news coverage. He argues that favorable media stories are so important to the Court that they cannot leave their media coverage totally to chance, or to reporters' discretion, as they have in the past. But consciously to pursue a media strategy has a major cost that may outweigh its advantage: The Court may no longer seem above the fray but rather just another political institution making political decisions. That the latter image is closer to reality does not change the fact that the former image is much more helpful to the Court in securing compliance with its rulings.

Press, Politics, and the Supreme Court
Richard Davis

The courts are a political institution, and we don't cover them as such. Washington Post *editor Bob Woodward*

THE COURT AND THE PUBLIC

... The U.S. Supreme Court is the most reclusive American political institution. In the past, the press has contributed to that reclusive nature, but the future may be a different matter. ...

SOURCE: From *The Press and American Politics: The New Mediator* by Richard Davis. Copyright 1992 by Longman Publishing Group.

The Court's continued success in gaining compliance with its decisions is contingent on the public perception that the Court is largely apolitical. ...

In the Court, the broader objective of its relations with the press is to perpetuate public confidence through maintaining its public image of aloofness from politics. No other governmental institution is as persistent nor as successful in accomplishing its objective. Individual presidents have achieved policy or personal objectives in press relations, and many members of Congress have been similarly successful, but for neither were the goals and accomplishments institutional in nature.

The Court possesses several distinct advantages over the other two branches of government in such a process. First, the small body of justices at any one time and the absence of innate and permanent factions such as divisions by political party aids in maintaining the public solidarity of the justices. And second, the continuity of the Court also supports institutional objectives. Where representatives, senators, and even the president must constantly look toward reelection challenges, the turnover of justices is usually extremely gradual and generally precipitated by choice on the part of the resigning justice.

On the other hand, the very small size of the Court and the independence of its members can lead to fragmentation. Fragmentation would mean each justice pursuing his or her own agenda in a manner potentially harmful to the court's ability to maintain public deference.

. . . The Court has even been generally successful in obtaining press cooperation in advancing Court objectives. The Court attempts to gain press coverage that reflects aloofness from politics and enhances public respect for the institution.

The press typically accepts the Court's objectives in regard to public perceptions, and this is reinforced by the language the press uses: the justices of the High Court, donned in their solemn black robes, "hand down" decisions. Two political scientists have argued that "journalistic language makes it less apparent to the public that nine unelected justices make policies as significant as those of the elected president and Congress."[1]

Also, the justices are successful in drawing attention away from themselves or the decision-making process and toward the decision itself. Almost none of the news coverage of the Court concerns the way the justices make decisions. Reporters rely on the authoritative Court sources, which fail to provide this information.

We learn of the structure of decision making—oral arguments, conferences, opinion writing, and final announcement—but the press does not examine that process in conjunction with specific decisions. The press does not because the Court has not made such reporting easy.

Hence, the Court's image as a body that proclaims the law with finality on the basis of legal factors is not undermined by an examination of the variables—legal or political—present in the process leading up to that decision.

JUSTICES' RELATIONS WITH REPORTERS

The justices of the U.S. Supreme Court individually have maintained their distance from journalists, traditionally, rarely giving inteviews to reporters and then usually only on a background basis. The justices do not hold press conferences except when retiring from the Court, and other employees of the Court are prohibited from talking with reporters.

As a result, news stories about the Court, [sic] rarely focus on the individual justices, personally or professionally. There is a great deal of coverage of the nominees to the Court. . . . However, once justices come on the bench, stories specifically about them are uncommon. Those that do occur tend to be reports on justices' health or occasional speeches.

Since the Court consists of only nine individuals, each of whom possesses an equal vote capable of shifting majorities and radically altering the direction of

Court decisions—since each justice is, in fact, one-ninth of a national political institution—this paucity of news coverage of the individual justices can only be a testament to the success of the justices' strategy of press relations.

The justices conduct press relations in order to preserve respect for the Supreme Court through which they can exercise political power. The potential weakness of the Court in the American political system necessitates active efforts to preserve the Court's revered position in national government. . . .

PURSUING MEDIA STRATEGIES

Recent years have provided indications that some of the justices intend, at least temporarily, to abandon that shared strategy of institutional aloofness for individual style. . . .

Although the justices still are far from media stars, this recent increased availability to the press suggests a possible change in the justices' relations with reporters and their attitudes toward the relationship between the Court and the press.

If a change has occurred, why? The justices may have opened up to the press in order to participate in the celebration of the bicentennial of the Constitution in the mid- to late 1980s. They would be ideally suited to explain the role of the Court in the expanded public discussion of the Constitution and the American system of government. The political environment is salient. The issues pushed to the Court in the 1970s and 1980s have been highly emotional ones unresolved by other political institutions. These have included, for example, abortion, school busing, affirmative action, and the death penalty.

. . . The justices also probably have been affected by the press's greater access to the other institutions of government. Since the 1970s, the press, including television has enjoyed largely unlimited access to congressional committee hearings. Floor proceedings are opened to live television coverage. While other institutions facilitated greater access for the press, the Court apparently has remained largely static.

Perhaps closer to home for the justices, lower courts have begun opening courtrooms to cameras. The Court has upheld the right of states to grant access to cameras.[2]

But the Court has been reluctant to follow suit itself. Former Chief Justice Warren Burger has suggested the justices might be distracted by the cameras and that highly selective coverage of all arguments, as the networks would provide, would give the public a distorted conception of the case.[3] Under Chief Justice William Rehnquist, the justices in November 1988 experimented with the televising of oral arguments. In late 1989, after polling his colleagues on the Court and finding a majority opposed to the presence of cameras, Rehnquist announced the Court would not change its policy.

One overriding issue in the debate over televising the Court, as with the televising of Congress, has been control of the television system. The justices desire power over the image and would demand control of the cameras. But the press responds, as one newspaper editorial, that "giving the Court such editorial control would be too high a price for public access."[4]

Less intrusive radio coverage has also been rejected, although three of the justices expressed support. Before retiring, Justice Brennan remarked that "There is no reason in my judgment why only those who gain entrance to the courtroom should be able to witness these proceedings."[5] ABC Radio requested such coverage for the oral arguments in the 1989 case of *Webster v. Reproductive Health Services* involving abortion, but Rehnquist denied it.[6]

... Some of the justice's [sic] new emphasis on individual visibility may be an attempt to pursue personal or policy objectives, however. Those who have made themselves most visible have been the justices viewed as liberals or centrists on the bench, such as Harry Blackmun, John Paul Stevens, and Thurgood Marshall. They have watched a more conservative majority form among the four Reagan-appointed justices and Justice Byron White, and they have seen their influence within the Court wane. They have watched the conservatives become more assertive on the Court and have observed changes external to the Court which favor the conservatives. The "liberal-centrists" may be pursuing an "outsider" strategy designed to bring public pressure on their colleagues or, at the least, to explicate their own roles.

If, however, these justices are using the press to achieve outside the confines of the Court what they have failed to achieve inside, it is not unreasonable to assume that debates within the Court's conference room will eventually begin to spill out into public view. If justices on both sides of an issue begin running to the cameras to air their sides of the issue, such activity would constitute a radical change in the justices' use of and dependency on the press. . . .

REPORTING THE DECISIONS

On the days when decisions are announced, the twenty-five reporters assigned to the Court full-time are at their busiest. This is so because when the press covers the Court, it reports its decisions. Only rarely are news stories not about the decisions. But the press is highly selective even in reporting decisions. One study of newspaper coverage of Court decisions in the late 1970s found that most decisions were never reported by local media, and that even a national newspaper never reported one-third of the decisions. According to another study, newsmagazine coverage of the Court decisions missed 80 percent of the decisions.[7] On the other hand, a few other decisions are accorded near saturation coverage for a short period. On the day of the announcement of the Webster case in July 1989, the television and radio networks went live for a half hour after the decision and then continued with periodic reports throughout the day. The decision received several pages of editorial space in the next day's major daily newspapers.

Another study suggested that press coverage concentrates on social policy such as abortion, school prayer, capital punishment, and civil rights and ignores other, more complex issues such as search and seizure and legal standing to sue.[8]

The explanation for press reporting of decisions rests with the way the Court releases its decisions as well as the way journalists approach reporting them. The Court offers extensive written explanations of their decisions. However, the justices do not make themselves available to reporters largely on their own to describe, explain, and analyze the decisions. As a result the journalists who cover the Court come to rely on non-Court sources, such as summaries of cases provided by legal groups and interviews with prominent legal scholars or representatives of affected interest groups.

Those decisions that are covered by the press tend to be reported briefly and sketchily, particularly by network news and non-elite daily newspapers. The effect of the decision on the parties involved may be reported, but for all except a handful of decisions little or no attention is paid to the decision's impact, to explanation of the decision-making process, to the context of the decision, or to the reaction of affected parties.

The press has frequently been criticized for serious errors in its reporting of Court decisions. Critics have argued that some reporters and many headline writers miss the subtleties of Court decisions. For example, David L. Grey documented misreporting of the 1962 school prayer case, and Frank J. Sorauf found news coverage of the Court's campaign finance rulings inaccurate and misleading.[9]

Who is to blame for sketchy and sometimes inaccurate reporting of decisions? Reporters complain that the fault lies with the Court. First, it speaks not to the public, but to a legal fraternity. The opinions are written in a style intended for a small group of attorneys, judges, and legal scholars. The Court does little to help reporters understand the opinions, which leaves much room for misunderstanding. Also, reporters say, the Court is to blame because it is unclear about its direction. Reporters say they cannot explain to the public the incomprehensible decisions of the Court. One reporter explained her dilemma in reporting a civil rights decision:

> It was literally impossible to decipher. All I could tell my readers is that the Court had done "x." I could not tell them why. One wire service hailed the decision as a great civil rights victory, while the other wire service called the decision a great civil rights defeat.[10]

... Another problem with Court coverage originates with the way the press treats news. The time constraints of the news business, primarily the speed of transmission and rapid-fire delivery, do not lend themselves to thorough digestion of decisions and thoughtful analysis. Reporters are handed the decisions as they are announced by the justices. They must read, understand, and be able to summarize accurately the decision, including dissenting and concurring opinions, before the next deadline. For network television reporters and national newspapers, that deadline may be only hours away. For the wire service reporters, whose stories will circulate more than any other print stories, the deadline may be only minutes away. In their reporting of the Webster decision, network reporters began live broadcasting two minutes after the decision was handed to the press.

The definition of news as what has occurred within the past 24 hours also prevents most of the press from returning to the decision the next day with longer, more reflective stories on the decision. Beyond the 24-hour period, the story of the latest Supreme Court decision is old news.

Where inaccuracy exists it is probably less the fault of reporters assigned to the Court, who have some familiarity with complex legal issues, than of editors and headline writers. Stephen Hess found that reporters assigned to the Court are more likely than their colleagues on other beats to disagree with editors over story language because of the technicality of legal terms.[11]

A more common and, indeed, a more subtle problem is reporter analysis of the decision. Most coverage of decisions consists only of a bare-bones description of the result, but when analysis is offered, the reporter determines its content. Reporters are free to frame the decision as they see fit, and the context a reporter sets for interpreting a given decision could be adherence to the Constitution, legal precedent, interest group pressure, or the personal values of the justices.

Reporters demand sources for stories, but since justices decline most requests for interviews, the press turns to non-Court sources. The choice of such sources is determined by reporters according to news values.

Reporters possess wide latitude in reporting decisions. A cross-media comparison of one decision on the constitutionality of sobriety tests for drunk drivers found wide variation in reporting.[12] One network evening news story focused primarily on the reliability of a breathalyzer, which was not a topic of the decision, and added conflict and skepticism to the story by highlighting problems with the breathalyzer. Two newspaper stories, however, seemed to reinforce the decision by including quotes from a supportive source, which in turn quoted generously from the majority opinion and minimized attention to any dissent.[13]

Why do reporters have such latitude? In part they do because the justices allow them to. Because of their own priorities—the need to maintain an apolitical and dignified image—the justices refuse to accommodate certain press priorities. Their reasoned arguments do not fit the media's needs for brevity and simplicity. If the justices explained their decisions in a format more suitable for the press, such as interviews and press conferences, reporters might gain a greater understanding of the decision. But, again, justices do not believe their decisions need to be explained more than they have already done in lengthy opinion, and they would run the risk of engaging in a post-decision fracas with legal scholars, interest group representatives and even with each other, which would only diminish the effect of the Court's decision. The Court's press officers might be capable of providing the analysis in a format desired by reporters. But press officers, probably in accordance with the wishes of the justices, have demurred at such requests. According to Supreme Court Public Information Officer Toni House:

> The justices spend anywhere up to nine months framing their opinions in the particular case. The idea that a press officer ... would then come along behind and say, "Well, in laymen's terms, this is what the Court really meant" is really mind boggling to me.[14]

Changes in the press have also affected the latitude that journalists who cover the Court claim. In the wake of the new journalism, reporters have tended to adopt a more interpretive role, one which treats Court decisions as parts of a larger context, interpreted by the reporter, rather than as stories unto themselves. Additionally, adversarial journalism has diminished reporters' deference toward the Court, as well as toward other national political institutions. The journalistic corps seems more inclined to regard the Court as a political institution than they once were.

COVERING A POLITICAL INSTITUTION

... Some journalists and scholars have urged that the press cover the Court more and treat it more as a political institution. They contend the Court too long has been handled by the press without the critical approach with which journalists view other institutions.

... Increased political coverage of the Court might well present greater difficulty for the Court as an arbiter of conflicts. The Court's position as a source of judgment aloof from political consideration would be undermined by coverage which emphasized political—even partisan—motivations or trends of the justices, and public deference for the Court, which is imperative to the maintenance of a significant role in national policy-making, might well decline.

Greater political coverage could in turn result in a more politicized body. The Court might be drawn into more political disputes with the president and the Congress, and perhaps urged to act in a more hasty manner with greatly reduced time for reflection.

The result eventually could be actual fragmentation of the Court mentioned earlier with each justice publicly pursuing independent individual objectives and seriously damaging the Court's ability to function as an institution.

Until recently, the Supreme Court has been the exception to the rule of increased dependency on the press by political institutions and processes. The Court has been relatively successful at keeping the press at arm's length in pursuit of the strategy of bolstering public deference.

However, that period may be closing if the trends continue. The Court may become more dependent on the press and the press will cover the Court from a more autonomous stance. Although the press will have a better story, it is not likely the nation would have a better Supreme Court.

NOTES

1. David L. Paletz and Robert M. Entman, *Media Power Politics*, New York: Free Press, 1981, p. 105.
2. *Chandler v. Florida*, 449 U.S. 560 (1981).
3. Eleanor Randolph and Al Kamen, "Chief Justice Considers Televising Supreme Court," *Washington Post*, April 12, 1986, p. 45.
4. "Light on the Supreme Court," *Washington Post*, April 22, 1986, p. A30.
5. Stuart A. Taylor, Jr., "Supreme Court Rejects Radio Coverage of Budget Argument," *New York Times*, April 20, 1986, p. 27.
6. "Supreme Court Officer Discusses Webster Case," *C-SPAN Update*, July 24, 1989, p. 8.
7. See David Ericson, "Newspaper Coverage of the Supreme Court," *Journalism Quarterly*, 54:605–607 (1977); and Michael Solomine, "Newsmagazine Coverage of the Supreme Court," *Journalism Quarterly*, 57:661–663 (1980).
8. Richard Davis, "News Media Coverage of American National Political Institutions," unpublished doctoral dissertation, Syracuse University, 1986, p. 135.
9. See David Grey, *The Supreme Court and the News Media*, Evanston, IL: Northwestern University Press, 1968; and Frank J. Sorauf, *Money in American Elections*, Glenview, IL: Scott, Foresman, 1988, pp. 223–225.
10. Mitchell J. Tropin, "What, Exactly, Is the Court Saying?" *The Barrister*, Winter 1984:14.
11. Stephen Hess, *The Washington Reporters*, Washington: Brookings, 1981, p. 3n.
12. Davis, "News Media Coverage," pp. 50–52.
13. Richard Davis, "Lifting the Shroud: News Media Portrayal of the U.S. Supreme Court," *Communications and the Law*, 9:50–52, 1987.
14. "Supreme Court Officer," p. 8.

DISCUSSION QUESTIONS

1. Does the Supreme Court need news coverage? Would it be able to operate and attain its goals if it rarely or never got into the news? Why?
2. Supreme Court decisions are frequently seen as the "final" determination of the question at stake. If reports of Court decisions build on the commentary of interested observers, including interest group representatives, is the "finality" of Court pronouncements thereby compromised? How so or why not?
3. Why shouldn't we expect the Supreme Court to issue an explanatory press release along with the text of their opinions in the cases they decide?
4. What can we learn from news coverage of the Supreme Court about the motives and rationales behind the Court's decisions? How much different would your view of the Court be if the news media explicitly reported the bargaining and negotiation that go on behind the scenes at the Court?
5. Would you be in favor of televising Supreme Court sessions? Why or why not? What effect would televising them have on Court procedures? On the public? On other interested parties?

17. GOVERNMENTAL BUREAUCRACY IN THE MEDIA

We don't see much in the papers about the way government agencies do their jobs. Oh, corruption stories and scandals, such as the flap at HUD and former Secretary Samuel Pierce, get a lot of play, but the day-to-day rule making and administration generate little coverage. Is it because executive agencies don't do many newsworthy things, or because the federal bureaucracy is so widespread that it is hard to cover? Stephen Hess argues that neither of these is the dominant factor. What makes the difference is the orientation the agency has toward the press. Whereas some agencies like to operate in virtual anonymity, others want to stimulate press attention. For some agencies, media coverage gets in the way of achieving their objectives; for others, getting in the news is an important way of accomplishing the agency's goals.

The Care and Feeding of the Fourth Estate
Stephen Hess

Variations in the responsiveness of press offices . . . depend on more than the status of news organizations and individual reporters. There are also institutional differences among government agencies that help determine their media strategies. Some agencies, such as those responsible for consumer protection, need attention; others may consider publicity counterproductive to their mission, as CIA director William Casey concluded when he eliminated his agency's separate press operation. Most are in-between. Note the implications about agency responsiveness that are contained even in the masthead format of the standard news release:

>Food and Drug Administration
>   Name of press officer
>   Office phone number
>   Home phone number
>
>Department of Transportation
>   Name of press officer
>   Office phone number
>
>Department of Defense
>   Office phone number
>
>Department of State

Another factor in official responsiveness is the age of an administration. In the beginning the career personnel, their new bosses, and the reporters are "trying to figure out where everyone's coming from so that, in some cases, even the simplest piece of information can become incredibly difficult [for the reporters] to get," says a veteran reporter. Another period, of course, usually comes a year into the administration, when the first sustained bout of bad publicity, combined with politically damaging leaks, produces a temporary damper on information.

Government agencies also can be diagrammed as a solar system that affects responsiveness. Its inner ring is the White House and the four original departments—State, War (Defense), Treasury, and Justice. All other departments and agencies, as in a schema developed by Thomas E. Cronin, constitute the outer government.[1] In general, reporters who cover the inner government are supplicants for information. In the outer government the officials are the supplicants if they wish attention. But, of course, some outer government agencies do not wish attention, which they may view as threatening to the status quo.

. . . The excesses of what government tells or fails to tell the press will most often occur when the relationship between the two institutions is most unequal—on either side: a supplicant agency may overreach to make news; a nonsupplicant agency may be overprotective of what should be news. News organizations, too, can suffer from arrogance or servility. Equals tend to have the healthiest fights and cohabitations.

Reporter/agency relations also depend on the type of news media involved. It is hardly surprising that the medium of choice for presidents has become television. Elected officials need to reach voters; diplomats, generals, and bureaucrats do not necessarily. I counted fifteen television cameras at

SOURCE: From Stephen Hess, *The Government/Press Connection: Press Officers and Their Offices*, pp. 101–106, copyright 1984 by the Brookings Institution.

one White House bill-signing ceremony and six cameras and twenty-seven people (mostly technicians) in the president's office for a routine photo opportunity. Because pictures dominate the planning and timing of White House events, the beat becomes less attractive to print journalists. The State and Defense departments, on the other hand, are essentially print beats. The Pentagon offers only one small room, partitioned into separate offices, for NBC, ABC, and CBS, with the CNN reporter's desk in the entryway; while talking with an NBC reporter, I could hear ABC and CBS reporters calling in their stories. "If I want privacy I go to a pay phone down the hall," one reporter commented. That the State Department now allows cameras into the daily briefings has not challenged the dominance of print on this beat; it merely gives the networks' diplomatic correspondents an extra visual angle that may help them sell a talking-heads story to their producers. With its reliance on pictures, television news is also at a disadvantage when sources insist on anonymity, almost always the case in national security affairs. Yet TV reporters have been helped by the world roving of recent secretaries of state; before John Foster Dulles, secretaries were a sedentary lot. Television also rates a higher priority at Foggy Bottom when the secretary of state is abroad, as is clear from the elaborate summaries of TV stories that headquarters cables to the traveling party—a service that is more perfunctory when the secretary of state is in Washington. As a rule of thumb, however, the more technical the work of an agency, the more specialized or "serious" the news media it favors. The deputy commissioner at the Food and Drug Administration says he takes calls only from reporters for trade and scientific publications; those from the mass media he refers to the public affairs office. But even at the FDA's public affairs office, a press officer says, "Broadcast people frighten me. I'm dealing with a stacked deck. They're performers."

Each government agency's strategy toward the press, which determines the news organizations or type of medium it will favor, partly depends on the reading or listening habits of those it wishes to influence. For instance, the *New York Times* is considered the publication that is most circulated within embassies and foreign ministries. At least, this is what the State Department must believe, because as I followed events from the government and press sides I sometimes felt that department officials were negotiating with *Times* reporters in much the same manner as they would with the diplomats of a sovereign nation. James Reston's interview with Alexander Haig on May 10, 1982, seemed more a meeting of potentates than a journalist questioning a foreign minister. I did not have the same impression of the State Department's relations with the other widely read paper: a Foreign Service officer praised a *Washington Post* reporter for being able to read the cables upside down on his desk as he conducted an interview—he seemed to find this enterprising, yet not really the way a gentleman should act.

There still remains among many State Department professionals what one press officer calls "the traditional nineteenth-century diplomat's view that ideally there should be no news at all." So there is within the department a sense of inevitability that, on balance, what gets published and broadcast is more likely to hinder U.S. foreign policy objectives than to help and that, therefore, the best press strategy is *damage limitation*. Or as Dean Rusk told Walter Cronkite in 1966, "You're interested in the drama of the news. What we are working for is the repose of solutions. . . . Our business is, in a sense, to get foreign policy off the front page back to page 8."[2]

At the same time, a certain ambivalence toward reporters creeps into the interstice between the professional and the political ranks of diplomacy, such as the noncareer assistant secretaries of state and the president's national security adviser. Zbigniew Brzezinski, for example, attacked the press for tending "either to sensationalize or oversimplify complex issues," and in the same interview bemoaned his administration's failure "to explain [its actions] to the public and to mobilize public support."[3] This too can be seen in the attitudes of most recent secretaries of state—with the exception of Henry Kissinger, who seemed to feel he could manipulate the press to his advantage. Most diplomatic correspondents do a fair-to-excellent imitation of Kissinger's efforts to cultivate reporters: *Your article, John, showed the best understanding.* Alexander Haig also worked hard at press relations, but I never met a reporter who thought that Haig liked reporters. This attitude of joyless obligation in dealing with the press trickled down from the seventh floor in 1982. The "chilling effect" in an agency that reporters talk about is usually nothing more than underlings' sensitivity to their bosses' attitude toward the press.

The Pentagon's press strategy could be characterized as *educating* (others would say *selling*). With huge budgets that need congressional approval and popular support and with a steady stream of proposed weapons systems, the press officers see themselves as having a positive mission in helping to maintain the military readiness of the nation. A naval officer walks over to a reporter: *"Let me educate you about. . . ."* This attitude permeates the news division, a large space without partitions where reporters stand around the press officers' desks. Press officers wander in and out of the newsroom, which is across the corridor. The press office has a bank of television sets tuned to each network (with the sound off) and a board that lists deadlines: "COB (close of business) Thursdays for *Aviation Week;* 1 p.m., *Christian Science Monitor;* 6 p.m., *Los Angeles Times.*" At the State Department the press officers and the reporters are also on the same floor, but on different corridors. Only three times in three months did I see a press officer in the newsroom. There are no television sets or notices of deadlines in the press office. The State Department officers' offices have doors.

. . . Despite shorthand notations of press strategies at the golden triangle—limiting damage, educating/selling, feeding the bears—most government agencies would be hard pressed to point to anything as grand-sounding as a strategy. There are campaigns from time to time, alerting the public to cuts in service that would result from a lower budget or the dangers of too much sodium in the diet or the value of treasury bonds. There are also officials who want their names and faces in the news and expect their press officers to satisfy this appetite. When career personnel complain of "politicizing," it often turns out to be the "personalizing" of information that they have in mind. I suspect, however, that most executives would be satisfied with a press strategy of *no surprises.* All their press officers need do to be doing their job is provide a rudimentary early warning system and issue routine announcements.

The modesty attached to the care and feeding of the fourth estate may come as something of a surprise: studies of government/press relations have tended to focus on the White House and election campaigns that lead to government service at the top, or on memoirs by reporters and officials of the presidents-who-have-known-me variety, or reporters' stories of the exceptional—a scandal, a crisis, or a remarkable official. But it needs to be noted again that only a few government agencies have newsrooms and a corps of regular reporters who spend part or most of each day inside specific buildings. Only eleven of the FDA's top nineteen officials turned out to be particularly interested in what the media was saying about them as measured by their attentiveness to the agency's excellent clipping service; one even admitted that he never read the daily clips. Judging from her telephone logs, there were days in October 1981 when only one or two reporters had anything to ask the Transportation Department's public affairs director. These are the parts of government where press coverage "is sporadic at best and nonexistent at worst," according to Lou Cannon,[4] and where the government likes it this way.

NOTES

1. Thomas E. Cronin, *The State of the Presidency,* Boston: Little, Brown, 1975, pp. 188–92.
2. See *Congressional Record,* March 25, 1966, p. A1738.
3. George Urban, "A Long Conversation with Dr. Zbigniew Brzezinski." *Encounter,* 56:14–15 (May 1981).
4. Lou Cannon, *Reporting: An Inside View.* California Journal Press, 1977, p. 196.

DISCUSSION QUESTIONS

1. Why do some agency personnel see journalists as intrusions and distractions, while others see them as part of the job? What differences among the agencies officials work for would help explain this pattern?

2. If you were an agency official, how would you go about attracting media coverage for something you were working on? How would you go about discouraging media coverage?

3. If Hess is correct when he suggests that some agencies discourage media attention, where would journalists find sources willing to speak with them about issues affecting those agencies? What implications can you draw from such a situation?

CHAPTER 6
Media and Law

The press is the only nongovernment institution to be explicitly protected by a constitutional provision: the First Amendment, which prohibits Congress and government generally from abridging the freedom of the press. Of course, the actual extent of the protection depends on the circumstances and on the Supreme Court's interpretation of that protection. For instance, how may government respond to the danger that publication of information may pose for law and order or for national security? How far may media go in criticizing public figures before they are liable for the damage that criticism causes? Is media access to sources and to locales where news is being made protected by the First Amendment? Finally, how one-sided may news reports and editorial comment be before media are required to give the other side an opportunity to respond? All these issues are explored in the selections in this chapter.

An overriding consideration seems to be that the operation of a free press is essential to the functioning of democracy in the United States. If government imposes restrictions on news organizations and news personnel, journalists may be inhibited from pursuing stories or reticent in their discussions of controversial issues. The losers in such instances are not reporters, editors, and publishers. Oh, they may suffer lower circulation or smaller audiences or enjoy lesser notoriety because they do not break new stories and raise new controversies. But the real losers are members of the public who do not hear about concerns that will affect their lives and who are therefore deprived of the opportunity to contribute to the ongoing public discussion about these issues. Democracy then is curtailed; it functions among those who have access to information but not among the rest of us who do not have alternative ways of finding out what is happening. The press is then protected to serve democracy, not to further the media's own interests.

Nevertheless, media issues do not arise in a vacuum. They arise in the context of conflicting values. Rarely does a case arise where an abridgement of press rights is the issue alone. Rather, it is press rights weighed against national security. Or it is press rights weighed against the need to have an effective law enforcement process. Or it is press rights weighed against the need to protect reputations from wanton and malicious comment. And although some Supreme Court justices may say that such weighing has been done by the framers of the First Amendment when they said that "Congress shall make no law . . ." limiting the press, the Court as a whole has generally taken very seriously the notion that other societal values cannot be ignored. The press is free, but it functions in a social and political context that must be taken into account. Or, at least, that is what the Supreme Court seems to be saying.

18. PRIOR RESTRAINT AND THE PRESS

If there is one point about government regulation of the media that courts have been rather consistent about, it is that any government action must follow, not precede, publication. In other words, action against the press for libel might be sustained, but preventing the libel by prohibiting publication in the first place invades press rights protected by the First Amendment (and extended to cover states' actions by the Fourteenth Amendment). In one case [*Near v. Minnesota,* 283 U.S. 697 (1931)], Minnesota applied a state law that allowed it to declare a newspaper a public nuisance for its scurrilous attacks on public officials and then to "abate" that nuisance by preventing it from publishing in the future. The newspaper in question, *The Saturday Press,* was particularly virulent in its anti-Semitism, and the fact that it loudly criticized Minneapolis city fathers probably helped its cause very little. The Supreme Court ruled that "prior restraint," or limiting the press before publication, was unacceptable under the First Amendment.

But sometimes matters of such concern to government arise that prior restraint seems to be the only way to prevent serious damage to national interests. In the early 1970s, Daniel Ellsberg managed to provide copies of a classified Defense Department study of U.S. entry into the quagmire of Vietnam to the *New York Times* and the *Washington Post.* The hope was that support for U.S. efforts in Vietnam would dissipate when the public knew how we got involved in the first place. After some indecision and study, the two newspapers began publishing long excerpts from those documents, known as the Pentagon Papers, including transcripts of secret cables and private conversations among government leaders. The embarrassment of top foreign policymakers was evident. What was also obvious was that some of the information could be seen as helpful to the North Vietnamese, to the Soviet Union, or to China. Whether it would be helpful, no one could tell. But the issue of national security weighed in the balance here against the interests of a free press. The Supreme Court decided rather hastily, resulting in an unsigned *per curiam* opinion for the majority and then a series of separate opinions written by the individual justices. Some excerpts give you the flavor of the dispute between the majority and the dissenters on the issue of prior restraint of publication in the area of national security.

New York Times Company v. United States, 403 U.S. 718 (1971).

Per Curiam

We granted certiorari in these cases in which the United States seeks to enjoin the New York Times and the Washington Post from publishing the contents of a classified study entitled "History of U.S. Decision-Making Process on Viet Nam Policy."

"Any system of prior restraints of expression comes to this Court bearing a heavy presumption against its constitutional validity." ... The Government "thus carries a heavy burden of showing justification for the imposition of such a restraint." ... The District Court for the Southern District of New York in the *New York Times* cases and the District Court for the District of Columbia and the Court of Appeals for the District of Columbia Circuit in the *Washington Post* case held that the Government had not met that burden. We agree. ...

Mr. Justice Black, with whom Mr. Justice Douglas joins, concurring.

I adhere to the view that the Government's case against the Washington Post should have been dismissed and that the injunction against the New York Times should have been vacated without oral argument when the cases were first presented to this Court. I believe that every moment's continuance of the injunctions against these newspapers amounts to a flagrant, indefensible, and continuing violation of the First Amendment.... In my view, it is unfortunate that some of my Brethren are apparently willing to hold that the publications of news may sometimes be enjoined. Such a holding would make a shambles of the First Amendment.

... In seeking injunctions against these newspapers and in its presentation to the Court, the Executive Branch seems to have forgotten the essential purpose and history of the First Amendment. When the Constitution was adopted, many people strongly opposed it because the document contained no Bill of Rights to safeguard certain basic freedoms. They especially feared that the new powers granted to a central government might be interpreted to permit the government to curtail freedom of religion, press, assembly, and speech. In response to an overwhelming public clamor, James Madison offered a series of amendments to satisfy citizens that these great liberties would remain safe and beyond the power of government to abridge. Madison proposed what later became the First Amendment in three parts, ... one of which proclaimed: "The people shall not be deprived or abridged of their right to speak, to write, or to publish their sentiments; *and the freedom of the press, as one of the great bulwarks of liberty, shall be inviolable.*" The amendments were offered to *curtail* and *restrict* the general powers granted to the Executive, Legislative, and Judicial Branches two years before in the original Constitution. The Bill of Rights changed the original Constitution into a new charter under which no branch of government could abridge the people's freedoms of press, speech, religion, and assembly. Yet the Solicitor General argues and some members of the Court appear to agree that the general powers of the Government adopted in the original Constitution should be interpreted to limit and restrict the specific and emphatic guarantees of the Bill of Rights adopted later. I can imagine no greater perversion of history. Madison and the other Framers of the First Amendment, able men that they were, wrote in language they earnestly believed could never be misunderstood: "Congress shall make no law ... abridging the freedom ... of the press...." Both the history and the language of the First Amendment support the view that the press must be left free to publish news, whatever the source, without censorship, injunctions, or prior restraints.

In the First Amendment the Founding Fathers gave the free press the protection it must have to fulfill its essential role in our democracy. The press was to serve the governed, not the governors. The Government's power to censor the press was abolished so that the press would remain forever free to censure the Government. The press was protected so that it could bare the secrets of government and inform the people. Only a free and unrestrained press can effectively expose deception in government. And paramount among the responsibilities of a free press is the duty to prevent any part of the government from deceiving the people and sending them off to distant lands to die of foreign fevers and foreign shot and shell. In my view, far from deserving condemnation for their courageous reporting, the New York Times, the Washington Post, and other newspapers should be commended for serving the purpose that the Founding Fathers saw so clearly. In revealing the workings of government that led to the Vietnam War, the newspapers nobly did precisely that which the Founders hoped and trusted they would do....

Mr. Justice Douglas, with whom Mr. Justice Black joins, concurring.

While I join in the opinion of the Court I believe it necessary to express my views more fully.

It should be noted at the outset that the First Amendment provides that "Congress shall make no law ... abridging the freedom of speech, or of the press." That leaves, in my view, no room for governmental restraint on the press....

The dominant purpose of the First Amendment was to prohibit the widespread practice of governmental suppression of embarrassing information. It is common knowledge that the First Amendment was adopted against the widespread use of the common law of seditious libel to punish the dissemination of material that is embarrassing to the powers-that-be. The present cases will, I think, go down in history as the most dramatic illustration of that principle. A debate of large proportions goes on in the Nation over our posture in Vietnam. That debate antedated the disclosure of the contents of the present documents. The latter are highly relevant to the debate in progress.

Secrecy in government is fundamentally anti-democratic, perpetuating bureaucratic errors. Open debate and discussion of public issues are vital to our national health. On public questions there should be "uninhibited, robust, and wide-open" debate....

Mr. Justice Brennan, concurring.

I write separately in these cases only to emphasize what should be apparent: that our judgments in the present cases may not be taken to indicate the propriety, in the future, of issuing temporary stays and restraining orders to block the publication of material sought to be suppressed by the Government. So far as I can determine, never before has the United States sought to enjoin a newspaper from publishing information in its possession.... [T]he First Amendment stands as an absolute bar to the imposition of judicial restraints in circumstances of the kind presented by these cases....

Mr. Chief Justice Burger, dissenting.
   So clear are the constitutional limitations on prior restraint against expression, that from the time of *Near v. Minnesota* until recently ... we have had little occasion to be concerned with cases involving prior restraints against news reporting on matters of public interest. There is, therefore, little variation among the members of the Court in terms of resistance to prior restraints against publication. Adherence to this basic constitutional principle, however, does not make these cases simple ones. In these cases, the imperative of a free and unfettered press comes into collision with another imperative, the effective functioning of a complex modern government and specifically the effective exercise of certain constitutional powers of the Executive. Only those who view the First Amendment as an absolute in all circumstances—a view I respect, but reject—can find such cases as these to be simple or easy....

Here ... the frenetic haste is due in large part to the manner in which the Times proceeded from the date it obtained the purloined documents....

It is not disputed that the Times has had unauthorized possession of the documents from three to four months, during which it has had its expert analysts studying them, presumably digesting them and preparing the material for publication. During all of this time, the Times, presumably in its capacity as trustee of the public's "right to know," has held up publication for purposes it considered proper and thus public knowledge was delayed. No doubt this was for a good reason; the analysis of 7,000 pages of complex material drawn from a vastly greater volume of material would inevitably take time and the writing of good news stories takes time. But why should the United States Government, from whom this information was illegally acquired by someone, along with all the counsel, trial judges, and appellate judges be placed under needless pressure? After these months of deferral, the alleged "right to know" has somehow and suddenly become a right that must be vindicated instanter.

DISCUSSION QUESTIONS

1. What does the Supreme Court seem to mean by "prior restraint"? Is it more than a slogan the Court uses when it disagrees with government's attempts to limit the press?

2. Does government realistically have any alternative to combat potentially harmful publications without running afoul of the "prior restraint" doctrine? How else could the government respond?

3. Is government helpless when secrets or damaging information are about to be published or aired? Is there a danger that government will claim a threat to national security when politically embarrassing information is about to be made public?

4. In this era of instantaneous communication, can government act quickly enough to prevent publication of damaging information, whether it would violate the "prior restraint" doctrine or not?

19. LIBEL AND THE LAW

Criticizing public officials is a favorite hobby of many of us. Comedians poke fun at presidents and senators; columnists rake members of the House over the coals; you and I share the latest joke about the mayor over our favorite beverages on Friday afternoon. More important, opposing candidates criticize each other so that the electorate can choose between them. Editors analyze strengths and weaknesses (and motivations) of policymakers and their policy proposals. Political cartoonists capture just the right, but ridiculous, image of the people who run our country or try to influence those who do. And sometimes the targets of these criticisms get angry.

Now, a longstanding rule of the common law is that the press is not free to damage someone else's reputation, and the best defense is that the press comment is true. And so, if my local media make disparaging comments about my teaching style, for instance, I could sue for libel, for the damage caused by the harm to my reputation. In *New York Times v. Sullivan,* 376 U.S. 254 (1964), the Supreme Court, however, reached the position that public figures should be treated differently in libel cases, because requiring the media to be able to *prove* their comments to be true places such a burden on free and open discussion of political matters and public figures that democracy in the United States itself would suffer. Such comments would be avoided, even if true, because one couldn't prove them true in court. The Court ruled that public officials could not collect damages for libel unless they could show that the damaging remarks were made with malicious intent, that is, knowing they were false or made with reckless disregard as to their truth or falsity. In the case here, the Supreme Court considered whether the Reverend Jerry Falwell, leader of the Moral Majority, could collect damages for intentional infliction of emotional distress from *Hustler* magazine because of a parody of him it published.

Hustler Magazine v. Falwell, 108 S.Ct. 876 (1988):
Chief Justice Rehnquist delivered the opinion of the Court.

Petitioner Hustler Magazine, Inc., is a magazine of nationwide circulation. Respondent Jerry Falwell, a nationally known minister who has been active as a commentator on politics and public affairs, sued petitioner and its publisher, petitioner Larry Flynt, to recover damages for invasion of privacy, libel, and intentional infliction of emotional distress. The District Court directed a verdict against respondent on the privacy claims, and submitted the other two claims to a jury. The jury found for petitioners on the defamation claim [libel], but found for respondent on the claim for intentional infliction of emotional distress and awarded damages. We now consider whether this award is consistent with the First and Fourteenth Amendments of the United States Constitution.

The inside front cover of the November 1983 issue of Hustler Magazine featured a "parody" of an advertisement for Campari Liqueur that contained the name and picture of respondent and was entitled, "Jerry Falwell talks about his first time." This parody was modeled after actual Campari ads that included interviews with various celebrities about their "first times." Although it was apparent by the end of each interview that this meant the first time they sampled Campari, the ads clearly played on the sexual double entendre of the general subject of "first times." Copying the form and layout of these Campari ads, Hustler's editors chose respondent as the featured celebrity and drafted an alleged "interview" with him in which he states that his "first time" was during a drunken incestuous rendezvous with his mother in an outhouse. The Hustler parody portrays respondent and his mother as drunk and immoral, and suggests that respondent is a hypocrite who preaches only when he is drunk. In small print at the bottom of the page, the ad contains the disclaimer, "ad parody—not to be taken seriously." The magazine's table of contents also lists the ad as "Fiction; Ad and Personality Parody."

... This case presents us with a novel question involving First Amendment limitations upon a State's authority to protect its citizens from the intentional infliction of emotional distress. We must decide whether a public figure may recover damages for emotional harm caused by the publication of an ad parody offensive to him, and doubtless gross and repugnant in the eyes of most. Respondent would have us find that a State's interest in protecting public figures from emotional distress is sufficient to deny First Amendment protection to speech that is patently offensive and is intended to inflict emotional injury, even when that speech could not reasonably have been interpreted as stating actual facts about the public figure involved. This we decline to do.

At the heart of the First Amendment is the recognition of the fundamental importance of the free flow of ideas and opinions on matters of public interest and concern. . . . We have therefore been particularly vigilant to ensure that individual expressions of ideas remain free from governmentally imposed sanctions. The First Amendment recognizes no such thing as a "false" idea. . . .

The sort of robust political debate encouraged by the First Amendment is bound to produce speech that is critical of those who hold public office or those public figures who are "intimately involved in the resolution of important public questions or, by reason of their fame, shape events in areas of concern to society at large." Justice Frankfurter put it succinctly in *Baumgartner v. United States,* when he said that "[o]ne of the prerogatives of American citizenship is the right to criticize public men and measures." Such criticism, inevitably, will not always be reasoned or moderate; public figures as well as public officials will be subject to "vehement, caustic, and sometimes unpleasantly sharp attacks." "[T]he candidate who vaunts his spotless record and sterling integrity cannot convincingly cry 'Foul!' when an opponent or an industrious reporter attempts to demonstrate the contrary."

Of course, this does not mean that *any* speech about a public figure is immune from sanction in the form of damages. Since *New York Times Co. v. Sullivan,* we have consistently ruled that a public figure may hold a speaker liable for the damage to reputation caused by publication of a defamatory falsehood, but only if the statement was made "with knowledge that it was false or with reckless disregard of whether it was false or not." . . .

Respondent argues, however, that a different standard should apply in this case because here the State seeks to prevent not reputational damage, but the severe emotional distress suffered by the person who is the subject of an offensive publication. . . .

Generally speaking the law does not regard the intent to inflict emotional distress as one which should receive much solicitude. . . .

Were we to hold otherwise, there can be little doubt that political cartoonists and satirists would be subjected to damages awards without any showing that their work falsely defamed its subject. Webster's defines a caricature as "the deliberately distorted picturing or imitating of a person, literary style, etc., by exaggerating features or mannerisms for satirical effect." The appeal of the political cartoon or caricature is often based on exploration of unfortunate physical traits or politically embarrassing events—an exploration often calculated to injure the feelings of the subject of the portrayal. The art of the cartoonist is often not reasoned or evenhanded, but slashing and one-sided. . . .

Despite their sometimes caustic nature, from the early cartoons portraying George Washington as an ass down to the present day, graphic depictions and satirical cartoons have played a prominent role in public and political debate. Nast's castigation of the Tweed Ring, Walt McDougall's characterization of James G. Blaine's banquet with the millionaires at Delmonico's as "The Royal Feast of Belshazzar," and numerous other efforts have undoubtedly had an effect on the course and outcome of contemporaneous debate. Lincoln's tall, gangly posture, Teddy Roosevelt's glasses and teeth, and Franklin D. Roosevelt's jutting jaw and cigarette holder have been memorialized by political cartoons with an effect that could not have been obtained by the photographer or the portrait artist. From the viewpoint of history it is clear that our political discourse would have been considerably poorer without them.

Respondent contends, however, that the caricature in question here was so "outrageous" as to distinguish it from more traditional political cartoons. There is no doubt that the caricature of respondent and his mother published in Hustler is at best a distant cousin of the political cartoons described above, and a rather poor relation at that. If it were possible by laying down a principled standard to separate the one from the other, public discourse would probably suffer little or no harm. But we doubt that there is any such standard, and we are quite sure that the pejorative description "outrageous" does not supply one. "Outrageousness" in the area of political and social discourse has an inherent subjectiveness about it which would allow a jury to impose liability on the basis of the jurors' tastes or views, or perhaps on the basis of their dislike of a particular expression....

We conclude that public figures and public officials may not recover for the tort of intentional infliction of emotional distress by reason of publications such as the one here at issue without showing in addition that the publication contains a false statement of fact which was made with "actual malice," *i.e.*, with knowledge that the statement was false or with reckless disregard as to whether or not it was true....

The Court of Appeals interpreted the jury's finding to be that the ad parody "was not reasonably believable," and in accordance with our custom we accept this finding.... [T]his claim cannot, consistently with the First Amendment, form a basis for the award of damages when the conduct in question is the publication of a caricature such as the ad parody involved here....

DISCUSSION QUESTIONS

1. One problem with the Court's *Sullivan* rule is how to determine if someone is a public figure. Attempt to define the concept for the application of the *Sullivan* rule. How broadly or narrowly should we think of the notion if the goal is a thriving democratic discourse?

2. Do you agree with the Supreme Court that the Reverend Jerry Falwell was a public figure under the *Sullivan* doctrine?

3. Sometimes campaign ads on television belittle the opponent. Do the candidates subjected to "mudslinging" in a negative campaign ad have any legal recourse? Should they?

20. OPPOSING VIEWPOINTS AND THE PRESS

It is pretty difficult nowadays to counter editorial positions the media may be taking. A newspaper's evaluation and commentary or a broadcast discussion on political issues and political leaders may affect how the public perceives them. Even if the media's commentaries do not change opinions, others may think that they do. But to neutralize such effects, one would have to be able to reach basically the same readership and the same audience. It doesn't do as much good to generate more favorable coverage in other media outlets, because that doesn't give one a chance to counteract the original message. The people exposed to the first won't necessarily hear the later. And not only is it extremely expensive to buy advertising to reach those people, advertisements are not taken as seriously as editorial commentary.

One response has been to seek the right of rebuttal. The underlying basis for such a right is the view that media monopolize channels of communication essential for public discourse. A variety of viewpoints should be heard through these channels, and specifically the viewpoints and people that are criticized should have an opportunity to respond in the same way to the same audience. The Federal Communications Commission required licensed radio stations to do so, but in 1964, one radio station refused to follow those rules. In *Red Lion Broadcasting Co. v. the Federal Communications Commission,* 395 U.S. 368 (1969), the Supreme Court held that the "fairness doctrine" under which the FCC required radio stations to allow rebuttals did not violate the free press clause of the First Amendment. When a similar case arose, under a state law that required a newspaper to allow rebuttal, the Supreme Court again acted. It may come as a surprise that the two decisions, only five years apart, reached opposite conclusions.

Miami Herald Publishing Company v. Tornillo, 418 U.S. 241 (1974):
Mr. Chief Justice Burger delivered the opinion of the Court.

The issue in this case is whether a state statute granting a political candidate a right to equal space to reply to criticism and attacks on his record by a newspaper violates the guarantees of a free press.

In the fall of 1972, appellee, Executive Director of the Classroom Teachers Association, apparently a teachers' collective-bargaining agent, was a candidate for the Florida House of Representatives. On September 20, 1972, and again on September 29, 1972, appellant printed editorials critical of appellee's candidacy. In response to these editorials appellee demanded that appellant print verbatim his replies, defending the role of the Classroom Teachers Association and the organization's accomplishments for the citizens of Dade County. Appellant declined to print the appellee's replies. . . .

The appellee and supporting advocates of an enforceable right of access to the press vigorously argue that government has an obligation to ensure that a wide variety of views reach the public. . . . It is urged that at the time the First Amendment to the Constitution was ratified in 1791 as part of our Bill of Rights the press was broadly representative of the people it was serving. . . . A true marketplace of ideas existed in which there was relatively easy access to the channels of communication.

Access advocates submit that although newspapers of the present are superficially similar to those of 1791, the press of today is in reality very different from that known in the early years of our national existence. In the past half century . . . [n]ewspapers have become big business and there are far fewer of them to serve a larger literate population. Chains of newspapers, national newspapers, national wire and news services, and one-newspaper towns, are the dominant features of a press that has become noncompetitive and enormously powerful and influential in its capacity to manipulate popular opinion and change the course of events. Major metropolitan newspapers have collaborated to establish news services national in scope. Such national news organizations provide syndicated "interpretive reporting" as well as syndicated features and commentary, all of which can serve as part of the new school of "advocacy journalism."

The elimination of competing newspapers in most of our large cities, and the concentration of control of media that results from the only newspaper's being owned by the same interests which own a television station and a radio station, are important components of this trend toward concentration of control of outlets to inform the public.

The result of these vast changes has been to place in a few hands the power to inform the American people and shape public opinion.... In effect, it is claimed, the public has lost any ability to respond or to contribute in a meaningful way to the debate on issues. The monopoly of the means of communication allows for little or no critical analysis of the media....

The obvious solution, which was available to dissidents at an earlier time when entry into publishing was relatively inexpensive, today would be to have additional newspapers. But the same economic factors which have caused the disappearance of vast numbers of metropolitan newspapers, have made entry into the marketplace of ideas served by the print media almost impossible. It is urged that the claim of newspapers to be "surrogates for the public" carries with it a concomitant fiduciary obligation to account for that stewardship. From this premise it is reasoned that the only effective way to insure fairness and accuracy and to provide for some accountability is for government to take affirmative action. The First Amendment interest of the public in being informed is said to be in peril because the "marketplace of ideas" is today a monopoly controlled by the owners of the market.

... However much validity may be found in these arguments, at each point the implementation of a remedy such as an enforceable right of access necessarily calls for some mechanism, either governmental or consensual. If it is governmental coercion, this at once brings about a confrontation with the express provisions of the First Amendment. ...

... [T]he Court has expressed sensitivity as to whether a restriction or requirement constituted the compulsion exerted by government on a newspaper to print that which it would otherwise not print. The clear implication has been that any such compulsion to publish that which "'reason' tells them should not be published" is unconstitutional. A responsible press is an undoubtedly desirable goal, but press responsibility is not mandated by the Constitution and like many other virtues it cannot be legislated.

... Faced with the penalties that would accrue to any newspaper that published news or commentary arguably with the reach of the right-of-access statute, editors might well conclude that the safe course is to avoid controversy. Therefore, ... political and electoral coverage would be blunted or reduced. Government-enforced right of access inescapably "dampens the vigor and limits the variety of public debate...."

Even if a newspaper would face no additional costs to comply with a compulsory access law and would not be forced to forgo publication of news or opinion by the inclusion of a reply, the Florida statute fails to clear the barriers of the First Amendment because of its intrusion into the function of editors. A newspaper is more than a passive receptacle or conduit for news, comment, and advertising. The choice of material to go into a newspaper, and the decisions made as to limitations on the size and content of the paper, and treatment of public issues and public officials—whether fair or unfair—constitute the exercise of editorial control and judgment. It has yet to be demonstrated how governmental regulation of this crucial process can be exercised consistent with First Amendment guarantees of a free press as they have evolved to this time. . . .

Mr. Justice White, concurring.

The Court today holds that the First Amendment bars a State from requiring a newspaper to print the reply of a candidate for public office whose personal character has been criticized by that newspaper's editorials. According to our accepted jurisprudence, the First Amendment erects a virtually insurmountable barrier between government and the print media so far as government tampering, in advance of publication, with news and editorial content is concerned. A newspaper or magazine is not a public utility subject to "reasonable" governmental regulation in matters affecting the exercise of journalistic judgment as to what shall be printed. . . .

Of course, the press is not always accurate, or even responsible, and may not present full and fair debate on important public issues. But the balance struck by the First Amendment with respect to the press is that society must take the risk that occasionally debate on vital matters will not be comprehensive and that all viewpoints may not be expressed. The press would be unlicensed because, in Jefferson's words, "[w]here the press is free, and every man able to read, all is safe." Any other accommodation—any other system that would supplant private control of the press with the heavy hand of government intrusion—would make the government the censor of what the people may read and know.

DISCUSSION QUESTIONS

1. Do you think newspapers ought to be allowed to take positions on candidates for office, given the advantage the press has in communicating with voters? If the First Amendment did not stand in the way, would you be in favor of limiting newspapers' right to endorse political candidates? Why?

2. How widely are unpopular or radical points of view communicated in your locality? Are your local media open enough to unconventional perspectives or does public discourse in your local media reflect only mainstream thinking? Is this a problem?

3. What alternative courses of action would you suggest to someone in Mr. Tornillo's situation who is denied access to the news columns to rebut unfavorable coverage? How can a person counter this kind of publicity?

21. NEWS GATHERING AND THE LAW

In the course of reporting the news, journalists cultivate relationships with a variety of sources. Sometimes, these sources will give reporters information they can get nowhere else or allow them to witness activities normally closed to them. Whistle-blowers may want to alert newspeople to mistakes being made by their supervisors. Others may want to stimulate publicity for their causes. And many times people will want to remain anonymous. However, reporters have found themselves in front of grand juries when their stories alerted authorities to unlawful activities that law enforcement officials want to prosecute. And so they are faced with violating the assurances of confidentiality they gave their sources or going to jail. Some states have passed so-called shield laws to protect reporters from this dilemma.

On the one hand, journalists are concerned that they will no longer be able to report on events that the public needs to know about because some kinds of information are only available if the sources are confident they can remain anonymous. Further, journalists worry about becoming tools of law enforcement, gathering evidence for police that police could not find themselves. On the other hand, government is concerned that journalists are treated differently from other people who have a duty to report their knowledge of criminal activity and to respond to legitimate law enforcement inquiries. A meter reader who sees marijuana growing in a basement must answer police questions about it, even if he promised the tenant he'd keep the information confidential. In the case here, the Supreme Court declined to adopt a reading of the First Amendment that would enshrine "shield law" protection in the Constitution:

Branzburg v. Hayes, 408 U.S. 665 (1972):

Opinion of the Court by Mr. Justice White, announced by the Chief Justice.

The issue in these cases is whether requiring newsmen to appear and testify before state or federal grand juries abridges the freedom of speech and press guaranteed by the First Amendment. We hold that it does not.

... Petitioners Branzburg and Pappas and respondent Caldwell press First Amendment claims that may be simply put: that to gather news it is often necessary to agree either not to identify the source of information published or to publish only part of the facts revealed, or both; that if the reporter is nevertheless forced to reveal these confidences to a grand jury, the source so identified and other confidential sources of other reporters will be measurably deterred from furnishing publishable information, all to the detriment of the free flow of information protected by the First Amendment.... The heart of the claim is that the burden on news gathering resulting from compelling reporters to disclose confidential information outweighs any public interest in obtaining the information. We do not question the significance of free speech, press, or assembly to the country's welfare. Nor is it suggested that news gathering does not qualify for First Amendment protection; without some protection for seeking out the news, freedom of the press could be eviscerated. But these cases involve no intrusions upon speech or assembly, no prior restraint or restriction on what the press may publish, and no express or implied command that the press publish what it prefers to withhold. No exaction or tax for the privilege of publishing, and no penalty, civil or criminal, related to the content of published material is at issue here. The use of confidential sources by the press is not forbidden or restricted; reporters remain free to seek news from any source by means within the law. No attempt is made to require the press to publish its sources of information or indiscriminately to disclose them on request.

The sole issue before us is the obligation of reporters to respond to grand jury subpoenas as other citizens do and to answer questions relevant to an investigation into the commission of crime. Citizens generally are not constitutionally immune from grand jury subpoenas; and neither the First Amendment nor any other constitutional provision protects the average citizen from disclosing to a grand jury information that he has received in confidence. The claim is, however, that reporters are exempt from these obligations because if forced to respond to subpoenas and identify their sources or disclose other confidences, their informants will refuse or be reluctant to furnish newsworthy information in the future. This asserted burden on news gathering is said to make compelled testimony from newsmen constitutionally suspect and to require a privileged position for them. It is clear that the First Amendment does not invalidate every incidental burdening of the press that may result from the enforcement of civil or criminal statutes of general applicability. Under prior cases, otherwise valid laws serving substantial public interests may be enforced against the press as against others, despite the possible burden that may be imposed....

A number of States have provided newsmen a statutory privilege of varying breadth, but the majority have not done so, and none has been provided by federal statute. Until now the only testimonial privilege for unofficial witnesses that is rooted in the Federal Constitution is the Fifth Amendment privilege against compelled self-incrimination. We are asked to create another by interpreting the First Amendment to grant newsmen a testimonial privilege that other citizens do not enjoy. This we decline to do.... [W]e perceive no basis for holding that the public interest in law enforcement and in ensuring effective grand jury proceedings is insufficient to override the consequential, but uncertain, burden on news gathering that is said to result from insisting that reporters, like other citizens, respond to relevant questions put to them in the course of a valid grand jury investigation or criminal trial.

This conclusion itself involves no restraint on what newspapers may publish or on the type or quality of information reporters may seek to acquire, nor does it threaten the vast bulk of confidential relationships between reporters and their sources. Grand juries address themselves to the issues of whether crimes have been committed and who committed them. Only where news sources themselves are implicated in crime or possess information relevant to the grand jury's task need they or the reporter be concerned about grand jury subpoenas.... The preference for anonymity of those confidential informants involved in actual criminal conduct is presumably a product of their desire to escape criminal prosecution, and this preference, while understandable, is hardly deserving of constitutional protection....

Thus, we cannot seriously entertain the notion that the First Amendment protects a newsman's agreement to conceal the criminal conduct of his source, or evidence thereof, on the theory that it is better to write about crime than to do something about it....

There remain those situations where a source is not engaged in criminal conduct but has information suggesting illegal conduct by others. Newsmen frequently receive information from such sources pursuant to a tacit or express agreement to withhold the source's name and suppress any information that the source wishes not published. Such informants presumably desire anonymity in order to avoid being entangled as a witness in a criminal trial or grand jury investigation. They may fear that disclosure will threaten their job security or personal safety or that it will simply result in dishonor or embarrassment.

The argument that the flow of news will be diminished by compelling reporters to aid the grand jury in a criminal investigation is not irrational, nor are the records before us silent on the matter. But we remain unclear how often and to what extent informers are actually deterred from furnishing information when newsmen are forced to testify before a grand jury.... We doubt if the informer who prefers anonymity but is sincerely interested in furnishing evidence of crime will always or very often be deterred by the prospect of dealing with those public authorities characteristically charged with the duty to protect the public interest as well as his. Accepting the fact, however, that an undetermined number of informants not themselves implicated in crime will nevertheless, for whatever reason, refuse to talk to newsmen if they fear identification by a reporter in an official investigation, we cannot accept the argument that the public interest in possible future news about crime from undisclosed, unverified sources must take precedence over the public interest in pursuing and prosecuting those crimes reported to the press by informants and in thus deterring the commission of such crimes in the future.

... We are admonished that refusal to provide a First Amendment reporter's privilege will undermine the freedom of the press to collect and disseminate news. But that is not the lesson history teaches us.... The existing constitutional rules have not been a serious obstacle to either the development of retention of confidential news sources by the press....

Mr. Justice Stewart, with whom Mr. Justice Brennan and Mr. Justice Marshall join, dissenting.

The Court's crabbed view of the First Amendment reflects a disturbing insensitivity to the critical role of an independent press in our society. The question whether a reporter has a constitutional right to a confidential relationship with his source is of first impression here, but the principles that should guide our decision are as basic as any to be found in the Constitution.... [T]he Court in these cases holds that a newsman has no First Amendment right to protect his sources when called before a grand jury. The Court thus invites state and federal authorities to undermine the historic independence of the press by attempting to annex the journalistic profession as an investigative arm of government. Not only will this decision impair performance of the press' constitutionally protected functions, but it will, I am convinced, in the long run, harm rather than help the administration of justice.

I respectfully dissent.

The reporter's constitutional right to a confidential relationship with his sources stems from the broad societal interest in a full and free flow of information to the public. It is this basic concern that underlies the Constitution's protection of a free press, because the guarantee is "not for the benefit of the press as much as for the benefit of all of us."

Enlightened choice by an informed citizenry is the basic ideal upon which an open society is premised, and a free press is thus indispensable to a free society. . . .

In keeping with this tradition, we have held that the right to publish is central to the First Amendment and basic to the existence of constitutional democracy. . . .

A corollary of the right to publish must be the right to gather news. The full flow of information to the public protected by the free-press guarantee would be severely curtailed if no protection whatever were afforded to the process by which news is assembled and disseminated. . . .

News must not be unnecessarily cut off at its source, for without freedom to acquire information the right to publish would be impermissibly compromised. . . .

The right to gather news implies, in turn, a right to a confidential relationship between a reporter and his source. . . .

. . . [T]he promise of confidentiality may be a necessary prerequisite to a productive relationship between a newsman and his informants. An officeholder may fear his superior; a member of the bureaucracy, his associates; a dissident, the scorn of majority opinion. All may have information valuable to the public discourse, yet each may be willing to relate that information only in confidence to a reporter whom he trusts, either because of excessive caution or because of a reasonable fear of reprisals or censure for unorthodox views. The First Amendment concern must not be with the motives of an particular news source, but rather with the conditions in which informants of all shades of spectrum may make information available through the press to the public. . . .

The error in the Court's absolute rejection of First Amendment interests in these cases seems to me to be most profound. For in the name of advancing the administration of justice, the Court's decision, I think, will only impair the achievement of that goal. People entrusted with law enforcement responsibility, no less than private citizens, need general information relating to controversial social problems. Obviously, press reports have great value to government, even when the newsman cannot be compelled to testify before a grand jury. The sad paradox of the Court's position is that when a grand jury may exercise an unbridled subpoena power, and sources involved in sensitive matters become fearful of disclosing information, the newsman will not only cease to be a useful grand jury witness; he will cease to investigate and publish information about issues of public import. I cannot subscribe to such an anomalous result, for, in my view, the interests protected by the

First Amendment are not antagonistic to the administration of justice. Rather, they can, in the long run, only be complementary, and for that reason must be given great "breathing space. . . ."

DISCUSSION QUESTIONS

1. How big a problem is the need for shield laws? Are journalists overestimating the risks involved?

2. This case deals explicitly only with journalists responding to grand jury subpoenas. Is there a real danger that this decision sets a precedent that could be expanded to require journalists to divulge their sources in other circumstances? In what ways would that be a problem?

3. What arguments can you make that the public would be better off if journalists were not required to identify sources to whom they have promised confidentiality?

CHAPTER 7
Media and Controversy

Controversies surround us. Conversations with friends over coffee sooner or later come around to the latest issues that engage us and divide us. Should the latest Supreme Court nominee be confirmed? Should the nuclear waste depository be located so close to our home town? Should stronger action be taken to deal with the federal budget deficit? Should states where acid rain originates be forced to help repair the damage it causes? For many of us, politics is controversy.

And we follow those controversies through the media. That is where we learn about the conflicts, that is where we discover what alternative positions are being attacked and defended, that is where we notice the possible implications for our own lives. And news media love controversy. Important issues that lead well-known people into conflict with each other wind up on the front pages of the nation's newspapers and as the lead stories on network news broadcasts. Both we as citizens and observers and the media as purveyors of information love the drama that political conflicts present. The recent Senate hearings into charges that Supreme Court nominee Clarence Thomas was guilty of sexual harassment entranced a nation for an entire weekend—no soap opera held the same appeal.

More than entertainment, however, media coverage of controversies potentially influences our own positions on the issues involved. How the issues are framed, how the alternatives are described, how the participants are characterized all may affect our perceptions of the conflict. More important, how the media report such controversies may define the nature of the debate about them. People with strong opinions on the question may find their positions reinforced by media coverage—or unexpectedly challenged. People without strong opinions may find themselves unconsciously discussing the issue along the lines of the news reports.

The selections in this chapter illustrate some points about media coverage of controversies. The first selection examines how the media treat abortion and antiabortion activists; the *Los Angeles Times* finds quite a disparity—to the disadvantage of abortion opponents. The second selection invites us to consider whether "live" coverage of ongoing events—such as the FBI's response to the Branch Davidian cult in Waco, Texas—makes it more difficult for government to act. The next two selections present some perspectives on media coverage of the Gulf War. The Gannett Foundation study delineates the strict ground rules under which the media were able to cover the war at all, and the study reports the dissatisfaction the media felt. The clear implication is that, given more freedom, the media would have reported much differently. The Andrews article places this controversy into historical context, arguing that military-press relations during the Gulf War were not much different from their relationship in the past. The Kurtz article describes how interest groups have been using advertising to influence President Clinton's health care proposals—and the public's reactions to them. Finally, Charles Clark raises some important questions about privacy and politics: What is acceptable commentary about the private lives of candidates for office?

Other issues will emerge in the future. We are likely to learn about them, too, through the media. Whether they are familiar issues in a new form or new controversies we have not considered before, how the media report them will significantly affect our responses to them—and how we as a nation ultimately decide them.

22. ANTIABORTION ACTIVISTS IN THE PRESS

One of the most heated issues being debated in the nation today is that of abortion. One side, calling itself "pro-life," equates aborting a fetus with taking a human life and staunchly opposes state and national policies that permit abortion. The other side, calling itself "pro-choice," considers it a woman's right to determine whether she will carry a pregnancy to term and vehemently objects to proposals to limit that right. Whichever position you hold, you probably object to my choice of words in depicting one or both sides of the issue. Descriptions of controversial issues are rarely neutral.

In the selection from the *Los Angeles Times* that follows, David Shaw explores the media's depiction of abortion opponents and finds that the press portrays antiabortion activists much more negatively than abortion rights supporters. Before we generalize too far from his evidence, we should ask whether historically proponents of a change in policy have been described as favorably as supporters of the status quo. It may be interesting to examine characterization of civil rights activists, Vietnam War opponents, the early "women's libbers," and the first environmentalists in the media during the periods when they first challenged existing policy. Whether Shaw's conclusions here about coverage of abortion foes are typical or atypical of coverage of those who seek policy changes, his conclusions nevertheless indicate a subtle orientation in media treatment worth taking into account.

Abortion Foes Stereotyped, Some in Media Believe

David Shaw

When abortion opponents picketed Turner Broadcasting System last summer to protest the showing of a film promoting abortion rights, TBS Chairman Ted Turner called the demonstrators "bozos" and "idiots."

Many in the anti-abortion movement say Turner was simply giving public voice to what many in the media privately think of their movement.

Some reporters agree.

Journalists tend to regard opponents of abortion as "religious fanatics" and "bug-eyed zealots," says Ethan Bronner, legal affairs reporter for the Boston Globe, who spent much of last year writing about abortion.

"Opposing abortion, in the eyes of most journalists . . . is not a legitimate, civilized position in our society," Bronner says.

Many journalists have vigorously denied having this view.

"There's a certain amount of newsroom debate about abortion," says Eugene Roberts, executive director of the Philadelphia Inquirer, "and my general impression is that . . . there's a good deal of respect for both sides."

Tom Bettag, executive producer of "The CBS Evening News," says CBS has "a large number of people . . . who feel very strongly on both sides" of the abortion issue and "that helps us cover it fairly. If we slip, someone inside tells us, 'Hey, that's loaded.' It's a very constructive, worthwhile debate, a very creative process of each side trying to check the other and report this in as open-minded a way as you can."

But several reporters who have written a lot about abortion agree with Bronner.

Cynthia Gorney, who covers abortion for the Washington Post, says she's troubled by the media's tendency to portray the anti-abortion movement as "dominated by religious crazies" and to "ignore what I think are the very understandable and reasoned arguments that are put forth by the pro-life side."

Susan Okie, medical reporter for the Post, says she herself "had a sort of mental image of the anti-abortion groups as all being extremists" before she began writing much about them.

But Bronner, Gorney and Okie have covered abortion extensively, and they've come to realize that there are intelligent, rational, sincere people on both sides of what is an extraordinarily complex issue. Few big-city reporters—or editors, television anchors or news directors—have the opportunity that these three have had, though. Abortion is but one of the many subjects they deal with every day, and because most of their colleagues, associates and friends generally share their support for abortion rights, it may be inevitable that they have a skewed view of abortion opponents.

"Reporters often say to me, 'Gee, you're reasonable,' as if all pro-life people are unreasonable," says Mirianne

SOURCE: Copyright, ©1990, *Los Angeles Times*. Reprinted by permission.

Rea-Luthin, president of the Value of Life Committee of Boston.

Reporters even try to perpetuate that stereotype, Rea-Luthin says, by asking her to "make sure you look angry" when she's being interviewed on television.

Abortion opponents say the media further stereotype them, not only as fanatics but as almost exclusively conservatives.

David Shribman of the Wall Street Journal, who has spent about 40% of his time writing about abortion over the past year, says the media is mistaken in perpetuating this stereotype. The anti-abortion movement is actually "one of the broadest political coalitions in American history," Shribman wrote on page 1 of the Wall Street Journal last summer.

Shribman pointed out that the movement includes feminists, opponents of the death penalty and people opposed to U.S. military involvement in Central America—all positions customarily associated with liberals.

Journalists insist they try to be fair to both sides, no matter how they feel about the people they cover. Much of the time, they are fair. In recent months in particular, abortion coverage has often been more evenhanded. Some news organizations have even tried, on occasion, to provide explicit balance in their coverage by selecting one aspect of the abortion controversy and providing opposing viewpoints and experiences on a given day.

The Philadelphia Inquirer did that after the U.S. Supreme Court issued its Webster decision a year ago Tuesday, giving states more latitude in regulating abortion. The Inquirer published stories on page 1 about activities at the offices of Minnesota Citizens Concerned for Life and at the National Abortion Rights Action League in Washington.

The Los Angeles Times has several times done something similar.

Twice last year, The Times published stories on women who had had abortions, and in each story, one woman told of deeply regretting her act while the other defended hers. The Times also published same-day stories on a women's health center where abortions are performed and on a crisis pregnancy center where women are encouraged to "deliver babies rather than seek abortions." On two other occasions, The Times has paired opposing abortion viewpoints on its opinion pages.

L. Brent Bozell III, chairman of the Media Research Center, a conservative media monitoring agency just outside Washington, says he doesn't think the media's choice of abortion opponents necessarily reflects the "pro-abortion bias" to which he thinks the media generally succumb.

"It has everything to do with agenda," he says. "I think it has everything to do with . . . journalism. The raunchier the quote, the better it is; the more fire and brimstone, the better the story comes out."

Television news executives deny being either biased or sensationalistic.

"We . . . bend over backward . . . to make sure that we don't go for the crazy on any particular issue," says Paul Friedman, executive producer of ABC's "World News Tonight." "One of the problems we sometimes have on that side of the issue is avoiding the people who will do damage to their cause because they're so extreme and so almost incoherent on the subject."

John Willke, president of the National Right to Life Committee, the largest anti-abortion organization in the nation, is probably the most frequent spokesmen [sic] for abortion opponents, and he is no extremist. As the Washington Post Magazine said in a cover story on him in April, "he clearly takes some pleasure in the country doctor aura and assumes in conversation a sort of kindly formality.... He does not inspire people to passion, or to civil disobedience."

But, like activists for any cause, many other abortion opponents are belligerent, even fanatical, and Susan Smith, the committee's associate legislative director, says bias—intentional or not—is the only way to explain why some in the media interview them instead.

Judie Brown, president of the American Life League, who opposes contraception and who says, "I've been described as a religious fanatic ... which I really don't mind," has often been chosen to represent the anti-abortion side, rather than someone from Willke's organization, which takes no position on contraception.

Randall Terry, a born-again Christian who likes to brandish a dead fetus in a tiny coffin and who founded Operation Rescue, which tries to blockade abortion clinics, is another frequent television guest.

But the abortion-rights position is often represented—and sometimes paired on television with either Terry or Brown—by Faye Wattleton, the calm, attractive president of Planned Parenthood of America. In fact, when abortion opponents complain of bias against them, they angrily point to the descriptions of Wattleton and Terry in the media.

Time magazine headlined its profile of Wattleton last December "Nothing Less Than Perfect" and said she was "self-possessed, imperturbable, smoothly articulate," "imperially slim and sleekly dressed ... a stunning refutation of the cliche of the dowdy feminist."

The New York Times Magazine put Wattleton on the cover last summer and described her as "relentlessly high-minded," "telegenic," "immaculately tailored," "a striking six-footer with an aristocratic bearing," "a tough, shrewd operator" and said, "Calmly, rationally, every hair in place, she will lead the faithful into battle...."

But Terry is almost always described as "a former used car salesman"; the Associated Press, New York Times, Los Angeles Times, Washington Post and Newsweek, among many others, have all referred to him that way.

The phrase suggests something "a little unscrupulous ... not quite trustworthy," says Eileen McNamara, who spent virtually all of 1989 covering abortion for the Boston Globe.

McNamara, who admits having used the "used car dealer" phrase herself in one story, says most reporters "try to be fair," but most support abortion rights, and "I think we were delighted to find out that he sold used cars."

Critics say the media's bias against abortion opponents is evident not only in the stature and characterization of the people they choose to interview but in their failure to identify some sources as proponents of abortion rights, thus leaving readers and viewers with the mistaken impression that the sources are impartial.

The Alan Guttmacher Institute in New York is probably the single-most widely quoted source for studies and statistics on abortion, for example, but except for the Washington Post, the media rarely point out that the institute is [a] special affiliate of Planned Parenthood of America, a major leader in the battle for abortion rights.

Even in the matter of numbers of sources quoted, the media often favor the abortion-rights side.

Counting the number of people quoted in a given story—or the number of inches or the number of photos used, as abortion opponents often do—is not necessarily the best way to evaluate fairness, of course.

As Sig Gissler, editor of the Milwaukee Journal says, "It's hard to be balanced, especially in a given story. There are a lot of subtle factors," including deadlines, the availability of sources and "what else is in the news that day." What a good news organization tries for, Gissler and others say, is "balance over time."

But over time—the first eight months of last year—the New York Times, Washington Post and three network evening news shows combined quoted abortion rights activists 60% more often than activists opposed to abortion, according to a study by the Center for Media and Public Affairs in Washington.

Kate Michelman, head of the National Abortion Rights Action League, and Molly Yard, head of the National Organization for Women, were quoted 76 times during this study period. Willke and Terry, the two most frequently quoted anti-abortion activists, were quoted 26 times. (President Bush, who also opposes abortion, was quoted 22 times.)

Sometimes, the media don't quote anyone on the anti-abortion side.

When the U.S. Court of Appeals in Washington ruled in April that a pregnant woman may refuse medical treatment even if that jeopardizes the survival of her fetus, the Los Angeles Times and New York Times each quoted a source praising the decision but no one critical of it. When the Louisville Courier Journal published a story on a Kentucky law requiring minors to get their parents' consent for abortions, it quoted several sources critical of the "extremely burdensome" nature of the law but quoted no one who favored the law.

Abortion opponents insist that this failure to give them "fair representation" is typical of the "double standard" the media apply to the abortion debate.

The media is generally careful, for example, to include comments from abortion-rights advocates in stories about abortion protests, but coverage of abortion-rights activities sometimes fail to include balancing comments from abortion opponents.

Moreover, the media rarely illustrate stories on abortion with photographs of aborted fetuses—or even, generally, of developing fetuses—claiming that to do so would be in bad taste and might offend readers. But no such concern inhibits the media from showing photos of starving, tragically bloated children in Ethiopia.

. . . [A]bortion opponents say the media often ignores—or are very late in covering—many issues and events that would receive thorough coverage if abortion-rights advocates or other liberal activists were involved.

When the National Organization for Women had its annual convention in San Francisco last week, the Los Angeles Times sent a reporter to cover it and made it the lead story in today's View section. But when the National Right to Life Committee had its annual convention in Sacramento last month, not a word about it appeared in The Times.

Nor did The Times—or most of the other major media—pay much attention to the discovery by Bob Woodward of the Washington Post last year that two justices who had played a major role in the 1973 Roe v. Wade decision legalizing abortion had conceded, in private memos, that they knew they were "legislating policy and exceeding [the court's] authority as the interpreter, not the maker of law," as Woodward wrote.

Abortion opponents had long made this very criticism of the Roe decision, and they are convinced that if a reporter of Woodward's stature had discovered private memos showing, say, that justices knew they were "exceeding the court's authority" in last year's Webster decision, the media would have swarmed all over the story. But except for a brief mention in Newsweek three months later, no major national media seem to have picked up Woodward's story.

Why not?

"There are more people in the news media than not who agree with the [Roe] abortion decision and don't want to look at how the sausage was made," Woodward says.

DISCUSSION QUESTIONS

1. Consider recent reports of controversies about abortion in your local media. Do you notice similar patterns as those Shaw recounts? Do these patterns occur only in the national media, or do the local media depict local antiabortion activists negatively, too?
2. To what extent does the pattern Shaw finds, do you think, result from the choices journalists make? To what extent do you think the pattern emerges from the activities of the participants in the abortion controversy themselves? Are journalists simply picking up the labels pro-choice activists use? Are anti-abortion activists more newsworthy when they seem more extreme?
3. Assuming that Shaw is correct about the depiction of abortion foes in the media, is the situation he describes an unusual one, or are there other occurrences where the media portray opposing sides in a conflict in similarly disparate ways? You might consider war supporters and opponents, capital punishment supporters and opponents, and gun control advocates and opponents as examples. Is the Nuclear Freeze movement (reading #9) also an example?
4. Rebut the argument that those who want existing policy to change are generally going to be depicted as more extreme and in less flattering terms by the media.

23. REPORTING NEWS AS IT HAPPENS

Reporters affect the news they report, simply by being on the scene. Even though they may wish to be neutral bystanders, not participating in the developments they are covering, newsmakers act differently in front of the media than do they otherwise. The effect is especially problematic when hostages have been taken, military action is being contemplated, or the forces of "law and order" are arrayed against lawbreakers. The problem is magnified when the coverage is broadcast live, and the targets of law enforcement action can watch the tactics and strategies of the police. In this selection from the *American Journalism Review,* Jeff Kamen explores the effect of live television coverage on the siege at David Koresh's Branch Davidian compound in Waco, Texas, in the spring of 1993. Notice

the conflict between the media's desire to report the news (and scoop its competitors) and their responsibility for the course of the events they report. How typical is this dilemma for journalists and public officials?

A Matter of "Live" and Death

Jeff Kamen

In its grim, closing hours, the Waco story was treated on television like a sports event with play-by-play reporting; perhaps that's all that could have been expected as the compound was quickly engulfed in flames. But the tragic outcome also raised questions about the way the press, especially television, had covered the previous 50 days, and whether the media's coverage had played a role in extending the siege and contributed to its horrific ending. Was Waco just another big story that should have been covered in the usual way? Or do events of this type demand new thinking and new policies from television news managers?

Many believe that from David Koresh's Ranch Apocalypse to the prison uprising at the Southern Ohio Correctional Facility at Lucasville, broadcast news had become too involved.

"I have not resolved in my own mind how we fulfill the public's desire, if not need, to know when something as dramatic as Waco is happening and not at the same time encourage someone who wants headlines to do something atrocious," says veteran CNN correspondent Mary Tillotson, expressing what many reporters and producers are feeling.

At Waco, television news provided Koresh the global audience he never would have had otherwise. By doing so the media may have unwittingly encouraged him to extend the confrontation, according to numerous hostage negotiators and cult experts. Frank A. Bolz Jr., who was a New York City police detective for 27 years and cofounded the department's hostage negotiation program, says Koresh did not want to surrender because that would have meant having to leave the stage. "[Koresh] might have come out right away but when he saw what great coverage he was getting, he figured, 'The hell with this. Let's keep this going!' " Bolz says.

... News executives defend their coverage.... Some broadcasters say that law enforcement is at least partially responsible for the coverage since it allowed cameras in the first place. Others defend their news judgment and say their coverage might have done some good.

One of the problems in covering an event like Waco, however, is that there are no rules or guidelines to help stations decide what is and is not appropriate. "I wish we had time to reflect in situations like these," says David Overton, news director at KXAS-TV in Forth Worth. "But we really don't. We're plowing new ground every time we get involved in a situation like this. And all situations are different. One thing we keep saying in our editorial meetings is that there are no rules."

Without guidelines, the competing agendas of the media and law enforcement authorities will ultimately shape

SOURCE: From "A Matter of 'Live' and Death," *The American Journalism Review*, June 1993, pp. 26–31. Reprinted by permission.

the news in ways that are unpredictable and possibly damaging to the interests of innocent victims. Police want to be portrayed uncritically as heroes who act with restraint; television wants to tell the story fast and dramatically, hoping for accolades and high ratings, but with little concern about the effect of overall coverage.

THE MEDIA AS PLAYER

Many experts in cult and terrorist psychology believe that broadcasters, as well as the government, need to take a hard look at how the media cover situations like Waco and the hostage crisis at Lucasville. In those circumstances, they say, the media becomes more than just an observer, it becomes a player.

Gary Weaver, who holds seminars for the FBI on hostage negotiations and is a communications professor at the American University's School of International Service, says television coverage of Waco was like the mob on the sidewalk chanting, "Jump! Jump!" to someone threatening to leap from the roof of a tall building. "You [televisions broadcasters] can say you didn't push [Koresh] and that's true," he says. "But on the other hand, you contributed."

Robert Kupperman, an often-interviewed terrorism expert, likens television's overall performance to "inciting a riot." Kupperman, senior advisor at the Center for Strategic and International Studies, believes that television news needed to be much more aware of the impact its coverage was having on Koresh's actions. "They were communicating with one man, amplifying his effects and promoting an incendiary situation which eventually led to the burning down of the compound. [It] was like yelling fire in a crowded theater; but all this was occurring in slow motion until the conflagration."

Indeed, a local television reporter in Waco has been accused of inadvertently tipping off Koresh to the initial raid on the compound during which four Bureau of Alcohol, Tobacco and Firearms (ATF) agents were killed. Dallas radio station KRLD read a statement written by Koresh just hours after the initial gunfire, and aired a 58-minute "sermon" by Koresh, after which he reneged on a promise to surrender following its broadcast. CNN was criticized for running a lengthy interview with Koresh.

Experts say that television news managers should have considered two issues when deciding how to cover the Waco siege: Koresh's potential reaction to what would be broadcast and the impending actions of the government agents. Beginning on the ninth day, the FBI cut electricity and used jamming devices, but many believed Koresh could still see or hear some live television broadcasts.

"Koresh had access to outside television when news media were broadcasting things that were not helpful to the overall negotiations," says FBI Special Agent Charles Mandigo. "They were broadcasting the government's intentions and some of our tactical movements, how [we were] setting up . . . operations." In addition to possibly giving away FBI and ATF tactics, Mandigo says the media massed at Waco—especially television—seemed to feed Koresh's hunger for attention to his own brand of apocalyptic philosophy: "He wanted publicity and knowing media was out there and wanting a story about him" may have contributed to the outcome.

Clinical psychologist Margaret Singer, a cult expert based in Berkeley, California, agrees. She says television news reports about Koresh and his Branch Davidian sect, especially negative comments, fed Koresh's ego and "confirmed" his followers' view that they were beleaguered by forces of darkness that they felt compelled to resist.

Pastor Richard Dowhower of All Saints Lutheran Church in Bowie, Maryland, has been studying cults and helping their victims for nearly 20 years. Dowhower believes that television news managers need to see themselves as potential players in this kind of situation. "I'm not sure that assembling an army of media standing behind the AFT and the FBI was helpful in defusing the situation," he says. "I think it hyped it up and escalated it to higher and higher levels of conflict." Dowhower also believes that the coverage made it more difficult for both sides to back down in the negotiations.

Not everyone in the media or the government agrees. David Bartlett, the television news industry's chief lobbyist and president of the Radio-Television News Directors Association, says, "There's no credible evidence that the news media contributed to that situation. To say that is childish at best, mean-spirited at worst and plain ignorant under any circumstances."

NBC's Executive News Director David Verdi adds that while he worries about individuals or groups who use dramatic or violent means to gain network coverage, he rejects the charge that television was a participant at Waco.

KRLD's Charlie Seraphin, who ordered his staff to broadcast some of Koresh's statements, has a different point of view. He says that those broadcasts led to the release of some of the cultists. At the same time, Seraphin believes that if ATF hadn't been worried about television coverage, the aborted raid on the compound might have gone forward, resulting in fewer deaths than occurred in the fiery ending to the standoff. "The media, in one sense, forced the standoff to a much longer length ...," says Seraphin. "If this event had happened without TV, [ATF would have] ended the standoff in a matter of hours, not days."

"We always have to be cautious when entering into these kinds of stories," Verdi says. "We were fortunate in that this time we remained outside observers throughout, which is ultimately what we want to do." Verdi says he assumed that Koresh was watching, but it didn't affect the way his network covered Waco. "We have worked with the military in the past ... to report within parameters to insure the safety of U.S. troops ...," he says. "We were never asked by the FBI to change the way we were reporting."

Some believe the FBI bears at least some of the responsibility for what television news broadcast from Waco since the bureau allowed the press within camera range.

FBI Special Agent In Charge Jeff Jamar, who was the on-scene commander at Waco, says he did not ask broadcasters to refrain from live shots. "I thought it was beyond our bounds to say to them, 'You can't use those cameras,' " says Jamar. "What we said was, 'Beware of what you're doing.' There was no way we could say, 'Hey! Turn the cameras off for the next hour.' That's beyond our bounds and beyond any expectation. That's obviously what we would have preferred but that's not the way things are done in this country. . . . I expect what we do to be given the closest scrutiny."

But television producer and former CNN Vice President Ted Kavanau believes the FBI's desire for good press may have also played a part in the bureau's failure to exercise full control over the media. "All the FBI had to do was control the air space and keep the press too far back to see and hold no press conferences until it's over. Case closed." Kavanau says. "But the FBI was too afraid of bad, angry press reactions to impose that kind of freeze. And although TV news hounds like me would have instinctively hated and fought that, it might have been the right thing to do and maybe should be tried in future circumstances, no matter how much we in the news business hate it and scream that it's unconstitutional."

Others, like Sen. Patrick Leahy (D-Vt.), wonders if the huge media presence and its daily output didn't indirectly pressure the FBI into taking action. "What got me about TV's role at Waco and the way it all ended," says Leahy, "is that I wondered how much pressure for action was caused by TV's constantly harping, 'Nothing's happened yet, nothing's happened yet,' as though it had to end with a big event."

Weaver has similar feelings. "I don't think [television] is capable of portraying a tragic reality where there are all kinds of in-betweens, gradations and shades," he says. "I think the story is dramatic, good guys and bad guys, black hats and white hats. . . . I know in law enforcement this is a common way of thinking. The media contributes to that and Koresh got caught up in it as well."

"That's a pretty astute portrayal of what happened," says Dave Overton, news director of KXAS-TV in Fort Worth. "Who [do] reporters drink beer with? It's their sources, their buddies, the cops. We as an industry have to examine our relationship with law enforcement. A lot of people down here believe law enforcement murdered those people in the compound and that we media people helped them. . . . Some of those who believe it are sane, thoughtful people who truly believe we were working for the FBI."

Special Agent Jamar maintains that "the existence of the cameras was in our minds but it didn't change what we did." He says the only potential danger television coverage posed to the FBI's operation was if there had been armed action. "What affected the decision was the negotiations going nowhere; we could have been there another year without any change."

GOING LIVE

A large part of the controversy over the media's role in unfolding, volatile events like those at Waco or Lucasville is the use of live versus tape-delayed coverage. The capability to transmit events as they happen has always posed problems and ethical dilemmas.

"The use of 'live' always comes under question," says CNN Vice President and Washington Bureau Chief Bill Headline, "because of your inability to edit and think, to have a complete idea of what you're dealing with; there are times when we in television should be restrained in our use of 'live' and we tend not to be."

"The question is, with all this technology, is it running the coverage or is the coverage going to use the technology for its own good?" asks NBC "Today Show" Executive Producer Steve Friedman. "Right now, the technology lets you go live anywhere, anytime and present it as it's happening with no editorial [control] function. In a lot of cases this [going live] is working against us."

. . . [Harry] Fuller [news director of KPIX-TV] was troubled by the networks' handling of Waco. "Much of the reporting was extremely naive," he says. "It was done as a cops and robbers story as opposed to what it really was—a psychodrama based on the mass delusional perception centered around Koresh and the people that followed him. . . .

"There was a perception that this was another hostage-taking where force and strategy matter. I didn't see [reporting] in the early days [of the siege about] the psychology of what goes on in a cult. In the end, some of the networks were pulling out their troops based on the fact that it didn't look like there was going to be a show-down, that it looked like it would go on forever, when in fact it was clear that at any moment there could have been a holocaust and in fact, there was."

But hostage negotiator Bolz believes there was another, more critical, dynamic taking place between Koresh and the television news media: "With all that money expended on putting [so many television crews] out there, [stations and networks] had to put something on the air to justify why you had them out and [Koresh] benefited from that constant, constant notoriety."

PRESS RESPONSIBILITY

Virtually no one in the media is eager to take responsibility for tragic outcomes in unpredictable situations. . . .

Overton of KXAS says with a situation like Waco, it's easy to get so caught up in producing a live shot that you can miss the obvious. "We don't have time to reflect on what we're doing. Early on, when we got our telephoto lenses onto the cameras [during live coverage of the first day], the next thing you know we're showing troop movements, the ATF on the roof, we're looking straight into the windows of the compound." Overton said it is frightening to him that it was only after an irate viewer called to complain that the station might be helping Koresh that he ordered a halt to the live shots.

NBC's Friedman warns that there are dozens of potential David Koreshes who watched the coverage and may have learned something from it. "Our industry has got to stop glorifying these guys . . . ," he says. "You can't treat these things as a normal story. We can't fall victims to the wackos of the world. You know: Kill someone, take hostages and we'll put you on TV."

DOING IT BETTER

Professor Weaver says police and reporters have to improve coverage next time. He recommends that law enforcement officials prohibit live coverage or the airing of live briefings to avoid the clash of egos that figured strongly in the 51 days at Waco. He also says television news should resist the lure of immediacy and urges news managers to use experts on hostage negotiation and cults to help steer coverage to keep their cameras from becoming a player in the crisis.

Some say network pools may be the answer. Hostage negotiator Bolz believes there should be an agreement among local stations and the networks to send a single pool camera crew and one pool correspondent, eliminating the competition and the need for dozens of reporters.

Rick Bradfield, news director of the CBS affiliate in Waco that was on the scene when the ATF raid took place, was amazed by the "astonishing amount of money" invested by stations and networks to "be in at the kill." To Bradfield, a network pool for such events "makes a lot of sense," but probably wouldn't work at a local level because of the competitive pressures.

Others say a lack of rules or guidelines about how to handle such situations is the problem. At KPIX in San Francisco, News Director Fuller says the television news business needs nationwide guidelines for future Wacos and Lucasvilles. "It needs to be understood going in that here are the ground rules and [the people behind the wall] can ask for whatever the hell you want and you either are or are not going to get it based on some guidelines."

Fuller believes that it's a mistake to leave decisions about coverage up to a police chief, a news director or the head agent of an FBI office. He would like to see Congress or another government agency like the Federal Communications Commission look into the issue.

That's hardly a popular idea, however. "God forbid," says Overton. "Congressional involvement in something like this would be a serious abridgement of freedom of the press." But he concedes that television has failed to deal effectively with creating voluntary guidelines. "We haven't had the guts to back away from this competitive aspect. Until news directors have the guts to say no to that, and establish our own guidelines, these things are going to get worse and worse and there very well could be a mass casualty directly because of the coverage."

Until that happens, and since hostage barricades and cult standoffs are such "good television," it is probably useless to argue against all live coverage. During hostage situations, the New York Police Department follows techniques Bolz helped create and has long offered broadcasters this advice, which is generally followed by New York stations:

- Always assume the hostage-taker is watching or listening to your broadcast. That is almost always true with terrorists, often with psychotics, and a clear possibility with the criminal who grabs a hostage after he's discovered in the act of his crime.
- Never include in your broadcast any tactical details such as, "The SWAT team has arrived and appears to be moving in," "Police snipers are on the roof across from the apartment where the people are being held hostage," or "Police have tapped the phone in the apartment, they're watching the gunman with surveillance cameras." In such instances the media can become the intelligent arm of the hostage-taker.
- Never describe the hostage-taker's state of mind or motive. Phrases such as, "Police believe the captor is a psycho" and "The hostage-taker went berserk after he discovered his neighbor in bed with his wife," are fine after the incident is over, but if such characterizations are heard by the perpetrators they could become additionally violent to others or themselves.
- Never reveal the condition of the wounded unless specifically authorized by police who are in touch with the hostage negotiators. Information about the wounded could cause the gunman to shoot again. If he's heard that one victim has died, he might think, "I'm already a murderer, so what've I got to lose by killing another?"

To raise media consciousness of its role in circumstances like Waco, cult expert Dowhower is calling for a simulated "war game" on cult standoffs conducted jointly by law enforcement, cult experts, the media and academics.

At Michigan State University, professor Frank Ochberg, who teaches psychiatry, journalism and criminal justice, is planning to establish a resource center to help reporters and government officials by providing consultation on how to cope with the sometimes conflicting interests of law enforcement and the media in covering a Waco-like crisis. Ochberg, a hostage negotiation and terrorism expert, says a way must be found to "defend the relationship between the media and the general public but look around for new ways to stop the [television and radio] signal from the outside world getting into the siege world."

Sens. Paul Simon (D-Ill.), Alfonse D'Amato (R-NY) and Leahy are among those members of Congress who want the television industry to meet with law enforcement and cult experts to examine broadcasting's role in Waco so that all parties can do a better job. "I'm in favor of a conference," says Simon, "so long as there is no suggestion of censorship."

Making decisions on how to report such stories puts tremendous stress on news executives, who want to make sure that doing their job doesn't contribute to the loss of life. NBC's Verdi admits to going home at night and "praying that the only thing I contributed to was excellent coverage of major stories."

DISCUSSION QUESTIONS

1. Would the siege at Waco have turned out differently if there had been less media coverage? How do you think events would have unfolded without the constant media presence?

2. Do you think the media should place a higher priority on the impact their reporting could have on the crisis they are covering or on providing the public with up-to-the-minute news? When should reporting the news give way to helping resolve the crisis?

3. Evaluate the guidelines for reporting live that the New York Police Department gives news stations; would following them eliminate the problems that we faced in Waco?

4. Do we place too much emphasis on "live" coverage just because technology makes it possible, or is "live" coverage preferable? What are the advantages to the public of delayed coverage?

24. THE MEDIA IN THE PERSIAN GULF WAR

The recent Gulf War was one of the most heavily reported military enterprises in history. Scores of journalists from many countries descended on Saudi Arabia and surrounding nations to witness events and file stories for news media around the globe. Having so many reporters so close to the theater of operations made many military leaders nervous. Many of the U.S. commanders remembered the old, but wrong, notion that the media lost the Vietnam war for the United States, and many thought that the restrictions on press access to military actions in Grenada and Panama had made a lot of sense. Accordingly, the Pentagon issued and then revised a set of regulations for covering the war.

The Gannett Foundation studied the role of the press in the Persian Gulf War immediately afterward. The study concluded that the press restrictions were generally broader than they needed to be, that they got in the way of legitimate news gathering, and that the restrictions reflected more a distaste for the press than a distrust of their reports. The selection from the report excerpted here concerns the requirement of pool reporting, where a small group of journalists is given access to a newsworthy event and expected to share their stories with reporters not in the pool. Not surprisingly, the media disliked the pool system intensely. But was there an alternative?

Pools and the Press in the Persian Gulf War
David Stebenne

When President Bush ordered U.S. troops dispatched to the Persian Gulf on August 8, 1990, Secretary of Defense Richard Cheney refused to allow reporters to accompany them. After intense criticism from the news media, Cheney relented. On August 13th, Assistant Secretary of Defense for Public Affairs Louis A. Williams ordered six press officers to accompany a 17-member press pool to Dhahran, Saudi Arabia. Those six officers established the Joint Information Bureau (JIB), the chief censorship unit in the combat theater, while the 17 American journalists became the first of their peers allowed to report from within it.

In response to persistent demands from the news media, Williams authorized the dispatch of a second wave of journalists, also grouped in a pool, only to run into resistance from the Saudi Arabian government. Saudi authorities have traditionally barred the presence of Western journalists, apparently out of fear that contact between the Saudi populace and American journalists could disturb the country's social structure as well as harmonious relations between its government and that of the United States. During the fall of 1990, an intense contest took place, with major U.S. media organizations on one side, the Saudi government on the other, and Williams and his staff in the middle.

The dilemma encouraged Williams to come up with a system for reporting that satisfied objections from all quarters. At a meeting held in mid-October, Williams and representatives of the major print and broadcast news organizations discussed the Defense Department's proposed restrictions on news reports from the war zone. Some of those restrictions had been devised to mollify the Saudi government, while others, Williams said, were intended to prevent the disclosure of information deemed vital to the security of U.S. forces in the Persian Gulf. The two sides proved unable to reach a consensus at that session, but Williams announced at its end that he would draw up a pool and censorship system, including ground rules and supplementary guidelines.

Williams and his staff eventually produced four different draft versions, consulting with press representatives on each one. Williams' superiors refused to accept one very important feature contained in the early drafts. In keeping with the Sidle Panel's recommenda-

SOURCE: From David Stebenne, "The Military and the Media: The Gulf Conflict in Historical Perspective," in the Gannett Foundation Media Center Report, *The Media at War: The Press and the Persian Gulf Conflict*, copyright 1991 by the Gannett Foundation Media Center, pp. 16–20. The Gannett Foundation has been renamed The Freedom Forum, and its operating program, The Gannett Foundation Media Center, has been renamed The Freedom Forum Media Studies Center.

tions with respect to press pools, Williams' early drafts proposed doing away with them as soon as independent coverage in the war zone became feasible; however, Williams' superiors excised that part from the drafts, and when he announced the final version on January 7, 1991, Williams made no promise to seek its restoration. Those restrictions thus contemplated that all American news media personnel would be subject to the pool system for the duration of the conflict.

The ground rules ... spelled out 12 categories of information that should not be reported. Restricted information included: (1) specific numbers of troops, aircraft, weapons systems, etc.; (2) details of future plans, operations or strikes, including those that had been canceled; (3) information or photographs that revealed specific locations of military forces or security at military locations; (4) rules of engagement details; (5) intelligence collection activities, including targets, methods and results; (6) specific information on friendly troop movements, tactical deployments and dispositions that could endanger operational security or lives; (7) identification of aircraft origin other than as land- or sea-based; (8) effectiveness or ineffectiveness of enemy camouflage, cover, deception, targeting, direct and indirect fire, intelligence collection or security; (9) specific identifying information on downed aircraft or ships while search-and-rescue missions were planned or underway; (10) the methods, unique equipment or tactics of special operations forces; (11) specific operating methods and tactics, such as angles of attack or speeds, but allowing general terms such as "low" or "fast"; and (12) information on operation or support vulnerabilities that could be used against U.S. forces, such as details of major battle damage or major personnel losses of specific units, until the military released such data. Descriptions such as "light," "heavy" or "moderate" would be allowed.

The supplementary guidelines spelled out how those rules would be enforced. When *gathering* news in the war zone, pool reporters were obliged to accept a military escort if U.S. military commanders deemed one necessary. The requirement meant, in effect, that reporters would have to conduct many of their field interviews with soldiers under the watchful eyes of public affairs officers. Although the guidelines stated that the requirement was intended to protect journalists' safety in combat areas, it also greatly increased the likelihood that soldiers would be inhibited from speaking openly to reporters.

The enforcement procedures related to news *reporting* were also quite strict. The guidelines provided that all copy pool journalists produced, including videotapes and photographs, would have to go through a security review system in which military public affairs officers screened such material prior to its transmission to news media organizations. If a journalist disagreed with the decision of a public affairs officer in the field, the journalist could file an appeal to the JIB, and then, if still dissatisfied, to Williams' office in Washington. If the head of the journalist's news organization still disagreed with the government's censorship demands, he or she could then choose to publish the material in question. Although that provision in theory left the final decision on publication in the hands of news organization executives, in practice that would likely not be the case. War news is often a perishable commodity, yet under the press restrictions journalists would be required to exhaust their appeals before a news organization could opt to publish material the military wanted censored. That time-consuming process would likely rob much of that information of its news value. Thus the outcome of the security review process, if a journalist chose to challenge it, would likely be a kind of *de facto* censorship.

The initial set of ground rules and supplementary guidelines, not surprisingly, came under immediate attack from the media. The requirement that all broadcast reporters participate in the pool system and the blanket security review provisions aroused the greatest press criticism, but to no avail. Williams did issue slightly revised ground rules and supplementary guidelines on January 14th, but the differences between the two versions were slight and did not address the principal complaints made by journalists and editors about the earlier version.... The only change in the revised ground rules was to state explicitly that all forms of imagery came within the security review procedure. The most significant change in the supplementary guidelines was the insertion of a passage stating explicitly that only journalists assigned to pools would be allowed into forward areas. And while Williams did promise orally that when the ground war began the other journalists would gain greater access to the front, they never did.

The beginning of hostilities on January 16 put the military's press ground rules and supplementary guidelines to an immediate test. From that date until February 23, when U.S. military and allied ground forces moved into Kuwait and Iraq, those press restrictions operated pretty much in the way their framers had intended. One should note in defense of the restrictions that they proved effective in preventing disclosure of information that would have endangered the safety of U.S. and allied forces in the combat zone.

On the other hand, only a small fraction of the journalists assigned to cover the war ever gained entry into the pools during the pre-invasion period of hostilities. An exact figure is hard to arrive at, because the number of journalists grew as the invasion date neared, and so, too, did the number of pools, largely in response to sustained pressure from news organizations. By the eve of the allied offensive into Kuwait and Iraq in late February, when those numbers peaked, more than 1,400 journalists, photographers and other news media personnel were in the region. Of that number, only 192 had been allowed to join military units through membership in one of the 24 press pools.

The pools' small size made the vast majority of the press corps heavily dependent upon official military briefings and pool reporters for news. Briefings proved only partially useful, given that such forums by their very nature tended to elicit only the military's official view of events. As for pool reporters, some took seriously their implied obligation to gather news useful to the press corps as a whole. Such reporters filed copy daily, even when their own employers did not require that kind of volume, wrote material of the sort that would be most useful to journalists outside the pools, and shared that copy freely. Journalists who behaved in that fashion functioned in effect as representatives of the press corps in its entirety, which was the only way in which the pools could serve, even in a limited way, the needs of the entire group. Other pool reporters, however, either unable or unwilling to refrain from the kinds of habits a competitive journalistic system tends to breed, refused to assume that kind of responsibility. Such reporters offended their peers outside the pools in several ways, either by writing only feature material, which was essentially useless to their peers, by filing only when their own publications required, or by refusing to share their work with other journalists.

Those kinds of newsgathering problems were compounded by the tight military supervision under which pool reporters were compelled to work. Visits to troops, military installations and the front all had to be arranged with the public affairs officers in advance, and, when they took place, reporters found themselves under almost constant military escort. As a result, reporters experienced great difficulty in trying to see or report on truly spontaneous and unrehearsed military activity. Interviews with GI's suffered, too, from the nearly ubiquitous and often inhibiting presence of the public affairs officers.

In addition to newsgathering problems came ones connected with news reporting. The security review system bred numerous delays, ones that afforded Pentagon officials the opportunity to break and thereby shape many of the most important news stories. Public affairs officers also edited copy on occasion in ways reporters found inappropriate given the existing ground rules and guidelines. Descriptions of soldiers' moods before and during battle, for example, were sometimes censored for reasons that appeared unrelated to military security.

All of these problems bred a great deal of dissatisfaction within the American news media. But despite their sometimes loud protests, and individual journalists' occasional efforts to go around the pool system, the Defense Department's press restrictions remained in effect throughout this period. A handful of reporters did go off on their own in search of news, but most were detained by the U.S. military, its allies, and, in one instance, by the Iraqis. The most that Pentagon officials would do in response was to increase gradually the number of pool slots. While that reform mollified the American news media somewhat, it did not address the problems created by the pool and security review systems' basic structure.

As difficult as the existing restrictions were for journalists before the allied ground offensive into Kuwait and Iraq began on February 23, matters thereafter grew even worse. Cheney announced as the invasion started that all press briefings were suspended indefinitely, and all pool reports as well. The success of the offensive soon led to a relaxation of that policy. Some 10 hours after pool reporters filed their first dispatches, the JIB in Dhahran began releasing some of them. Long delays remained the norm, however, until the conclusion of the fighting on February 27. After General Normal Schwarzkopf, the American field commander, gave his first briefing on the offensive around that same time, more junior officers also began to resume press briefings. Even so, press restrictions during the short period of ground fighting were even more serious than had existed during the five weeks preceding it.

The military used the news media effectively during the period immediately before the ground invasion to spread disinformation to the Iraqis. During that time, military officials fed news-hungry journalists false information about how it would be carried out. Endless reports based on those briefings soon appeared in the press. The most notable instances involved erroneous reports about plans for an amphibious assault on Kuwait and the allies' decision to concentrate their troops for a frontal asault at the Saudi-Kuwaiti border. Thus, in the end, Pentagon officials succeeded not only in censoring media coverage of the gulf war but also in making what coverage there was inaccurate in ways that suited the military's purposes.

A few journalists such as CBS' Bob McKeown and ABC's Forrest Sawyer did elude the pool restrictions and provide spot news on the ground during the allied offensive, but most either complied with the ground rules and were censored, or failed in their efforts to escape the government's restrictions. The quick allied victory rendered the issue of changes in those restrictions moot, and left unanswered the question whether continued fighting would have led to a collapse of the pool and security review systems, or at least to drastic changes in them.

During the brief period of ground combat the press did report one story that military officials later described as a breach of the ground rules. News reports about Air Force tactics used to locate and destroy Iraqi tanks, General Colin L. Powell, chairman of the Joint Chiefs of Staff, later said, offered information useful to the Iraqis in dealing with that challenge. That one complaint aside, however, senior Pentagon officials pronounced themselves satisfied with the reportage produced under the press ground rules and accompanying guidelines—and so, too, did the majority of the public, as measured by the most reputable public opinion surveys.

Those in the news media, on the other hand, gave themselves a much lower grade. Howell Raines, who had represented the *New York Times* during the fall 1990 discussions about the proposed press restrictions, described the ultimate result in these terms: "We lost. They [Pentagon officials] managed us completely. If it were an athletic contest, the score would be 100 to 1." Editors and correspondents at other leading print and broadcast news organizations tended to share that bleak assessment. In the end, media coverage of the gulf war was shaped far more by the military's concerns with achieving a decisive victory than the media's paramount goals of comprehensive and accurate reporting. American citizens will have to decide for themselves whether that result best served the public interest.

DISCUSSION QUESTIONS

1. Were the Pentagon's pool reporting requirements appropriate? In what ways do you think they could have been less restrictive? In what ways do you think they should have been more restrictive?

2. In part, the Pentagon restricted reporters to protect their safety. What do you think public response would have been had reporters roamed relatively freely and been killed, injured, or taken captive by Iraqi forces?

3. The Pentagon said that reaching Allied objectives would be harmed if the press had unlimited reporting privileges during the Gulf War. How much deference to military judgment is appropriate on decisions about press access to the theatre of operations?

4. CNN reporting from Baghdad provided U.S. officials with important information about the accuracy of their first bombing raids on Iraq. Do you think that media reports from Saudi Arabia on Allied preparations could have been a source of information for the Iraqi government? What leads you to say so?

25. THE PENTAGON AND THE PRESS—ANOTHER VIEW

The tense relationship between journalists and the armed forces during the Gulf War was nothing new. Reporters and the military had rarely seen eye-to-eye. For one, information is a weapon to be used to achieve its goals. For the other, information is to be gathered, reported, and communicated as news. For the military, restricting access to some information and limiting access to the rest makes good sense—information is used strategically. For the media, choosing from as much information as possible is the goal, and conditions that limit media access interfere with freedom of the press.

Since the Vietnam war, the military has generally viewed the media skeptically, distrustfully. For its part, the press has treated the military with detached amusement, almost with disdain. As a result, neither institution was comfortable dealing with the other, but the military had prepared a strategy for news management, a strategy tested in Grenada and Panama. Here Peter Andrews explores the historical roots of military-media relations in the United States and argues that the Pentagon got the better of the exchange during the Gulf War.

The Media and the Military

Peter Andrews

After more than 130 years, the fundamental dispute between the American media and the American military has changed hardly at all. The essential argument is still about access. How much should the press be allowed to know and see of the conduct of battle? Access was the question posed by the eighteen hundred media personnel accredited to cover Operation Desert Storm in Iraq... when fewer than three hundred were permitted onto the field in press pools so carefully escorted and monitored that one correspondent likened

SOURCE: Reprinted by permission of *American Heritage* Magazine, a division of Forbes, Inc., ©Forbes Inc., 1991.

them to "excursion tours for senior citizens."

Access was all Florus Plympton of the Cincinnati *Commercial* wanted in September 1861 when he arrived at Gen. William Tecumseh Sherman's command in Kentucky with a sheaf of letters of introduction from Sherman's military superiors and a request for an interview. Sherman, who hated the press with a devouring flame, ordered the newsman to take the next train back to Louisville. When Plympton protested that he had come only to learn the truth, Sherman flew into a fine rage.

"We don't want the truth told about things here," Sherman exploded. "...We don't want the enemy any better informed than he is."

With varying degrees of acrimony, that conversation has been going on ever since.

Gen. H. Norman Schwarzkopf, the victor in the Persian Gulf, claims an affection for the writings of Sherman, and several times during the Gulf War he quoted the old general more aptly and accurately than many military historians have. More important, Schwarzkopf and his forces paid honor to Sherman's memory not only by conducting a flanking action reminiscent of Sherman at his best but by accomplishing something Sherman never did. Thanks to careful planning and meticulous execution, as well as the kind of good luck that goes with such planning and execution, they managed to control the press to a degree not seen in our history. With few meaningful exceptions, the words and the pictures were entirely those approved by the military command.

If the media were as well disciplined and given to conducting extensive critiques of their performance as the military is, there would be a large group of high-level news personnel huddled around a sand table at the Columbia Journalism School right now, rerunning the exercise and trying to discover what went wrong. It is important to find out, for while an unfettered press may sometimes be nettlesome, a tame, obedient press is always dangerous. If ever there was an object lesson in this, it was demonstrated by Saddam Hussein, who, immediately after the cease-fire, threw foreign journalists out of Iraq so he could go back to slaughtering his own people without letting them read about it in the papers.

It is not in their natures for the military and the media to be entirely comfortable with each other. The disciplines are too disparate. The military requires subservience of the individual to the needs of the group, while the media prize independent initiative above all else. The same elements that make a good reporter would likely make for a poor field commander. At their best the media and the military work together in roughhewn harmony, providing sound military leadership and an independent source of information that helps the public (which provides the troops and pays the bills) to know what it's getting for its expenditure of blood and money. At their worst the military wraps itself in the flag and the media wrap themselves in the First Amendment and neither party listens to the other.

... Freedom of the press as guaranteed by the Constitution is a particularly American concept. While the American press is not impervious to control or attack, it is afforded legal protections not available elsewhere. During World War I, Winston Churchill seriously suggested that *The Times* of London be commandeered and turned into an official government publication, to be used as "a sure and authoritative means of guiding public opinion."

By this time the press had become an unpleasant fact of life for the military. If correspondents could not be kept off the field, however, it was essential that they be controlled. The British press and army censors acted in concert to keep the horrors of trench warfare out of new accounts. Late in December 1917 Prime Minister David Lloyd George confided to the editor of the Manchester *Guardian*: "If the people really knew, the war would be stopped tomorrow. But of course they don't know and can't know."

As before, American correspondents...had to concern themselves with access. The United Press's Westbrook Pegler, twenty-three years old and the youngest accredited reporter in France, tried to get an interview with the American commander, Gen. John J.

Pershing. The interview consisted in its entirety of Pershing's saying, "Pegler, get the hell out of my office."

... A sorry estrangement developed between the top military and civilian levels in Vietnam and the media. As a rule of thumb reporters like to go to the highest-ranking official they can find who has good information. But correspondents were becoming increasingly uncomfortable with the rosy predictions being given out at the top and worked their way down the command level to junior combat officers who had a bleaker view. In effect, many correspondents became rogue reporters working a different side of the story from the official one. When Joseph Alsop, the pundit's pundit, arrived in Saigon in 1969 and grandly declared that he never talked to anyone under the rank of colonel, he became an object of derision. "We had gotten to the point," remembers Kevin Buckley, *Newsweek*'s bureau chief in Vietnam, "that we hardly talked to anyone *above* the rank of colonel."

... The war in the Persian Gulf was the media's Cannae, and the press played Varro to Schwarzkopf's Hannibal: the military's victory over the press was total and devastating. The media were essentially reduced to being a conduit for official information offered by commanders who could scarcely disguise their scorn for the delivery system they were forced to use. It is a truism of war that to create a victory as massive as Cannae, it takes two generals, a smart one on one side and a stupid one on the other. In the almost twenty years since Vietnam the military has been working on its media problem while the press has been sitting on its First Amendment rights.

The new system is right out of a Madison Avenue manual for a publicity blitz. If you want pictures, you will get more than you can possibly use, but they will be our pictures. If you want quotes, you will get them by the hour, but they will be our quotes. If you want access, you will be personally escorted to the front, but we will determine where and when you get there.

Make no mistake about it, the military has become extremely sophisticated in the way it handles public relations. Death by friendly fire is one of the most horrible things that can happen in combat. For troops to die in the face of enemy action is one thing. To have them killed by their own gunfire is grotesque. But it has happened ever since armies first started throwing iron into the sky. The service used to go to extraordinary lengths to cover up such stories, but when it happened in the Gulf, high-level officers came forward almost immediately and acknowledged the mistake. The incident showed how well the services had mastered the dictum that it is better to break bad news yourself than to have it broken for you. It also displayed an extraordinary confidence in the public's capacity to accept that kind of loss. If is unfortunate the military's confidence in the public did not extend further.

In controlling the words and pictures that came out of the Gulf, the military had an unbeatable hole card that it played to the hilt and somewhat beyond—the argument that the lives of the troops must not be endangered by the unwarranted disclosure of information. Fair enough. But demonstrably, much that was done in the name of security was simply an attempt to help sell the war to the home audience. Field interviews with the troops were closely monitored by officers, pictures showing soldiers in distress were suppressed, and television coverage of flag-draped coffins arriving at Dover Air Force Base was banned altogether. The military did not allow the media a view of the conflict as much as it gave them the bum's rush through the desert.

The public, watching on television, loved it. And why not? The media had been begging for it. Since Vietnam the military has been a favored whipping boy of the media; brass hats go on brass heads, men and materiel are just boys with their toys, and the Pentagon doesn't know how to buy a toilet seat. The military has routinely been subjected to the kind of comic abuse you would expect to find in the sports section. . . .

The press is free to write what it wishes. But it should not be surprised if it finds that its subjects resent being patronized. Nor should it be surprised if the military, whose business is the management of violence, strikes back. In Vietnam the daily press conferences in Saigon were called "the five o'clock follies," and the briefing officers were frequently given a rough going-over by the press. In a picture-perfect demonstration of how those who bear the sword may also perish by it, the military turned the tables on the press in the Gulf briefings. Watching the media in action is never pretty, but looking in on a press conference is the worst possible view. There are too many people asking too many questions from too many angles for the sessions to be coherent. I have been told the military was so certain the press would act badly at the briefings that it was written into the public affairs scenario that televised press conferences would show the American public how important it was to muzzle the media. It is certain that the press played into the military's waiting hands. "Saturday Night Live" took time off from its traditional political targets to do a devastating parody of the sessions, with the reporters cast as buffoons. The satire was nothing, however, to the scorn heaped on the press by its own fellows. Peter Braestrup, who covered Vietnam for *The New York Times* and *Washington Post* and is now director of communications at the Library of Congress, was withering in his commentary on the press in the Gulf:

> They're ahistorical: they can't remember any precedents for anything. They keep discovering the world anew. They either concentrate on high-tech stories or on what an ABC producer described to me as "boo-hoo journalism," that is, asking How do you feel? not What do you know? They're looking for that little emotional spurt. They don't know what the wider vignette means. They're yuppies in the desert.

. . . It is an unhappy rule of journalism that the bigger the story, the less expert is the general coverage, at least at first. This is true regardless of the subject matter. The number of reporters covering professional golf quintuples during the Masters Tournament. This is not because there are suddenly five times as many members of the press who know something about golf. It's because the Masters is a big sports story and a pleasant one to cover in early April. Thirty years ago, when I was sent to Cape Canaveral to cover the start of America's manned space program, I had so little scientific background I didn't know how a doorbell works. For that matter, I'm still not certain. When the Gulf War exploded, the ranks of the press were suddenly swollen by correspondents who, in one veteran's downright phrase, "don't know a tank from a turd."

In time the press would have shaken itself out. There would have been the laggards, because there are always those who prefer to cover combat from the confines of the saloon. In the Western command of the Union Army, they were known as "Cairo correspondents" because that was as close to the field as they ever got. And there would have been those who learned their craft and did their jobs, and doubtless some of them would have been killed doing so.

Mercifully there wasn't time.

So now the media are on the defensive and deserve to be. Talking about how freedom of the press is protected by the First Amendment is like hiding behind your mother's skirt. It may be a warm and comfortable place to be, but it's not much good in a fight. As Bill Kovach, curator of the Neiman Foundation for Journalism at Harvard University, said, "A huge industry has grown up to shape public opinion by controlling what goes into the media in the last twenty years and in all that time, the press doesn't seem to have thought about the problem at all. We tend to be a responsive apparatus that reacts to whatever comes along."

When the siren went off in the Gulf, the American media were caught flatfooted. With few exceptions, military beats had been poorly covered for years. There was always room for a five-hundred-dollar hammer story but little about the people who were going to be responsible for any future military action. "We covered the politics of the military," says Kovach, "but not its mission." It is time to play some catch-up ball, and a good place to start may be that the media should begin to take a somewhat less cosmic view of themselves. It is difficult enough to learn what American politics are and to report on how they are being carried out. It is asking a great deal for the media to act like emissaries from The Hague sitting in judgment.

No story as big as Desert Storm can stay bottled up forever. As brief as the action was, there were signs the steel-tight control over the media was loosening up. Reporters were starting to hook up with units on their own and filing good stories. Subsequent information on bombing runs took some of the high-tech gloss off the stunning television pictures that showed ordnance making its unerring way into doorframes and the like. After the cease-fire Air Force officers announced that only 7 percent of the 88,500 tons dropped on Iraq and Kuwait were so-called smart bombs. The rest were ordinary unguided bombs, most of which missed their targets. The military shrewdly played this kind of information tight to the vest, knowing the clatter of a victory parade drowns out the complainers.

Soon after the American troops started to move toward the desert, media attention began to focus on the arresting personality of "Stormin' Norman" Schwarzkopf. An indication of how poorly the media have been covering the military beat for the last twenty years is the scant information the public had on Schwarzkopf when he took command. In a perceptive article in the *Washington Monthly,* Scott Shuger pointed out that the press, which was so interested in getting a line on the judicial thinking of the Supreme Court nominee David Souter that it dug up his college thesis, didn't know anything about the military philosophy of any of the top brass and seemed not to care. This situation is changing now that the media are interested in generals again, and General Schwarzkopf, riding a tidal wave of popularity, may learn to miss the days when he led a life of relative obscurity. The dust had hardly settled in the desert when negative stories about the general began to circulate. He is an attention grabber who thinks he planned Desert Storm all by himself. He is loath to give credit to his field commanders and quick to relieve any staff officer who disagrees with him. A joke going around the planning staff in Riyadh a few weeks back ran:

"Who is the second most hated man in the Middle East?"

"Saddam Hussein."

None of this is necessarily a mark against Schwarzkopf. It is the inevitable backlash that goes with prominence. Certainly, when compared with the kinds of stories that were circulated about Sherman and Grant, these are small potatoes. Politicians understand such things. Generals don't.

Within days of the cease-fire, the surefooted Schwarzkopf made his first bobble in traversing the treacherous shoals of politics. In the last days of Desert Storm, coalition forces were smashing up elements of the fleeing Iraqi army. This is known as gathering up the fruits of victory. Killing the enemy's men and destroying his equipment is one of the chief reasons why you fight a battle in the first place. The totality of the victory, however, seemed to sit uneasily on the consciousness of the television analysts. Jim Lehrer of the "MacNeil/Lehrer Newshour" suggested that the coalition forces were "shooting fish in a barrel," and a local New York television poll declared that America was playing the bully. The next day President Bush called off the operation. In a television interview with David Frost, General Schwarzkopf made it clear that he had wanted to carry on the pursuit of Iraqi forces. Schwarzkopf was swiftly and publicly rebuked by the White House and recanted.

It was an old scenario. First he said it. Then he said he didn't say what he said. Then he said it was all the media's fault for asking him to say what he said in the first place.

The beat goes on.

DISCUSSION QUESTIONS

1. Do the media and the military ever share perspectives and strive for common goals? What would be some examples of that?

2. What alternatives did journalists have during the Gulf War, do you think, to counter the military's attempt to control their reporting? How necessary was it to have reporters "at the scene?"

3. Is Andrews right, that the military was as concerned with "selling the war back home" as it was with protecting U.S. interests in the war with Iraq? Was their concern with what Iraqis would learn or with what Americans would learn?

4. Both warfare and communications have changed markedly in the last half-century. Wouldn't we expect the military-media relationship to have changed over that period, too? How do you think that relationship has changed since World War II? You may want to go to your library to read war correspondents' reports from the front during World War II in old newsmagazines or newspapers.

5. Andrews suggests that the press should have covered military commanders and future military commanders routinely over the past several

decades. Do you think that is a good idea? Would that coverage have been "newsworthy" at the time? Why or why not?

26. INTEREST GROUPS USING THE MEDIA

When government considers actions that will affect some segments of society more than others, the interest groups involved will rarely stand idly by. When lobbying needs to be reinforced with favorable public opinion, various organizations will use the media to put their point of view forward, and these organizations will buy advertisements to make sure their messages reach the public. At the same time, groups hope that policymakers will also take the groups' perspectives into account. If the decision makers themselves see the issue as a group sees it, that group gains a big advantage in the policy-making process.

When Hillary Rodham Clinton's Health Care Task Force was meeting during the spring of 1993 to formulate proposals to revamp the nation's health care system, drug manufacturers, medical associations, insurance companies, and other interest groups took out advertisements to put forward their reading of the issues involved. One might say that they were attempting to "frame" the issue, that is, trying to focus attention on the points they favored and away from the ones they opposed. Howard Kurtz surveyed many of these advertisements for the *Washington Post Weekly Edition* to summarize their perspectives and place the ads in the relevant context. Notice how many seemed less than forthright about their own economic interests!

Take Two Ads and Call Me in the Morning: The Media Blitz Aimed at Hillary's Health Care Task Force

Howard Kurtz

The magazine ad casts the health care question in highly personal terms. There is a picture of a balding, genial-looking fellow with the headline: "Ask Mike what he'd do if you took away the ulcer drug that's saving him from a $25,000 operation."

This is the pitch of the Pharmaceutical Manufacturers Association, one of several trade groups, corporations and lobbying organizations that have launched an advertising blitz about health care reform. Although the ad

SOURCE: ©1993 *The Washington Post.* Reprinted with permission.

touts the "cost-saving power" of prescription drugs, it neglects to mention that the industry spends $1 billion more each year on advertising and lobbying than on developing new drugs.

The recent media offensive is reminiscent of last year's presidential campaign, which sweeping claims about solving the health care mess and snappy slogans about protecting consumers. This time, however, the object is not to win public office but to influence the recommendations of Hillary Rodham Clinton's health care task force.

As in political ads, the agendas of these organizations are not always made clear. All proclaim themselves strongly in favor of "reform" and insist that preserving their particular financial interest somehow will lower health costs. Some make questionable or misleading assertions.

"The secret of advocacy advertising is that the target audience is a tiny universe of highly influential people," says Jay Severin, a New York political consultant. "A group like the American Medical Association is saying to its opponents: 'We're prepared to wage a fight that could get ugly and expensive for you.'"

Many of the ads, targeting Beltway decision-makers, appear in The Washington Post, Congressional Quarterly and Roll Call. Others are in such national publications as Time, Newsweek, U.S. News & World Report and The New York Times Magazine. One series of spots has aired on local television in Washington.

Here is an analysis of eight recent ads and what their sponsors are trying to accomplish:

AMERICAN MEDICAL ASSOCIATION

The Pitch. "Price controls didn't work in the Nixon Administration. They didn't work in the Carter Administration. Why should anyone believe they'll work now? We asked 12 of America's leading economists, including Nobel Laureates and deans of leading business schools, for their views on price controls and the rising cost of medical care. The response was unanimous. Price controls on health care would be a *costly* mistake."

Another AMA ad says limits on health care spending "could also result in long lines and loss of patient choice."

The Background. The AMA does not mention that "price controls" would mean limits on physicians' fees or that the average salary for doctors is $170,000. The group's warning about "long lines" and "loss of patient choice" is aimed at preserving a system in which doctors have the greatest autonomy.

AMA Vice President Steven V. Seekins says the point of the ads is "positioning with the Congress and the administration to make sure they knew what we stood for." Borrowing a campaign tactic from Bill Clinton, the ads invite readers to write for a copy of the AMA's health plan, and 1,500 have done so.

PHARMACEUTICAL MANUFACTURERS ASSOCIATION

The Pitch. "Ask Katie's parents what they think of the asthma drug that's saving her trips to the emergency room." Another ad says: "What we're doing to hold down the high cost of cancer. Leading the way in the search for relief is the pharmaceutical industry, with 126 medicines currently in development for cancer. It's part of the industry's $12.6 billion R&D investment in 1993 alone."

The Background. President Clinton has been denouncing drug companies for "unconscionable" profiteering on childhood vaccines. The ad tries to neutralize White House charges that drug profits have been rising at four times the rate of those at Fortune 500 companies.

PMA Vice President Jeffrey Warren calls the ads "a response to some of the misinformation that's been put out" by the president and Congress. "We're spending more on R&D than any industry in the country," he says.

COMMITTEE FOR NATIONAL HEALTH INSURANCE

The Pitch. Against the backdrop of an American flag, this group says that "health care reform in America . . . just won't fly" without certain "principles," such as "people want to choose their own doctor" and "private insurance should play a role." The committee touts its proposal as "the only plan created by respected health experts, after years of careful work."

The Background. The group is headed by former United Auto Workers president Douglas Fraser, which is disclosed in the ad, and supports the AFL-CIO's effort to protect union-negotiated health benefits. It is funded by organized labor, and 20 union presidents sit on its board. Director Melvin Glasser says the group is "largely in agreement" with the Clinton plan, particularly on such points as cost controls and the need for public-private partnerships.

HEALTHRIGHT

The Pitch. [Television narrator:] "Claire Love's son was diagnosed with cancer last year." [Love:] "I really don't know what you can do, because we thought we were all covered. We all had insurance. Even with good insurance, you're stuck with massive medical bills. I had to sell the house." [Visual:] HealthRight: Because health care is a right, not a privilege.

The Background. HealthRight is a coalition of such groups as the National Association for Home Care, National Council of Senior Citizens, Child Welfare League and American Federation of State, County and Municipal Employees. This TV ad, one of several involving ailing patients, uses an emotional appeal to underscore the limits of health insurance. HealthRight organizer Val Halamandaris says the group has interviewed thousands of people "to put faces on the problem" but has no legislative agenda, other than supporting greater emphasis on preventive and long-term care.

AMERICAN OCCUPATIONAL THERAPY ASSOCIATION

The Pitch. "Occupational therapists help millions of people of all ages recover from illnesses and injuries or adapt to disabling conditions. And over 80 percent of those treated return to their homes, work, schools or resume active retirement. . . . Rehabilitation can save $11 for each dollar invested."

The Background. The figure is from a 1986 industry survey and may be suspect, as it is in the providers' interest to claim large benefits from their work. The group's aim is to make sure that coverage of services provided by its 46,000 members does not change.

"If anyone is not in the benefits package, they're in trouble," says Fred Somers, the group's lobbyist. "Some folks may not automatically think of rehabilitation services as being part of a standard benefits package."

PRUDENTIAL INSURANCE CO.

The Pitch. [Picture of baby in intensive care] "For around $70,000, her life could be saved. For around $700, she'd never have been in danger. Her parents' health care plan didn't cover the few hundred dollars they needed for prenatal care.... That's why, at Prudential, we strongly support the wider use of managed-care programs that put an increased emphasis on preventive medicine."

The Background. Prudential is one of several large insurance companies that promote managed care because they have entered the managed-care business. Company spokeswoman Elaine Cinelli says Prudential is running managed-care health plans in at least 45 cities. Managed care is controversial because nonphysicians make decisions about patient care. Prudential's profits would be more directly squeezed by price controls, which the company opposes.

AMERICAN SPEECH-LANGUAGE-HEARING ASSOCIATION

The Pitch. "Making Health Care Reform Look Like All of America. 42 million children and adults in this country have a speech, language or hearing disorder.... With diagnosis and treatment by a qualified audiologist or speech-language pathologist, millions of Americans live independent.... All Americans deserve access to basic health care, including rehabilitation services."

The Background. The ad does not mention that private and federal insurance does not cover many outpatient and other services that the group wants to make part of Clinton's standard benefits package. "This is an opportunity for us to get certain things covered that are not covered," spokeswoman Mona Thomas says.

UNITED STATES SURGICAL CORP.

The Pitch. "An Open Letter to President and Mrs. Clinton On Containing Health Care Costs. New surgical technology is reducing our national health care costs by billions of dollars while improving patient care and adding billions of hours to American productivity.... Medical technology, properly used, can be a major factor in reducing the total costs of health care in America."

The Background. Many experts, including some on Clinton's task force, say that excessive use of medical technology is a major factor in rising health care costs. "Our whole point is that high tech doesn't necessarily mean high cost, and we didn't want that message to get lost," company spokesman Steven Rose says.

DISCUSSION QUESTIONS

1. Watch your daily newspaper for advertisements in support of interest group positions. When you find some, consider what position the group wants you to take and why they favor that position.

2. Have interest groups been more or less active in trying to influence public opinion since the Clinton health care proposal has been sent to Congress? Would you expect to see more or fewer advertisements to influence

public opinion the closer a controversial policy proposal comes to a final vote in Congress?

3. Why don't more groups use advertising to try to get public opinion on their side? What conditions lead to greater success in doing so?

27. PRIVACY, PUBLIC OFFICIALS, AND THE PRESS

Candidates for office and people who may be appointed to public office come under intense media scrutiny. Reporters pored over Geraldine Ferraro's husband's complicated finances. Journalists wondered out loud about people smoking marijuana when they were younger after Douglas Ginsburg's nomination to the Supreme Court was withdrawn. Were all the social security taxes paid on the nominee's baby-sitters? Is there a history of sexual harassment? Indeed, as Garry Trudeau had a character ask in "Doonesbury": Were income taxes paid on frequent flyer awards? Newpeople seem to thrive on exploring the blemishes on the records of public officials, trivial or serious.

Even candidates' sex lives have come under scrutiny. Gary Hart dropped out of the 1984 presidential race when his affair with Donna Rice became public knowledge. Bill Clinton had to answer Gennifer Flowers's claims that they had been long-time lovers. But shouldn't there be limits to the press's digging? After all, don't public officials retain some privacy? In this selection, Charles S. Clark considers the difficulties journalists face when allegations of sexual improprieties surface. Does the public have a right to know? Or should reporters shield public officials from invasions of their privacy? Lurking in the background is the implicit question whether such concentrated examination of one's personal life deters otherwise qualified people from public service. How many among us would pass such scrutiny?

Politicians and Privacy

Charles S. Clark

THE ISSUES

Hillary Clinton took shelter in what she called a "zone of privacy" during an ex-

SOURCE: From "Politicians and Privacy" in *The CQ Researcher,* Vol. 2, No. 15, April 17, 1992, pp. 339–343, pp. 354–355. Reprinted by permission.

traordinary "60 Minutes" interview in January [1992] about the adultery allegations dogging the presidential campaign of her husband, Arkansas Gov. Bill Clinton. But judging from the flood of news coverage of the candidate and an ex-cabaret singer named Gennifer

Flowers, privacy is a prerogative that politicians no longer enjoy.

Displayed that week in the *Star*, a supermarket tabloid, were partial transcripts of a telephone conversation Flowers said she had secretly taped between herself and the governor. The flirtatious dialogue, the partially deleted references to sex and the vague discussions of a strategy for fending off reporters were offered as proof of Flowers' claim that she had a 12-year love affair with Clinton.

"Sex, Lies and Audiotape" screamed front-page headlines in both the *New York Daily News* and *New York Newsday*. In marked contrast, *The New York Times, The Washington Post* and the *Los Angeles Times* relegated their stories to inside pages.

... The news media immediately showed signs of sharp disagreement over the coverage. Flowers' story is "a shabby accusation," said Al Hunt, Washington Bureau chief for *The Wall Street Journal*. "I'm ashamed for my profession," said *New York Times* Executive Editor Max Frankel. "Newspapers are behaving like a bunch of dominoes," said *Miami Herald* Editor Doug Clifton, who years earlier had spied on presidential candidate Gary Hart. ... "Some low-rent publication publishes damning information with dubious sources and credibility, and then the 'higher' publications give up their independence."

But defenders of the coverage—and they were not confined to "rumormongers" in the tabloid press—saw the story as an indicator of Clinton's character. "If Anita Hill's stories about Clarence Thomas were judged relevant to his nomination for the U.S. Supreme Court, then why shouldn't Flowers' claims about Clinton be aired as well?" wrote *New York* magazine media critic Edwin Diamond.[1] "There's a woman standing there," said *Des Moines Register* Editor Geneva Overholser. "Is [the skepticism] because of her questionable morals, her peroxided hair? It's because we're uncomfortable with the subject."

The lack of consensus on the newsworthiness of the Clinton-Flowers story is the latest question mark in a conundrum the press has yet to resolve for itself: how to balance sound news practices and respect for privacy with the competitive demands that arise with a mesmerizing sex scandal.

The current preoccupation with the private lives of public figures—what perennial tabloid target Sen. Edward M. Kennedy, D-Mass., called political journalism "honed through the prism of *People* magazine"[2]—is a trend that dates from the late 1960s and early '70s. A generation of reporters egged on to aggressiveness by the Watergate scandal combined with new revelations about past presidents ... to produce a cynical curiosity about the sex lives of politicians.

Suzanne Garment, author of the recent book *Scandal,* points out that the period also bred an alliance of old-fashioned morality with feminist disdain for men who womanize. "On the one hand we were seeing new habits of explicitness and a growing market for news about sex and public personalities," she writes. "On the other side we saw a growing hostility toward women who made a sexual display of themselves and an increasing disapproval of personal immorality in politicians."[3]

The media go through cycles of style and fashion, notes Dom Bonafede, a professor of communications at American University in Washington. In contrast with the 1960s, when film stars' visits to a president's hotel suite were winked at and ignored by reporters, there's more subjective analysis now. "In this day and age, if President Bush invited Madonna to go swimming with him, it would be reported," Bonafede says.

At the same time, the decline in the influence of political parties in the past two decades has magnified the importance of journalists in determining the fate of candidates. "No individuals are so entrusted with enormous yet nearly unchecked influence as are newspersons," University of Virginia government Professor Larry J. Sabato writes in *Feeding Frenzy*, his recent book on press excesses. "The abuses painfully visible during feeding frenzies damage the political fabric of America by cheapening public discourse, trivializing the campaign agenda, breeding cynicism and discouraging people from seeking public office."[4]

Newspaper editors struggling with declining readership are aware of the limits of the public's attention span for such topics as the federal budget deficit or affordable health care. The appetite for "inside dope" about sex among the rich and famous is obvious from the popularity of the tabloid press and its more recent cousin—tabloid TV. "The public goes for simplicity," says Duke University political scientist James David Barber. "They don't know what *deficit* means but they know what *adultery* means."

On a conscious level, however, the public seems to side with those who argue that a politician's private life should remain so. Only 25 percent of those responding to a recent poll agreed that voters should be informed about extramarital affairs and other private aspects of presidential candidates.[5]

When an intimate detail of a candidate's life suddenly barrels its way into publication, the public often takes its cue from the importance assigned the story by the media. Hence there is irony in the press' own confusion. *New York Times* Deputy Metropolitan Editor Michael Oreskes summed it up in a 1991 symposium on campaign coverage:

When you pick a president, the most important thing you are picking is ... someone whose judgment and strength and will are things that you respect and can count on.... But somehow, we twisted that idea, a good idea, and an idea that would be really helpful in understanding who we elect as president into a license to ask all sorts of questions about fundamentally unimportant things.[6]

As scandals and phony scandals play out on the campaign trail, here are some of the key questions being asked about politicians and privacy:

Are the news media too aggressive in probing the private lives of politicians? Mainstream journalism reached the pinnacle of its pursuit of the adultery issue when it dug into the private life of Democratic presidential hopeful Gary Hart in May 1987. The coverage of Hart broke new ground in two important regards. A team of *Miami Herald* reporters spent hours furtively staking out Hart's Washington townhouse in order to verify the overnight presence of Donna Rice, a young woman who was not Hart's wife and whom the reporters had followed on a flight from Miami. Secondly, the evasive give-and-take that followed between Hart and the press gave *The Washington Post*'s Paul Taylor his opening to ask Hart, after a series of questions of morality: "Have you ever committed adultery?"

Both Taylor and the *Herald* drew heavy criticism. "The notion was to put a citizen under surveillance," said Bill Kovach, then-editor of *The Atlanta Journal-Constitution*.[7] "That is a technique for police, not journalists." A poll showed that 63 percent of the *Herald*'s own readers thought the coverage was excessive. Several *New York Times* columnists accused Taylor of deliberately trying for titillation, wondering whether reporters would soon be asking candidates about masturbation or impotence.

Defenders responded by noting that only weeks before the stakeout, Hart had vehemently denied rumors of womanizing and had actually dared reporters to follow him around. In the subsequent debate over "the character issue," many argued that Hart's deception showed poor judgment and a disturbing compulsiveness that voters should be informed of even if it made reporters feel sleazy. "Sometimes this job demands that we raise questions we'd rather not ask," Taylor said. "What I did was ask Gary Hart the question he asked for."[8]

The Hart affair also made editors and reporters wary of missing the next scoop. "This paper has tended to be very conservative about rumors," said *Rocky Mountain News* reporter Pam Maples. "After the Gary Hart story broke, there was guilt among some of the editors and reporters. You know, he was the hometown boy. Shouldn't we have been doing that story?"[9]

Politically, the legacy of the scandal was that syndicated columnist Charles Krauthammer called the "Hart Rule on Infidelity: For the offense to be fatal, it must be compulsive and current."[10]

As far as is known, that is not the situation with Bill Clinton. But that hasn't stopped assignment editors around the country from dispatching teams of reporters to sift through Clinton's past in search of women willing to kiss and tell. It is a trend that many journalists frown upon. "When the press is confronted by such [sexual] behavior in a presidential candidate, it has no choice but to report it," wrote veteran *Washington Post* political reporter David S. Broder. "But the press has no such obligation to go rummaging in the closets of White House contenders for any past indiscretion that may fall out."[11]

But others argue that the press wasn't tough enough in ferreting out the extent of the scandal. The media are "letting Clinton lie," charged media watchdog Reed Irvine of the Washington-based Accuracy in Media. "If Gennifer Flowers had turned the tapes over to *The Washington Post* instead of the supermarket *Star,* Clinton would be finished as a presidential candidate."[12]

Author Garment confesses to some ambivalence on the coverage of Clinton, noting that if he indeed had affairs, they apparently happened a long time ago. But she also was startled that the press dropped the issue so quickly. "I don't think journalists have terrific self-confidence in this story," she says. "Clinton is the Democrat reporters think has the best chance to beat Bush, and they're hoping for a good race. Many can't be reporting it with enthusiasm, because they're of the same generation as Clinton and lived through the heyday of the sexual revolution."

The general public is as divided as the press over coverage of Clinton and the adultery issue. In a January poll by the Times Mirror Center for the People and the Press, 53 percent of the respondents said that if they headed a news organization they would report the Clinton-Flowers story, while 43 percent said they would not.

Nonetheless, the public does *not* appear to believe journalists who say they reported the story because it helped voters learn about Clinton's character. A full 73 percent of those responding to the Times Mirror poll said news organizations were driven more by the belief that the Clinton stories would draw large audiences. . . .

Is news coverage of sex scandals lowering standards of fairness and accuracy? When tabloids report on Elvis sightings or the breakup of Prince Andrew's marriage to Sarah Ferguson, their "sources" can be as wispy as a rumor—an item printed in an obscure publication or a tip from a notorious liar. The mainstream press traditionally has required more rigorous verification.

In recent years, however, newspapers going for sassy "personality journalism"—as well as publications subject to manipulation by media-savvy political operatives—have unwittingly helped to spread "stories" later found to be false or unprovable. In *Feeding Frenzy,* Larry Sabato cites such examples as a 1988 story on vice presidential candidate Dan Quayle's purported drug use in the early 1970s (the source was a prisoner serving 50 years for drug smuggling and domestic terrorism) and a 1989 rumor that House Speaker Thomas S. Foley, D-Wash., was a homosexual (a story now known to have been generated by his political enemies).

"The new permissive approach," wrote *Time* magazine's Walter Shapiro, allows leading newspapers and the television networks "to write and broadcast artfully crafted stories about the rumors themselves, thereby spreading calumny while piously decrying it."[13]

According to Sabato, that's how the press went overboard in covering this year's claims against Clinton. Its first mistake, Sabato says, was printing references to unsubstantiated rumors about Clinton and marital infidelity even before Flowers came forward. The second was using the Flowers information simply because the *Star* had published it.

Clinton's hometown paper, the *Arkansas Democrat-Gazette,* took the restrained approach. "On the whole," said Editor John Starr, "I'd rather get beat on a story like this than scoop the world and be wrong."[14]

The potential harm from publicizing unverified charges was dramatized in a recent study by University of Virginia researcher Daniel Wegner. In an experiment demonstrating what is called the "innuendo effect," he showed that consumers of news, who in their haste often pay only partial attention to news reports failed to distinguish among three very different headlines: "Smith linked to mob; Is Smith linked to Mob? Smith Not linked to Mob."[15]

The use of rumors can also backfire and prevent a reporter from unearthing verifiable facts. Queries based on rumors are more easily dismissed by press spokesmen seeking to protect their candidates. "When people asked me a general, vague question like, 'Gee, we hear there are rumors,' " recalls Kathryn Bushkin, who was Gary Hart's press secretary in 1984, "I'd say 'Fine, if you can come back with something specific, then maybe there's something to talk about.' "[16]

The trend toward reporting rumors does not disturb all media-watchers. When it comes to sex, after all, there usually are only two witnesses. Editors nowadays may ease their requirements for multiple sources for every fact if they want to keep up with a breaking story that, for reasons beyond titillation, is becoming relevant to public discourse.

Press analyst Stephen Hess, a senior fellow at the Brookings Institution in Washington, says the current "short-term blip" toward reporting rumors is no worse than the situation in the 19th century, when newspapers were much more partisan. The Gary Hart stakeout, he says, shows "we have brought the standards of factual journalism to what used to be rumors."

Defending his paper's coverage of the Clinton-Flowers episode, *Washington Post* Managing Editor Robert G. Kaiser distinguished between investigative reporting and a need to report other breaking developments on campaigns. "If we didn't pay attention to the fact that Clinton's private life, subject of rumor or gossip for years, had become news," he said, "it would feed the anxiety among our readers that we know lots of things we don't share with them because of some conspiracy...."[17]

OUTLOOK
A Call for Restraint

When politicians feature their families in brochures in order to get votes, "they are inviting the press into their private lives," said George Reedy, former press secretary to President Johnson. The trouble is, the absence of clear boundaries between the private and public spheres often means that informed political debate gets overwhelmed by a carnival atmosphere in which all bedroom doors are flung open.

At a news conference in January [1992], Gennifer Flowers was asked by a radio show prankster whether she and Gov. Clinton had used a condom. In 1987, Donna Rice endured an embarrassing fishing expedition from reporters at the Miami airport: "Have you slept with Gary Hart? 'No.' Do you want to? 'No.' Has he ever asked? 'No.' "[18]

Time's Hugh Sidey says he is troubled by the trend toward asking about private matters and wonders whether it might not deter good candidates from running for political office. Sidey recalls the old saying: "The search for perfection is the enemy of what is just good." When it comes down to it, he adds, "Jefferson and Lincoln were very odd people."

Surveys cited by the Sex Information and Education Council of the United States show that in as many as 50 to 80 percent of marriages, at least one partner will have an affair at some point in the relationship. Combine that with the aphrodisiac effect of political power, and one can understand the estimate of the late political reporter Theodore H. White, who covered national campaigns from the late 1940s to the mid-1970s. In his memoirs, White wrote that he had met only three candidates who had not succumbed to casual sex on the campaign trail—Truman, George Romney and Jimmy Carter.[19]

... To many political and journalistic observers, sex habits will continue to be seen as an indicator of character, and hence fair game for the press. "It's precisely when editors decide at Page 1 meetings," writes media critic Diamond,

that inquiries into the candidate's finances, for example, are important, while those about the candidate's sex life are not, that the short-circuiting of civic education begins. How can anyone argue that something is not relevant to the presidency until you know what that something is—compulsive sex, drug-taking, beating the draft?

Others says interest in the issue may die off "In a strange way, this election may be a turning point," says the Brookings Institution's Hess. "Clinton has had everything thrown at him. If he wins, he could do for adultery what JFK did for Catholicism and Nixon did for campaign losers, which is to provide a sort of journalistic inoculation.

What the press should strive to do, says Duke University's Barber, is present individual traits of candidates "not just as a blip" but in the larger context of their overall lives. In *The Wall Street Journal*'s 1987 profile of presidential candidate Marion G. (Pat) Robertson, for example, the titillating fact that his first child was born less than nine months after he was married appeared not in the headline but well into the story. Such restraint requires confidence on the part of editors.

"If newspapers can say, 'I don't care what the competing publications are doing, this is what we do,' then it can be done on a higher plane," says *Miami Herald* Editor Clifton.

Larry Sabato offers a set of guidelines for minimizing press "feeding frenzies." He would have the press cover health questions that affect a politician's performance; incidents that reach police blotters or courts; sex with staff (coercion); sex that is compulsive; ongoing alcohol or drug abuse; and any illegal abuse or condoning of drug abuse, perhaps within the past decade. Sabato would have journalists avoid coverage of non-legal matters involving candidates' underage children; current extramarital affairs as long as it is discreet, non-compulsive and not involving minors or staff; sexual orientation unless it is compulsive or with minors; and drug or alcohol abuse that is at least a decade old.[20]

But as Paul Taylor has written, journalism is "too unwieldy, untidy and plural a profession for rules." (The Code of Ethics of the Society of Professional Journalists pays heed to both a "right to privacy" and the "public's right to know.") News judgments are made case by case.

The recent concentration on reporting adultery is clearly the result of a trend that could taper off. Columnist Carl Rowan has called for editors who advocate questioning candidates about adultery to sign affidavits swearing that they themselves have never sinned.

"Was there really anything wrong 30 years ago—and is there anything wrong today—with respecting the privacy of politicians if personal conduct is not distorting public performance?" asks veteran TV journalist Bill Monroe. "The alternative is to get comfortable with the idea of sinful editors exposing sinful politicians, with the journalists emerging as the more dedicated hypocrites."[21]

NOTES

1. Edwin Diamond, "Crash Course: Campaign Journalism 101." *New York*, February 17, 1992, p. 28.
2. Quoted in *Washington Journalism Review*, May 1988, p. 38.
3. Suzanne Garment, *Scandal*. New York: Times Books, 1991, p. 175.
4. Larry J. Sabato, *Feeding Frenzy*. New York: Free Press, 1991, p. 23.
5. The poll was conducted in January by Yankelovich Clancy Shulman for *Time* magazine.
6. "Reporting the Presidential Campaign of 1992: Lessons from 1988," Marist Institute for Public Opinion, 1991, p. 18.
7. Quoted in *Time*, May 18, 1987.
8. Letter to the editors of *The New York Times*, quoted in Paul Taylor, *See How They Run*. New York: Knopf, 1990, p. 70.
9. Quoted in *Time*, July 10, 1989, p. 53.
10. Column in *The Washington Post*, January 28, 1992.
11. Column in *The Washington Post*, January 28, 1992.
12. *AIM Report*, February-B [sic], 1992.
13. *Time*, May 18, 1987, p. 33.
14. Quoted in *Editor & Publisher*, February 8, 1992, p. 8.
15. Reported in *The Washington Post*, March 16, 1992.
16. Quoted in Sabato, *Feeding Frenzy*, p. 77.
17. Quoted in *The Washington Post*, January 28, 1992.
18. Jack Germond and Jules Witcover, *Whose Broad Stripes and Bright Stars?* New York: Warner Books, 1989, p. 198.
19. Theodore H. White, *In Search of History*. New York: Harper and Row, 1978, p. 529.
20. Sabato, *Feeding Frenzy*, p. 218.
21. Column in the *Washington Journalism Review*, June 1991, p. 6.

DISCUSSION QUESTIONS

1. Would you run for office, knowing that all your past indiscretions would be investigated by the media for all to consider? How many of us do not have skeletons in the closet? Will good people choose to run if this kind of media reporting continues?

2. Is it the media's responsibility to discover candidates' fitness for office? If so, how should the media fulfill this responsibility? If not, whose responsibility is it?

3. What would you say to the argument that all this is nothing new—except that in the past, this kind of information was spread by rumor and word-of-mouth? Is the situation today enough of a problem that we need to deal with it?

4. You are an advisor to a political candidate whose past disreputable escapades have been leaked to the media. What strategy would you suggest the candidate adopt to minimize the damage? What is the likelihood you will be successful in your efforts to keep the damage in check?

CHAPTER 8
Conclusion

I have left you hanging. I argued in the introduction that media bias tends to be of the structural sort, a product of media practices and norms, rather than intentional bias. Yet the readings in the last section strongly suggest otherwise, that in some very important policy areas, media personnel make conscious choices that affect the very nature of the political process they report on. It strains our credulity to think that journalists are blissfully unaware of the impact of their reporting. And if journalists are not oblivious to the effects news may have, it is hard not to conclude that their reports reflect their positions, their perspectives, and their preferences. Only the naive would conclude that reporters gather news, air stories, and publish articles without knowing that these actions affect the very events being reported.

However, do we have any evidence that journalists report as they do to build support for a particular perspective or to undermine other points of view? It is hard to argue from effect to motive: Just because an outcome has occurred, we cannot assume that there was an intent to produce that outcome. Just because incumbents suffer from stories about political corruption is no evidence that the articles were published in an attempt to undermine incumbents' electoral support. We cannot conclude anything about the attitudes of reporters from the effects of their stories. Perhaps newspeople reflect many of the same attitudes you and I hold; perhaps they subscribe to beliefs somewhat different from ours. Perhaps in their reporting they simply build on presuppositions and assumptions without ever being aware of them. But they may be guided by considerations that have little, if anything, to do with those values and attitudes. Their lodestone may be news value rather than political effect.

Nevertheless, media have an impact. In elections and in government, political leaders base their decisions on their perceptions of the media's likely response. Sometimes they seek publicity—of almost any kind, as do challengers in congressional races. Sometimes they seek publicity—but only of their choosing, as do presidents and presidential candidates. Sometimes they avoid publicity—negotiation and compromise work best out of the limelight. But the likelihood of news coverage and the probable nature of that coverage become important factors in the strategic calculations of political activists at all levels and in all areas of politics and government. Despite the media's attempts to be objective and to report but not influence events, the media affect events around them, and affect them profoundly.

That makes them an essential element in the U.S. political system. But by law they are private institutions with no official standing and, therefore, are not limited by the sorts of restrictions under which political parties and government institutions operate. The First Amendment provides them with protection from government influence—at least of a direct and obvious sort—and those protections are predicated on the notion that media represent citizen voices and provide citizens with the political information they need to function effectively. But if media are in fact political institutions, not formally part of government but essential to political processes in the United States today, it may make more sense to think of media more as we do political parties: private institutions with quasi-public functions. And it may be time, controversial as such an attempt may be, to reconsider the legal status of mass media in the United States.

That won't happen in the near future. For one thing, attempts to regulate media as quasi-public institutions will unavoidably be interpreted in political terms. If a conservative suggests it, liberals will oppose it; if a liberal makes the argument, conservatives will defend the free press. For another, the media will use their considerable powers to defend the U.S. system as they see it. They have been much more likely, for example, to report Supreme Court decisions dealing with freedom of the press than similar decisions dealing with other aspects of the Bill of Rights. And the media will see any attempts to treat them as quasi-public institutions as an invasion of First Amendment rights. Finally, even if we all agree some changes are necessary (and that is by no means likely—I, too, have my doubts), we are most unlikely to agree on the specific changes we can support. Lacking consensus on changes to adopt, we are likely to muddle through with the way things are.

But I urge you to consider this question carefully: Does it make sense to treat institutions with the significant political impact of the media, institutions that have become essential to the way political power is exercised by elected and unelected officials alike, as if they were individual pamphleteers bartering in the marketplace of ideas? No longer can people easily start a newspaper or magazine to provide competing points of view. No longer do most cities have several morning and daily newspapers taking contrasting positions on public issues. Selling news is now a highly concentrated function.

At the same time, candidates, government officials, and the public depend more on the media to disseminate information than ever before. Alternative modes of communication are either unavailable or too cumbersome. Political parties no longer function as effective channels of communication between officeholders and citizens, and officials can meet too few members of the public directly, given our growing population.

Leaders have to resort to the media as a way to reach the citizenry, and the public needs the media to discover what they need to know about the issues that will affect them and the performance of the people who govern them. The media play a more central role in our political system than ever before.

Yet we still think of the media the same way: as private institutions protected by the First Amendment performing a useful public function. But as the nature and impact of media have changed, perhaps our way of thinking of them should change as well. Maybe we should recognize the media for what they are: significant and indispensable actors in an increasingly complex political system. Rather than treat them legally as outside the realm of government and therefore of regulation, it may be time to reconsider their legal status. They are, after all, in the middle of things.

Index

ABC, 18, 23, 70, 85, 119, 123, 130, 153, 172
abortion, 8, 42, 121, 123–124, 151–156
Accuracy in Media, 182
Addis Ababa, 24
Admiral, 70
adversarial model of press and government relations, 103, 126
advocacy journalism, 143
affirmative action, 123
AFL-CIO, 177
Africa, 24–25
Africare, 24
agenda-setting, 3, 10, 55, 77, 81, 96, 104–106, 181
AID, 24
Air Force, U.S., 168, 173
Alan Guttmacher Institute, 154
Albuquerque, New Mexico, 38
Alford, John, 68
Alsop, Joseph, 171
alternative media, 60
America Online, 116–117
American Federation of State, County and Municipal Employees, 177
American Life League, 154
American Medical Association, 176
American Occupational Therapy Association, 177
American Speech-Language-Hearing Association, 177
Anderson, Paul, 30
Andrews, Peter, 151, 169
Angotti, Joseph, 23
apartheid, 21
Arabian Gulf, 1
   see also Persian Gulf

"The Arsenio Hall Show," 4, 82, 84–85, 115
Arterton, F. Christopher, 67, 75–76
Arvey, Joseph, 70–71
Associated Press, 117, 154
Atlantic Monthly, 100
audience, 56
   targeting of, 82–85

balance, journalistic, 12, 13, 84
Baltimore Sun, 114
Band-Aid, 24
Barber, James David, 181, 184
Bartlett, David, 159
Baumgartner v. United States, 139
BBC, 23
Beard, Charles, 30
Beirut, Lebanon, 21
Bennett, Charles, 98
Bennett, W. Lance, 37
Berlin, 27
Berlin Wall, 27
Bettag, Tom, 152
bias, media, partisan, 9, 79, 186
bias, media, structural, 9, 79, 186
Biden, Joseph, 119
Bill of Rights, 135, 142, 187
   see also First Amendment, free speech, and freedom of the press
Blackmun, Harry F., 124
Blaine, James G., 140
Blumenthal, Sidney, 97, 114
Bolz, Frank A., 157, 161, 162
Bonafede, Dom, 180
Bosso, Christopher J., 10, 20–21
Boston, Massachusetts, 25, 64

Boston Globe, 152, 154
Bower, Bill, 117–118
Bozell, L. Brent III, 153
Bradfield, Rick, 161
Braestrup, Peter, 172
Branch Davidians, 8, 150, 156–161
Brazil, 24
Breindel, Eric, 93
Brennan, William, 123
Brinkley, David, 17–18
British Central Television, 23
Broder, David S., 182
Brokaw, Tom, 22–23, 25
Bronner, Ethan, 152
Brown, Edmund G. (Jerry), 63, 81–82
Brown, Judie, 154
Bryan, Tracy, 120
Bryan, William Jennings, 84
Brzezinski, Zbigniew, 131
Buchanan, Patrick, 63
Buckley, Kevin, 171
Buddhists, 15
Buerk, Michael, 23
Bureau of Alcohol, Tobacco and Firearms (ATF), 158–159, 161
bureaucracy, federal, 97, 128–132
Burger, Warren, 123
Burger King, 32–33
Bush, George, 1, 63–64, 84, 112, 115, 117–119, 155, 164, 174, 180, 182
Bushkin, Kathryn, 183
business, 7
Byrd, Robert, 100

cable television, 83, 98
California, 116–117
campaign strategy, 77–78, 86
campaigns, congressional, 86–91, 99
  gubernatorial, 89
  media in, 4, 67–68, 67–95 *passim*
  presidential election, 4, 67, 76–81, 82–86, 89, 176
  U.S. Senate, 89
Campari Liqueur, 139
Campbell, James, 68
candidates, congressional, 4, 68, 86–91
  see also incumbents *and* challengers

candidates, congressional (*Cont.*):
  presidential, 4, 59–60, 67–69, 74–82, 86, 179–185, 186
  vice-presidential, 69, 179
Cannon, Lou, 132
capital punishment, *see* death penalty
Capitol Hill press corps, 99, 101–106
Carlson, James M., 45, 47
Carter, Jimmy, 29, 57, 81, 110, 116, 184
Casey, William, 129
Catholic Relief Services, 22–23
CBS, 22–23, 70, 130, 152, 161
censorship, military, 165–166, 170
Center for Media and Public Affairs, 155
Central America, 25
Central Park, 38, 40
Chad, 21, 24
challengers, 68, 86–91, 186
Charlotte Observer, 85
Chase Manhattan Bank, 32
Chattanooga, Tennessee, 117
Chautauqua circuit, 83–84
Cherry, Richard, 164, 167
Chicago, Illinois, 64, 70–71, 87
Child Welfare League, 173
Churchill, Winston, 170
Cincinnati, Ohio, 88
Cincinnati Commercial, 169
Cirelli, Elaine, 178
civil rights, 121, 124
civil rights movement, 42, 151
Clark, Charles S., 151, 179
Clifton, Doug, 180, 185
Clinton, Hillary Rodham, 175–176, 178–179
Clinton, William, 6, 63–64, 68, 82–85, 97, 113–120, 151, 176–179, 182, 184
CNN, 60, 83, 115, 130, 157–160
Coffin, William Sloan, 40
Cohen, Bernard, 3
Collins, Gail, 94
"Comedy Channel," 83
Committee for National Health Insurance, 177
Committee on the Present Danger, 39, 42

committees, congressional, 99–101, 106
  conference, 6
Commager, Henry Steele, 30
common law, 138
CompuServe, 116
confidentiality of sources, 145–149
Congress, 5–7, 24, 36, 47, 99–107, 109, 112, 127, 133–134, 162, 177
  members of, 6–7, 36, 48, 88–91, 96–109, 121
  see also House of Representatives, Senate
congressional hearings, 1, 6
Congressional Quarterly, 176
Connecticut, 4, 63, 116–117
Constitution, U.S., 123, 125–126, 135, 139, 142, 145–147, 170
Conus Communication, 105, 115
Cook, Timothy, 96, 98
Coolidge, Calvin, 4
Cosby, Bill, 72
criminal justice system, 52, 121, 145–149
Cronin, Thomas E., 129
Cronkite, Walter, 130
C-SPAN, 7, 98, 115, 117
Cuba, 117
cultivation theory, 47, 50

Dakota Radio Network, 116
Dallas, Texas, 87
D'Amato, Alfonse, 163
Davis, Richard, 97, 121
Deakin, James, 111–112
death penalty, 123–124, 153
Deaver, Michael, 118–119
debates, candidate, 81
Defense, Department of, 13, 129–131, 134, 163–165, 167–168, 172
Democratic Congressional Campaign Committee, 118
Democratic National Committee, 71, 73
Democratic Party, 16, 69–74, 82
Desert Storm, 169, 173–174
Dhahran, 164, 167
Diamond, Edwin, 69, 92, 180,184
Dinkins, David, 92–94
Dionne, E.J., 85
disinformation, 33
Dover Air Force Base, 171

Dowhower, Richard, 159, 162
Downs, Anthony, 22, 25
Duberstein, Kenneth, 109
Dukakis, Michael, 93
Dulles, John Foster, 130

Easterbrook, Gregg, 100
Easton, David, 48
Edelman, Murray, 36
editorials, 46, 56–58
editors, 7, 58
800 numbers, 68
Einstein, Albert, 29
Eisenhower, Dwight D., 112
elections, 4, 67
  city, 92–94
  congressional, 86–91
  presidential, 4, 60, 64, 67, 75–81, 81–86
elites, 35–36, 39, 41–43, 46, 55, 58, 98, 108, 111
Eller, Jeff, 116–119
Ellsberg, Daniel, 134
Emerson, Ralph Waldo, 30
EMILY's list, 84
endorsements, 69, 92–94
Entman, Robert, 35, 46, 55
Ethiopia, 10, 21–25, 155

fairness doctrine, 16, 142
Falwell, Jerry, 138
famine, Ethiopian, 10, 20–25, 155
Federal Bureau of Investigation, 158–160
Federal Communications Commission, 16, 142, 162
Federalist Papers, 115
Federation of American Scientists, 36
Ferraro, Geraldine, 179
Fifth Amendment, 146
First Amendment, 8, 133–135, 139, 141–143, 145–149, 170–171, 173, 187–188
  see also Bill of Rights
Florida, 116–118, 142–144
Flowers, Gennifer, 179–180, 182–184
Flynt, Larry, 139
Foley, Thomas S., 183
Food and Drug Administration, 130, 132

Ford, Gerald R., 5, 57
Forsberg, Randall, 36, 40, 43
Fort Worth, Texas, 87, 157
Fourteenth Amendment, 134, 139
Fowler, Don, 72
framing, 10, 34–43, 84, 125, 150–156, 175
France, 170
Frankel, Max, 180
Frankfort, Kentucky, 88
Frankfurter, Felix, 139
Franklin, Aretha, 72
Fraser, Douglas, 177
free speech, 121 see also Bill of Rights
freedom of the press, 133–137, 169–170
see also Bill of Rights
Friedman, Paul, 120, 153
Friedman, Steve, 160–161
Frost, David, 174
Fulbright, J. William, 16
Fuller, Harry, 160–161

Ganges, 21
Gannett Foundation, 151, 163
Garment, Suzanne, 180, 182
Geldorf, Bob, 24
George, David Lloyd, 170
Georgia, 70
Gerbner, George, 49, 51, 53
Ginsburg, Douglas, 179
Gissler, Sig, 154–155
Gitlin, Todd, 37–38
Glasser, Melvin, 177
"going public," 96, 108–112
Goldberg, Arthur, 16, 18
Goldwater, Barry, 13
Gonzalez, Juan, 94
"Good Morning America," 83
Gore, Al, 68
Gore, Tipper, 116
Gorney, Cynthia, 152
governors, 7
Graham, Billy, 29
grand juries, 145–148
Grant, Ulysses S., 174
Greenberg, Stanley, 119
Grenada, U.S. invasion of, 163, 169
Grey, David L., 125
Ground Zero, 36–39
Ground Zero Week, 37, 39
Grunwald, Molly, 120
Gulf of Tonkin, 12–15
Gulf War, 1, 8, 64, 151, 163–174
see also Iraq and Kuwait
gun control, 42

Haig, Alexander, 130–131
Haiti, refugees from, 117
Halamandáris, Val, 177
Hallin, Daniel C., 9, 11, 46
Hanoi, 13, 15, 17
Harriman, W. Averill, 16, 70–71
Harrison, Michael, 61
Hart, Gary, 119–120, 179–184
Headline, Bill, 160
health care policy, 175–178
Healthright, 177
Heckler, Margaret, 73
Helms, Jesse, 111
Hemion, Dwight, 72
Henry, Keith, 68
Herbert, Bob, 94
Hess, Stephen, 97, 101–102, 125, 128, 183–184
Hill, Anita, 180
Hoagland, Peter, 88
Hoge, Michael, 93–94
Holocaust, 10
Homestead Air Force Base, 117
Hopper, Kim, 116
horse-race coverage, 80–81, 84, 90
Hosler, Karen, 114–115
hostages, coverage of, 156–163
House, Toni, 126
House Democratic Caucus, 99
House of Representatives, 1, 34, 96, 98–107
see also Congress
Housing and Urban Development, Department of, 128
Humphrey, Hubert H., 16–18, 118
Hunt, Al, 180
Hunter, Ruth, 118
Huntley, Chet, 18
Hussein, Saddam, 170, 174
Hustler Magazine, 138–140

ideology, 56–58, 62
Illinois, 70

incumbents, congressional, 4, 68, 86–91, 109
independence, journalistic, 11–12
Independents, 62
"infomercials," 82
"infotainment" politics, 60
interest groups, 3, 175–178
Iran, 33
Iranian hostage crisis, 33
Iraq, 1, 166–170, 173
Irvine, Reed, 182
Isenberg, Steven, 93

Jackson, Jesse, 74
Jamar, Jeff, 159–160
Jefferson, Thomas, 30, 144, 184
Jennings, Peter, 18
Johnson, Lyndon B., 12, 14, 17, 109, 116, 184
Johnson, Robert M., 93
journalist as adversary, 17
journalistic norms, 2, 89, 91
Judiciary Committee (House), 99
Justice, Department of, 118, 129
Justices of the Supreme Court, 121–127, 134–135

Kaiser, Robert G., 183–184
Kalikow, Peter, 92
Kamen, Jeff, 156
Kansas, 30
Kavanau, Ted, 159
Kefauver, Estes, 70–71
Kehler, Randy, 36
Kennedy, Edward, 24, 36, 180
Kennedy, John F., 184
Kentucky, 88, 155
Kernell, Samuel, 96, 108
King, Coretta, 40
Kirkpatrick, Jeane, 73
Kissinger, Henry, 131
Kline, David, 22–23
Klurfeld, Jim, 93
Koch, Ed, 92–94
Koresh, David, 156–161
Kovach, Bill, 173, 181
Krauthammer, Charles, 182
Kupperman, Robert, 158
Kurtz, Howard, 151, 175
Kuwait, 1, 166–167, 173

"Larry King Live," 60, 68, 82–83, 114–115
Lawrence Livermore Laboratory, 38
Leahy, Patrick, 160
legislative process, 6, 100–107
legislators, state, 90
Lehrer, Jim, 174
Lexington, Kentucky, 88
libel, 8, 136, 138–139
Libya, 21
Limbaugh, Rush, 60, 63
Lincoln, Abraham, 84, 140, 184
London, 23
Longworth Building, 118
Los Angeles, California, 87–88, 117
Los Angeles *Daily News,* 117
Los Angeles Times, 88, 117, 150–151, 153–155, 180
Louisville, Kentucky, 88, 169
Louisville Courier Journal, 155
low information campaigns, 89
Lucas, C. Payne, 24
Lucasville, Ohio, 157–158, 160–161

McAlary, Mike, 94
McCurry, Mike, 73
McDougall, Walt, 140
McKeown, Bob, 167–168
McNamara, Eileen, 154
McNamara, Robert S., 15
"MacNeil/Lehrer Newshour," 174
McPherson, M. Peter, 24
Madison, James, 135–136
Madonna, 180
majority leader, Senate, 6
Mali, 24
Manchester Guardian, 170
Mandigo, Charles, 158
Manhattan, 4, 118
Manilow, Barry, 72
Mansfield, Mike, 13
Maples, Pam, 182
Mark Goode Enterprises, 72
Marshall, Thurgood, 124
mayors, 90, 92–94
media, local, 6, 92–94
media effects, 49–50, 55, 59, 62–63, 156–163, 186
media expectations, 4, 76
media intent, 2, 186

media market-district fit, 4, 68, 86–89
media markets, 4, 77
Media Research Center, 153
media technology, 82–85, 116–118, 160
Mencken, H. L., 72
Mengistu regime, 24
Miami, 117
Miami Herald, 117, 180–181
"Miami Vice," 51
Michelman, Kate, 155
military and media, 163–168, 169–174
Miller, Perry, 30
Milwaukee, Wisconsin, 115
Milwaukee Journal, 154
Minneapolis, Minnesota, 134
Minnesota, 134
Minnesota Citizens Concerned for Life, 153
Missouri, 70
mobilizing information, 59
Molander, Roger, 36–41
Monroe, Bill, 185
Mozambique, 23
MTV, 68, 82–84, 114

name recognition, 4, 87–88
"narrowcasting," 83–85
Nashville, Tennessee, 117–118
Nast, Thomas, 140
National Abortion Rights Action League, 153, 155
National Association for Home Care, 177
National Council of Senior Citizens, 177
national nominating conventions, 4, 67, 69–75, 84
National Organization for Women, 155
National Right to Life Committee, 153, 155
national security, 134, 164–168, 171
NBC, 18, 22–24, 70, 130, 159–161
Near v. Minnesota, 134, 137
Nebraska, 86, 115
Nevius, Allan, 30
New Hampshire, 63
New Jersey, 4
New Left movement, 41

New York City, 4, 36–41, 64, 82, 87, 92–94, 157
New York Daily News, 92–94, 180
New York magazine, 69, 180
New York *Newsday,* 92–94, 180
New York Police Department, 162
New York Post, 92–94
New York state, 63, 70
New York Times, 12–13, 15, 18–19, 23, 35, 37–38, 41, 43, 83, 92–94, 101, 115, 130, 134–137, 154–155, 168, 172, 180–181
New York Times Magazine, 154, 176
New York Times v. Sullivan, 138, 140
Newfield, Jack, 93–94
news analysis, 14
news conventions (routines), 13, 103
news spin, 6–7
newsgathering, 145–149, 165–168, 186
newspapers as businesses, 8, 142
Newsweek, 115, 154, 156, 171, 176
newsworthiness criteria, 2, 6, 10, 14, 78, 83, 87, 89–90, 101–103, 105–106, 150, 186
Nickelodeon cable network, 83
Niger, 24
"Nightline," 119
Nimmo, Dan, 67, 69
Nitze, Paul, 39
Nixon, Richard M., 5, 29, 99, 110, 118, 184
nominations, 4
North Vietnam, 12, 14–18
nuclear freeze movement, 35–40

objectivity, 2, 9, 11–19, 57–58, 84–86, 187
Ochberg, Frank, 162
Ohio, 81
Okie, Susan, 152
Omaha, Nebraska, 88
Omaha World-Herald, 88
O'Neill, Thomas P. (Tip), Jr., 98
open-seat races, 87, 90
Operation Rescue, 154
Orange County, California, 87–88
Oreskes, Michael, 181
Ortega, Katherine, 73
Overholser, Geneva, 180

Overton, David, 157, 160–162
Owen, Diana, 46, 59
Oxfam International, 23

Pakenham, Michael, 93–94
Panama, 163, 169
Panetta, Leon, 116
Parenti, Michael, 51
Paris, 18
party platforms, 69
Patterson, Philip, 82
PBS, 23
Pegler, Westbrook, 170–171
Pentagon, *see* Defense, Department of
Pentagon Papers, 134
People Magazine, 24, 180
Perot, H. Ross, 60, 63–64, 68, 82–85
Pershing, John J., 170–171
Persian Gulf, 1, 163, 170
Pharmaceutical Manufacturers Association, 175
Philadelphia Inquirer, 152–153
Philco, 70
Physicians for Social Responsibility, 36
Pierce, Samuel, 128
Planned Parenthood of America, 154
Plate, Tom, 93
Plympton, Florus, 169
Podhoretz, Norman, 39
policy-makers, 96–97, 108, 175–176
political culture, 3, 45
political discourse, *see* public discourse
political participation, 35, 37–38, 40–41, 43, 46, 59, 61–62, 64
political parties, 5, 67, 69, 187
political socialization, 3, 45–53
    agents of, 48–50
pool reporting, 164–168
populism, 62
Postman, Neil, 10, 27
Powell, Colin L., 168
president, U.S., 5, 13–14, 32–33, 47–48, 96–97, 108–121, 127, 129–130, 177, 180
press, partisan, 11
press conferences, 6, 13, 77, 111, 114, 117, 122, 172

prestige press, 17
primacy principle, 48–49
primaries, 4, 63, 69–70, 76, 80–81
priming, 10
prior restraint, 8, 134–137, 146
priorities, media, 2
privacy, 151, 179–185
Prudential Insurance Company, 178
public agenda, 20, 46
public discourse, 27, 30, 60, 65, 83–85, 133, 139–143, 148
public figures, 138–141
public information officers, 129–132, 165, 167
public opinion, 3, 21, 25, 46, 55–58, 60, 106–111, 141–143, 150, 168, 170, 175
public relations, 3–4, 110–111
publishers, 7–8, 92
Purdue, 117

Quayle, Dan, 83, 183

Radio-Television News Directors Association, 159
Raines, Howell, 168
Rangoon, Burma, 16
Ravitch, Richard, 92
Rayburn, Sam, 71
Rea-Luthin, Mirianne, 152–153
Reagan, Ronald W., 24–25, 37, 39–40, 42, 109–110, 112, 114–115, 117–120, 124
Reagan Administration, 36, 38–39, 42–43
Red Lion Broadcasting Co. v. Federal Communications Commission, 142
Reedy, George, 184
Rehnquist, William, 123–124
Reinsch, J. Leonard, 71
Republicans, 62–63
Republican Party, 16, 69, 71–74, 82
Reston, James, 130
Rice, Donna, 179, 181, 184
right of rebuttal, 8, 142
Roberts, Eugene, 152
Robertson, Marion G. (Pat), 184
Robinson, Michael, 100

Roe v. Wade, 155–156
Rojecki, Andrew, 35
Roll Call, 176
Romney, George, 184
Roosevelt, Franklin D., 84, 140
Roosevelt, Theodore, 140
Rose, Steven, 178
Rosenthal, Jack, 93
Rostow, Eugene, 39
Rowan, Carl, 185
Rusk, Dean, 16, 130
Russell, Bertrand, 28
Russell, Richard, 70

Sabato, Larry J., 181, 183, 185
Sacramento, California, 117, 120, 155
Sacramento Bee, 117
Saigon, 171–172
San Diego, California, 117
San Francisco, California, 87, 117, 155
San Francisco Chronicle, 117
San Francisco Examiner, 117
San Jose, California, 117
San Jose Mercury, 117
The Saturday Press, 134
Saudi Arabia, 1, 163
Save the Children Fund, 22–23
Sawyer, Forrest, 167–168
school busing, 123
Schwarzkopf, Norman, 167, 170–171, 173–174
Seekins, Steven V., 176
Selassie, Haile, 21
Select Committee on Committees (House), 98
Senate, 6, 100–101 *see also* Congress
Senate Foreign Relations Commitee, 16
Seraphin, Charlie, 159
Severin, Jay, 176
Sex Information and Education Council of the United States, 184
Shakespeare, William, 30
Shapiro, Walter, 183
Shaw, David, 151
Sherman, William T., 169–170, 174
shield laws, 145–145
Shreveport, Louisiana, 115
Shribman, David, 153

Shuger, Scott, 173
Sidey, Hugh, 184
Simon, Paul, 163
Sinclair, Barbara, 109
Singer, Margaret, 158
"60 Minutes," 179
Smith, Dorrance, 119
Smith, Gary, 72
Smith, H. Allen, 30
Smith, Hendrick, 100
Smith, Larry David, 67, 69
Smith, Susan, 154
Smith-Hemion Productions, 72–73
Snow, Tony, 119
Solicitor General, 135–136
Solomon, 28
Sorauf, Frank J., 125
sound bites, 68, 84–85
Souter, David, 173
South Africa, 21
South Vietnam, 15, 18
Southeast Asia, 12
Southern Ohio Correctional Facility, 157
Sowers, Fred, 177
Spencer, F. Gilman, 92–94
Sphere of Consensus, 11, 16–17
Sphere of Deviance, 11, 16–17, 46
Sphere of Legitimate Controversy, 11, 16–17, 19
Star, 180, 182–183
State, Department of, 97, 129–131
state legislatures, 7
Stephanopoulos, George, 119–120
Stevens, John Paul, 124
Stevenson, Adlai, 70–71
Streisand, Barbra, 72
structuring principle, 48–50
Sub-Saharan Africa, 21
Sudan, 23
Sulzberger, Arthur O., 93
Supreme Court, U.S., 8, 97, 121–127, 133–149, 153, 180, 187
Supreme Court Public Information Office, 126

talk shows, 4, 46, 59, 68, 90
Talkers, 61
Taylor, Paul, 119–120, 181–182, 185

television crime shows, 46–47
television in court, 123
Terre Haute, Indiana, 117
Terry, Randall, 154–155
Tet, 18
Thomas, Clarence, 150, 180
Thomas, Mona, 178
Thoreau, Henry David, 30
Tillotson, Mary, 157
Time Magazine, 35, 37, 39–41, 43, 115, 154, 176
The Times (London), 170
Times-Mirror Center for the People and the Press, 59, 63–64, 182
"Today," 83, 160
Tokyo, 27
Transportation, Department of, 132
Treasury, Department of, 129
Trout Unlimited, 84
Trudeau, Garry, 179
Truman, Harry S, 70–71, 84, 112, 184
Tsongas, Paul, 118
Turner, Frederick Jackson, 30
Turner, Ted, 152
Turner Broadcasting System, 152

UNICEF, 22
Union of Concerned Scientists, 36
Union of Soviet Socialist Republics, 24, 36–37, 39–40, 134
United Airlines, 32
United Nations, 16, 18, 36, 40
United Press, 170
United States Surgical Corporation, 118
USA Today, 23
uses and gratifications theory, 62
US News and World Report, 176
US Newswire, 116

Value of Life Committee of Boston, 153
Verdi, David, 159, 163
Vietnam War, 11–19, 46, 110, 134, 136, 163, 169, 171–172
Village Voice, 94
violence in media, 51
Virginia, 70

Waco, Texas, 8, 150, 156–163
Wall Street Journal, 115, 153, 180, 184
war reporting, restrictions on in Gulf War, 165–168
Warren, Jeffrey, 177
Washington, George, 140
Washington, D.C., 5, 7, 24, 82, 89–90, 96–97, 99, 102, 104, 108–112, 130, 176, 181
Washington Post, 13, 23, 85, 115, 119, 130, 134–136, 152, 154–155, 172, 176, 180–182
Washington Post Magazine, 153–154
Washington Star, 115
Watergate, 99, 180
Wattleton, Faye, 154
Weaver, Gary, 158, 160–161
Webster v. Reproductive Health Services, 124, 153, 155
Weekly Compilation of Presidential Documents, 117
Wegner, Daniel, 183
Welles, Orson, 40
Westinghouse, 70
White, Byron, 124
White, Theodore, H., 184
White House, 100, 108, 112–120, 129–131, 177
White House beat, 5
White House press corps, 5, 96, 108, 113–114, 117–119
White House Press Office, 5, 114–120
Wicker, Tom, 12–14
Wilkins, Lee, 82
Williams, Louis A., 164
Willke, John, 153–155
Willse, Jim, 94
Wired, 116
Wolpe, Harold, 22
Woodward, Bob, 121, 155–156
"World News Tonight," 153
World War I, press and military in, 170–171
Wyoming, 30

Yard, Molly, 155